GOD   REMEMBERS

A. Dale Stohre   4/15/84   - from Dad

GOD REMEMBERS

A Study of Zechariah

by
CHARLES LEE FEINBERG, Th.D., Ph.D.
Dean Emeritus, Professor of Semitics and Old Testament
Talbot Theological Seminary
La Mirada, California

MULTNOMAH
PRESS
Portland, Oregon 97266

Third edition 1977, Multnomah Press, Portland, Oregon 97266.

Library of Congress card number: 77-18362

ISBN: 0-930014-18-9

TO
ANNE PRISCILLA
MY BELOVED WIFE

PREFACE

I HAVE never felt an apology necessary for a new exposition of any part of God's Word. The truth revealed is final and authoritative, but our comprehension of it is partial and progressive. "For we know in part, and we prophesy in part."

One who has never attempted a commentary on a book of the Bible cannot know the feeling of inadequacy that overwhelms a writer who has completed such a task. But the benefits of such an experience are incalculable. To fellowship with the mind and heart of a writer who was wrought upon of the Spirit of God is an unforgettable experience of lasting value. May God grant spiritual refreshing to the reader as he searches the riches of this inexhaustible mine.

Every commentary is of necessity written from a definite theological approach to the Scriptures. The author maintains throughout this volume the orthodox, traditional viewpoint of the Bible. His interpretation of Holy Writ is the premillennial and dispensational. This position is adhered to after years of intensive study of the Bible with special reference to the prophetic portions.

The substance of the material incorporated in this volume has been taught to my initial classes in Hebrew exegesis, first at the Dallas Theological Seminary, then at the Los Angeles Bible Theological Seminary, and now at Talbot Theological Seminary. The prophecy was treated by the writer in a series of exegetical studies which appeared in *Bibliotheca Sacra* from 1940-46, and numerous messages from the book have been given in various Bible Conferences throughout the United States of America, Canada, and abroad.

The Tetragrammaton, *YHWH,* has been rendered "Jehovah." This is not entirely satisfactory to the author, but was chosen as less confusing to the reader. Diacritical marks have been omitted in the transliterations of the Hebrew and Greek words because of the labor and expense involved. The reader will soon become aware that many cross references dot the pages of this volume. No thorough treatment of the Old Testament can be hoped for without them. All the references have been carefully checked and are vital for study.

The author wishes to express his appreciation to the following for permission to quote: The University of Chicago Press (D. D. Luckenbill, *Ancient Records of Assyria*); Charles Scribner's Sons (J. H. Breasted, *A History of Egypt*);The John S. Hopkins Press (W. F. Albright, *Archaeology and the Religion of Israel*); and Our Hope Publishers (A. C. Gaebelein, *Studies in Zechariah*).

Special thanks are due to Dr. Wilbur M. Smith for reading the entire manuscript at the request of the publishers and for offering valuable suggestions; and to my wife for proofreading the entire manuscript, for the index of Scripture, and, above all, constant encouragement, help, and inspiration. The dedication of this volume to her is a small token of my appreciation for making the volume possible.

The author invites helpful comment on any part of the book. He commends it to the blessing of God.

CHARLES L. FEINBERG

La Mirada, California

TABLE OF CONTENTS

PAGE

PREFACE vii

EXEGETICAL OUTLINE OF THE BOOK xi

INTRODUCTION 1

COMMENTARY ON ZECHARIAH 15

INDEX OF SCRIPTURE REFERENCES 265

INDEX OF SUBJECTS 277

SELECTED BIBLIOGRAPHY 281

ix

EXEGETICAL OUTLINE

I. An Exhortation to Repentance, 1:1-6.

II. The Prophet's Night-Visions, 1:7-6:15.

    a. The Vision of the Horses, 1:7-17.

    b. The Vision of the Horns and Smiths, 2:1-4 (Hebrew).

    c. The Vision of the Surveyor, 2:5-17 (Hebrew).

    d. The Vision of Joshua the High Priest and the Angel of Jehovah, 3:1-10.

    e. The Vision of the Candlestick and the Two Olive Trees, 4:1-14.

    f. The Vision of the Flying Roll, 5:1-4.

    g. The Vision of the Woman in the Ephah, 5:5-11.

    h. The Vision of the Four Chariots, 6:1-8.

    i. The Coronation of Joshua, 6:9-15.

III. The Question and the Answer concerning Fasting, 7:1-8:23.

    a. The Question, 7:1-3.

    b. The Rebuke, 7:4-7.

    c. The Warning from the Past, 7:8-14.

    d. The Restoration of God's Favor, 8:1-17.

    e. The Abrogation of the Fasts, 8:18-23.

IV. The Future of the World Powers, Israel, and the Kingdom of Messiah, 9-14.

    a. The First Burden, 9-11.

        1. Judgment on the Land of Hadrach, 9:1-8.

        2. Israel's King of Peace, 9:9,10.

        3. The King's Mission in Relation to Israel, 9:11-17.

        4. Additional Blessings for Israel, 10:1-12.

        5. The Rejection of the Good Shepherd and the Rule of the Wicked One, 11:1-17.

    b. The Second Burden, 12-14.

        1. Israel's Conflict and Deliverance, 12:1-14.

        2. Israel Cleansed of Her Sin, 13:1-6.

        3. The Shepherd Smitten and the Sheep Scattered, 13:7-9.

        4. The Great Consummation: Israel's Deliverance and God's Earthly Kingdom, 14:1-21.

INTRODUCTION

IF ANY portion of the Old Testament has come in for undeservedly scant attention, it has been the minor prophets. In the Hebrew Testament these books are called simply The Twelve and form a part of the *nebhi'im 'aharonim,* the latter prophets. Among the major messages of the minor prophets Zechariah is probably preeminent. He is undoubtedly the greatest of the postexilic prophets. In the introductory word we purpose to treat the book from several angles.

I. THE PROPHET ZECHARIAH

Of the personal history of Zechariah very little is known. His name, *Zekharyah* "he whom Jehovah remembers," or "Jehovah remembers," is a common one in the Scriptures, for more than twenty different persons in the Old Testament had the same name. Attempts have been made to identify our prophet with Zechariah mentioned in Isaiah 8:2, but without sufficient evidence. Like his predecessors, Jeremiah and Ezekiel, he was of priestly lineage, the son of Berechiah and grandson of Iddo (1:1, 7). He was born in Babylon and with his grandfather was in the company of exiles who returned to Palestine with Joshua and Zerubbabel (Neh. 12:4). His father evidently died young, for Zechariah is named as the immediate successor of Iddo in the priestly office under Joiakim, who succeeded Joshua (Neh. 12:12-16). This may explain why the prophet is called the son of Iddo in Ezra 5:1 and 6:14. (This argument cannot be conclusive in itself, because, as is known, there is no specific word in Hebrew for grandson, the same

1

word as for son being used.) Zechariah began his prophetic ministry in the second year of Darius Hystaspes, two months after Haggai, his contemporary (cf. Hag. 1:1 with Zech. 1:1). The length of his ministry is uncertain, but the final prophecies of the book are of a later period. Jewish tradition credits him with being a member, along with Haggai, Malachi, Ezra, and Nehemiah, of the Great Synagogue; but though not contrary to the possibilities of the case, there is no clear testimony for it. It has been inferred by many from 2:8 (Hebrew) that he was not a full-grown man at the beginning of his prophetic ministry. The term *na'ar,* youth, lad, or young man, does not mark any specific age. (Cf. Gen. 41:12 with 41:1, 46 of Joseph at twenty-eight; Benjamin and Absalom had households of their own, Gen. 43:8; 46:21; II Sam. 18:5; 14:27.)

II. The Historical Background

Before entering upon the subject matter of the prophecy we do well to note the historical circumstances surrounding the ministry of Zechariah. The historical background furnishes in the first instance the reason for his prophetic labors. When Cyrus sent forth his decree in 536 B.C. (II Chron. 36:22, 23; Ezra 1:1-4) there were 50,000 who returned from Babylon. Their enthusiasm was high and their one thought was to rebuild the temple of God and resettle in the land. Immediately they began to work and in the second month of 535 B.C. laid the foundation (Ezra 3: 11-13). The Samaritans, having been denied participation in the work, began to oppose the work, and succeeded even in Cyrus' reign (Ezra 4:5). For nearly fourteen years the work was at a standstill. In 521 B.C. Darius Hystaspes came to the throne. The prophets, Haggai and Zechariah, assuming that the decrees of the former king were void, aroused their coreligionists to undertake the task once more.

The work went forward under the leadership of Joshua and Zerubbabel; but was again interrupted by the inquiry of Tatnai, the Persian governor west of the Euphrates, as to the purpose of the work. When the matter was referred to Babylon, where search brought to light the original decree of Cyrus, Darius confirmed the permission in the second year of his reign, thus removing all outward obstacles.

But a change had taken place in the hearts of the people. With the opposition to the rebuilding of the temple, they had turned to the pursuit of their affairs. They saw in the hindrances to the work the hand of God restraining them from furthering the work. Haggai and Zechariah arduously sought to bring the people from their indifference. God prospered them in this ministry, and the building was completed in 515 B.C., the sixth year of Darius' reign and twenty-one years after the beginning of the work in 536 B.C. All the dates in Zechariah (1:1, 7; 7:1) come within the period of work on the temple. It would be untrue to suppose, however, that all his earlier prophecies were directed to the completion of the temple alone. Haggai's chief purpose is the rebuilding of the temple; but Zechariah goes farther, beginning where his older contemporary had left off, to bring about a complete spiritual return of the people to the Lord. The historical position in the second to the fourth years of Darius supplies the background for the prophecies, but by no means limits the scope or interpretation of the prophecies.

III. THE STYLE OF THE BOOK

The book, often called the Apocalypse of the Old Testament, makes much use of figurative and symbolical language. At times its statements are quite brief and succinct. What former prophets revealed at length, Zechariah epitomizes for us in terse sentences or even clauses. The messages of the prophecy

are given sometimes in direct prophetic speech, sometimes in the
narration of visions, and sometimes in the setting forth of symbolical acts. It was contended at one time that the prophecy
reveals the marked presence of Chaldaisms. It is now a matter
of general agreement that the Hebrew is pure. The contention
that Zechariah was indebted to Persian theology for his presentation of truth, such as the doctrine of angels, has been proved
to be entirely baseless.

IV. The Interpretation of the Prophecy

We heartily concur in Dods' pronouncement that "To
interpret prophecy has at no time been found easy." Those who
have made a study of the prophetic Scriptures will know of
what we speak when we distinguish two extremes in prophetic
interpretation: (1) There is the critical position. The advocates
of this view begin with their fundamental axiom: a prophet
always spoke out of a definite historical situation. At the most
they allow the possibility of an immediate future fulfillment.
This leads them to a fantastic twisting of the prophecies to make
them fit the age of the prophet or the time immediately subsequent to it. (2) At the other extreme is the position taken by
some conservatives. One such writer, in speaking of the prophecies of another prophet of the Old Testament, claims we may
read the future even in the past, so that while the prophet
mentions a nation of the past, "we must discern one of the
future." After this fashion they make the primary sense of almost
all prophecy entirely or principally future. This destroys, we
believe, the effectiveness of the prophet's message for his contemporaries. If the prophecy had no real relation to the prophet's
generation, then why need it have been uttered at that particular
time and under just such circumstances?

Let us illustrate with the prophecy in the seventh chapter
of Isaiah. The historical background must be taken into account,

namely, the Syro-Ephraimitic coalition against Judah. The Messianic prophecy uttered in verses 14 to 16 served a real purpose to the nation of that day. But it was not thereby exhausted. The terms of the prophecy are such that, although it ministered to the quieting of terror-stricken Judah, it could only be fulfilled in a future coming of the Messiah of Israel. The critical view seeks to find a solution in the time of the prophet with the birth of Isaiah's son (8:3). Such an interpretation would serve a purpose in the national life of the time—although not a very unusual sign, to be sure—but how well does it fit with the content of the prophecy? It does not answer the demands of the prophecy at all. On the other hand, those who would disassociate the prophecy from the historical background, cannot explain why it was given at just that time and what good was accomplished by it in Judah's plight. Our position is simply this: we note the historical background of each prophecy and relate the setting to the message; when the prophecy cannot thus be accounted for by an immediate reference, then a future fulfillment is to be sought for.

As to the interpretation of Zechariah specifically, many have been the complaints as to its obscurity. Hengstenberg quotes the Jewish commentator, Abarbanel, as saying, "The prophecies of Zechariah are so obscure that no expositors, however skilled, have 'found their hands' (Psa. 76:5) in the explanations." From Jarchi he gives this word, "The prophecy of Zechariah is very abstruse, for it contains visions resembling dreams, which want interpreting. And we shall never be able to discover the true interpretation until the teacher of righteousness (the Messiah, Joel 2:23) arrives."[1] Although Jerome expressed himself similarly, the difficulty in the minds of the

---

[1] E. W. Hengstenberg, *Christology of the Old Testament*, Vol. III, p. 269.

Jewish rabbis can be traced to a subjective cause; the book is so full of the portrayal of a Messiah, other than they have pictured Him to be.

It is Hengstenberg again who has pointed out the method of a sane interpretation. He calls attention to two aids for the student of the book: "At the same time, it must not be overlooked that, although the obscurities are much greater in Zechariah than in the other prophets on account of the predominance of symbolical and figurative language, yet there are two circumstances which facilitate the interpretation of the prophecies. In the first place, there is no prophetic book in the study of which we can obtain such decisive results, from a careful comparison of parallel passages, as we can in that of Zechariah, who rested so much upon the prophets who had written before him. And, secondly, since he lived after the captivity, his prophecy does not move over nearly so extensive a field as that of his predecessors."[2] Since Zechariah is a prophet of the restoration, much that was future to the pre-exilic prophets is now history for him. Prophecies of future glory cannot be explained as the return from Babylon, for that has already been accomplished. The restriction of the sphere of the vision serves to diminish the chance for error. As for the parallel passages, many have pointed out the evident allusions in the book to the prophecies in Isaiah, Jeremiah, Micah, Hosea, Amos, the Psalms, and Joel.

V. The Importance of the Book

If the prophecy is difficult of interpretation, it has not lost in importance thereby. This portion of the prophetic Scriptures is so important in the realm of revealed truth that Luther called it *Der Ausbund der Propheten,* or, the model, pattern, quintes-

---

[2] *Ibid.,* p. 270.

sence of the prophets. If the prophecy be viewed from one angle alone—that is, its contribution to the field of Messianic prophecy—this statement will be seen to be well substantiated. Zechariah seems to delight to give in concise and epitomized form that which the former prophets set forth concerning the person and work of the Messiah of Israel. He is the Epitomist of Messianic prophecy. Note the fulness of his word. He relates the Messiah to the predictions of Isaiah and Jeremiah by designating Him as the Branch who will remove the iniquity of the land in one day. He is also the Stone upon whom there are wondrous engravings conducive to its beauty. In a later prophecy Zechariah foretells that the Branch will sit as priest upon His throne, combining in Himself the sacerdotal and regal offices; and will build the temple of Jehovah, in which the Gentiles will have their part.

In the first prophecy of the latter part of the book, Messiah is seen coming as King, in lowliness yet endowed with salvation, to speak peace to the nations and to extend His kingdom universally. The prophet foresees the Shepherd ministry of the Messiah, the ingratitude of His people for His service, the severing of relations with them, their contemptuous estimation of His worth at thirty pieces of silver, His deliverance of them into the hands of a foolish shepherd. In the twelfth chapter Messiah is seen returning to penitent Israel who look upon Him whom they have pierced, mourning the great tragedy of their national history in rejecting Him. Immediately the forgiveness and cleansing of Israel are accomplished by the fountain opened long since potentially, but now actually, for them. The last prophecy but one reveals the Father smiting His Equal, the Son, and scattering the sheep. The concluding Messianic prophecy predicts the coming of the Messiah to the Mount of Olives for the rescue of His surrounded and beleaguered people in Jerusalem,

this appearance being followed by the consummation wherein
Jehovah shall be King over all the earth. Where else in all the
range of prophetic revelation can we find such abundant detail
concerning Messianic truth in such small compass as here?
But that is not all. Our prophet has much to say of the
important Day of Jehovah. The return of a portion of Israel
to their land in unbelief; their passing through the furnace of
affliction in the days of great tribulation; the siege of Jerusalem
by the great confederated Gentile powers in the last days; the
distress of Israel and their returning to the Messiah; their deliverance through the visible appearance of their King Messiah; the
fulfillment by Israel of God's intended mission for them wherein
they are a kingdom of priests and a holy nation, leading the
peoples of the earth to the knowledge and worship of God—
these events are all clearly predicted by the prophet through the
Spirit, who knoweth the end from the beginning. We can do
no better than to conclude with the statement with which
Hengstenberg begins his comments on the prophet Zechariah:
"The Messianic prophecies of Zechariah are only second to those
of Isaiah in distinctness and importance. In this, the last prophet
but one, the prophetic gift once more unfolded all its glory, as a
proof that it did not sink from the exhaustion of age, but was
withdrawn according to the deliberate counsel of the Lord."[3]

VI. The Critical Question

The critical question with reference to the book is an interesting, important, and lively one. It is only second in importance,
possibly, to the critical attack on the Mosaic authorship of the
Pentateuch, the authorship of chapters 40-66 of Isaiah, the
Danielic authorship of the book bearing his name, and the question of the alleged priority of Ezekiel to the Priestly Code. To

---

[3]E. W. Hengstenberg, *op. cit.*, p. 264.

enter into all the ramifications of this vital and fascinating problem is wholly without the range of our. purpose in this introduction to the book. Those who are interested can find ample material to satisfy them. [4] The critics deny that chapters 9-14 are Zecharian; conservative scholars defend the Zecharian authorship of the whole. Among the former are Eichhorn, Vatke, Gesenius, Driver, Knobel, and many others; among the latter are Hengstenberg, DeWette (in the first three editions of his *Einleitung* he took the critical position, but in the fourth came back to the traditional view), Keil, Kliefoth, Pusey, and many others.

Those who reject the traditional authorship of the last six chapters are again divided into two distinct camps: those who hold to a pre-exilic date, and those who maintain a post-Zecharian date. The critics differ on the date, some assigning it to the time of Uzziah, Jotham, Ahaz, or Hezekiah; while others contend for the time of Alexander the Great, or Antiochus Epiphanes. We heartily agree with Pusey in his pronouncement upon the critical dilemma: "Criticism which reels to and fro in a period of near 500 years, from the earliest of the prophets to a period, a century after Malachi, and this on historical and philological grounds, certainly has come to no definite basis, either as to history or philology. Rather, it has enslaved both to preconceived opinions." [5]

The critical position rests on several arguments of which we chose the three most weighty: (1) the reference in Matthew

[4] Able treatments of the subject can be found in D. Baron, *The Visions and Prophecies of Zechariah*, pp. 261-282; E. B. Pusey, *Minor Prophets*, Vol. II, pp. 327-338; Lange, *Commentary on Zechariah*, pp. 11-16. For a competent discussion of the critical position, see S. R. Driver, *Introduction to the Literature of the Old Testament*, pp. 344-355. See also pp. 117 and 154 below.

[5] *Op. cit.*, p. 329.

27:9, 10 which assigns Zechariah 11:12 to Jeremiah; (2) the contrast in style between the two parts of the prophecy (chapters 1-8 and 9-14); (3) the subject matter of the respective parts. Not only can these arguments be met, but additional proof can be brought forward to show the unity of authorship of the prophecy. As for the first argument, the Talmud specifically states (*Baba Bathra*) that Jeremiah was arranged by the Jews in their canon as the first of the prophets. In this way Jeremiah lent his name to all the prophetic books, and Matthew so treats it. The contrast in style can be explained by the difference of subject under discussion. This argument holds good for the Pentateuch, the book of Isaiah, and other attacked books of the Old Testament, as Dr. Melvin Grove Kyle, the eminent archaeologist, demonstrated many times. The difficulty with regard to the subject matter can be traced to the critical animus to predictive prophecy. With them this is ruled out beforehand as an impossibility, because it is supernatural. Prophecy is relegated to the place of history written *post eventum*. If Zechariah mentions Greece, and he assuredly does in 9:13, then the prophet is not speaking predictively of the future conquests of the Greeks under Alexander the Great; but he must, of necessity and from the very nature of the case, be writing in the time of Alexander, chronicling his victories around the land of Palestine. So say the critics. We maintain it is impossible to confine or restrict the Spirit of God in His revelatory purposes. If He cares to predict an event three centuries off, He is sovereign; and if it pleases Him to foretell the plan of God a millennium before its materialization, He is just as sovereign. We emphasize this because we believe it to be the *sine qua non* of reverent, acceptable interpretation of Biblical prophecy.

But we have suggested that there are lines of evidence that definitely point to the unity of the book. We turn to this briefly. Our

Lord Jesus received all The Twelve as the Scripture of God,
and from Josephus and others we know the book of Zechariah
was included just as we have it. Both parts of the book show a
considerable knowledge of the writings of the pre-exilic prophets. Both divisions contain the expression *me'obher umish-
shabh* (7:14; 9:8), which occurs besides only in Ezekiel 35:7, and
there it is not the identical construction. In both sections of the
book the Messiah is referred to as the King of Israel whose coming brings final rejoicing to His people. Throughout the book
the whole nation is referred to in its specific parts. (Cf. 2:2; 8:13
[in the Hebrew, for the two versions divide differently] with
9:10, 13; 10:6; 11:14.) In both portions God's earthly, temporal
gifts are offered to Israel for obedience (8:12; 10:1) together
with promises of the overthrow and utter annihilation of Israel's
foes (2:4 [Hebrew]; 14:12; *et al.*). The untenableness of the
critical view and the definite testimony for the unity of the book
bring us to the inexorable conclusion that the prophecy is post-
exilic, and by Zechariah and none other.

VII. The Plan of the Prophecy

The contents of the book may be summarized as: (1) eight
night-visions (including the introduction and the closing symbolical act), chapters 1-6; (2) two answers, chapters 7 and 8;
(3) two burdens, chapters 9-14. Most students of the prophecy
divide it into four divisions. After an introductory admonition
to return to the Lord (1:1-6), the prophet relates his eight
night-visions seen in one night, concluding with a symbolical
act and its prophetic import (1:7-6:15). In reply to the question
put by the deputation from Bethel relative to the continuance
of the fasts, Zechariah answers both negatively and positively
(7 and 8). At a later time the prophet delivers two burdens
from his ideal (not actual) standpoint of the victories of Alex-

ander, bringing us up to the consummation of all things prophetic, the dispensation of the fullness of the times (9-14). In
the night-visions it is necessary to remember that although the
prophet begins from his actual standpoint (the time of the
restoration from Babylonian Captivity), he goes on to the very
end of God's dealings with Israel and the Gentiles. The main
objective of the prophet throughout the visions and burdens,
and indeed even in the answers to the questions about fasts,
is to console and comfort weary and worn Israel. May God
by His blessed Spirit give us full and satisfying insight into
this rich portion of His incomparable Word.

PART ONE

CHAPTER I

AN EXHORTATION TO REPENTANCE
(1:1-6)

THE FIRST six verses of the book are an introduction, not only to the first chapter or the series of eight night-visions, but to the entire prophecy of Zechariah. The gist of the message is: do not repeat the disobediences of your fathers, but rather learn from past experience. Is not this the burden of the Apostle Paul's recital of the disobediences of Israel in the wilderness as recorded in I Corinthians 10? He says plainly: "Now these things happened unto them by way of example; and they were written for our admonition, upon whom the ends of the ages are come" (v. 11). Especially is this true in the study of the remnant in Israel of the restoration period, because they so often portray morally the position of believers now awaiting the return of the Lord.[1]

Since the book is mainly one of consolations and hope, some may be inclined to ask: Why does it begin with a charge to repent? The purpose, no doubt, is to preclude any false security on the part of the ungodly in Israel who might think themselves to be the recipients of the blessings and promises of God regardless of their spiritual condition. To the superficial student of Old Testament prophecy the transitions of the prophets—often quite abrupt—from promises of blessings to threats of judgment and *vice versa,* these changes, I say, strike them as

---

[1] E. Dennett, *Zechariah The Prophet,* p. 3.

15

unnecessary and uncalled for. Divine wisdom, however, is here, for while the prophet pours out condemnation and warning of judgment, he takes care lest the godly be overcharged with misgivings and despair. So he passes on to the prediction of future blessings for the godly. On the other hand, while delineating the surpassing glories of the future, he is diligent to give the ungodly no ground for baseless and false security, so he warns of the righteous judgment of God upon the wicked. The understanding of this great principle will aid, not only in the interpretation of the introduction and entire message of this prophecy, but of all the revelation of the prophets.

Zechariah's first word places his prophecy as to time and assures of its divine origin: "In the eighth month, in the second year of Darius, the word of Jehovah came to Zechariah the son of Berechiah, the son of Iddo, the prophet, saying" (v. 1). By a comparison of this verse with Haggai 1:1 it will be seen that Zechariah uttered this prophecy two months after Haggai began his ministry to the remnant. The date here given is most significant, for it serves to the discerning student more than a mere chronological notation. If the books of the Old Testament prophets be compared, it becomes immediately evident that those who date their prophecies (and not all do so) invariably do so according to the reign of a king in Israel or Judah or both. To this rule (holding good even for the exilic prophet Daniel, who, though classed with the Hagiographa in the Hebrew canon, deserves a place among the prophets, which our Lord accorded him in Matthew 24:15) there are but two exceptions—Haggai and Zechariah. Their prophecies are dated according to the reign of the Gentile monarch, Darius Hystaspes. Why? Words could express no more clearly the actuality and the reality of the truth that the times of the Gentiles were then in progress as they are to this very day. Israel has been shorn of her glorious dynasty, but not forever. For the times of the Gentiles run from the reign of Nebuchadnezzar, called king of kings (Dan. 2:37), to the reign of the Lord Jesus Christ, the King of kings and the Lord of lords (Rev. 19:16). Cf. Luke 21:24. As for the names of the prophet, his father, and his grandfather, there is precious truth here as has been noted by many others. We can find warrant in the Word for such procedure for the Spirit Himself unfolds truth from the name of Melchizedek (Heb. 7:1, 2). The names together signify that Jehovah remembers, and He will bless at the set time, a message which contains in germ the theme of the book.

The prophet's word from the Lord is both solemn and sobering: "Angry was Jehovah at your fathers with [great] anger" (v. 2). The verse begins with the verb *qatsaph* and ends with its cognate noun *qetseph,* the position of both being for emphasis. The LXX adds the words *'orgen megalen.* The Hebrew word in its root sense appears originally to have meant breaking out in long-controlled indignation. "It expresses vehement displeasure, almost to the extent of abhorrence."[2] Confirmation of this pronouncement can be seen in the magnitude of God's wrath: their pleasant land desolated, the holy places desecrated and defiled, the enslavement of the very choicest of the people of the land, and the cessation of all Levitical ministrations. The words *qatsaphti me'at* of verse 15 ("I was angry but a little") of this chapter do not contradict this verse. Verse 2 reveals the intensity of the wrath, while verse 15 points to its duration ("but a little while"). How can those who cannot bear to think of a God of love having indignation and wrath explain this concise and pointed declaration? If God were the God of love and nothing more, then it were beside the point to speak of our God as a consuming fire (Heb. 12:29); yea, more, then the

---

[2] D. Baron, *The Visions and Prophecies of Zechariah,* p. 10.

whole plan of redemption were unnecessary and unwarranted. Israel must know of the severity of God's wrath, so the prophet clearly stirs up their minds by way of remembrance.

Note that the prophet does not dwell on the Lord's displeasure against Israel, but goes on from that to speak of His tender love in the form of an invitation: "And thou shalt say unto them, Thus saith Jehovah of hosts, Return unto me, saith Jehovah of hosts, and I will return unto you, saith Jehovah of hosts" (v. 3). The prominence of the name of Jehovah throughout the book is remarkable (8 times in 1:1-6). In this verse we find it three times, lending authentication and authority to the words of invitation. The word *shubh* is comparable to the New Testament *metanoeo* and there is more in mind than just the building of the temple. True, the nation had returned to God in a measure, but there was necessity for a more complete turning unto God. We are reminded that for the child of God in this time the exhortation of the Spirit is: "Draw nigh to God, and he will draw nigh to you" (Jas. 4:8). Positionally, we have been made nigh (Eph. 2:13), but experientially we need to be ever more near. With us, as with them, there is first the exhortation, then the expectation or the promise. This call to return dare not be passed over lightly, for it is the basic and fundamental plea of God throughout the Bible to all sinful men. Zechariah, then, like John the Baptist and our blessed Lord Himself at a later day, comes with the message: *Repent.*

Since there was danger that with Israel then as with their fathers formerly, this gracious invitation would go unheeded, Zechariah warned: "Be ye not as your fathers unto whom the former prophets cried, saying, Thus saith Jehovah of hosts, Return ye, I pray, from your evil ways and from your evil deeds; but they did not hear nor did they give heed to me, saith Jehovah" (v. 4). Evil example is always strangely infectious (Mic.

6:16; Psa. 78:57). In the short compass of about two dozen
words we have the gist of all the messages of the pre-exilic
prophets, *hannebhi'im hari'shonim.* They were essentially preach-
ers of righteousness, and these words characterize their prophecies. To be sure, these words do not sum up all that these
men of God said. One of the many such instances will suffice:
"Say unto them, as I live, saith the Lord Jehovah, I desire not the
death of the wicked, but that the wicked return from his way
and live; return, return from your evil ways, for why will ye die,
O house of Israel?" (Ezek. 33:11; see also particularly Jer. 3:6-4:4;
7:3, 5; 18:11; 26:13). The summary of Israelitish pre-exilic history is to be found in II Kings 17:7-23; that of the Judean, in
II Chronicles 36:14-16. Zechariah, more succinctly still, says, "and
they did not hear nor give heed to me." *'Elay* (to me) shows
that it was not a matter of refusing to hear the words of the
prophets, as though they spoke from themselves, but Israel did
not hearken to God, hence the gravity of the offense.

Whereas verse 4 sets forth the message of the prophets and
the reaction of Israel to it, the next verses reveal the consequences of the disobedience of God's people. In order to bring
the full force of God's dealings home to them, the prophet
couches his next words in two pointed questions :"Your fathers,
where are they? and the prophets, do they live for ever?" (v. 5).
The first question in its abruptness seems to point to an abrupt
and unexpected close to the lives of their fathers. The fullness
of expression *'ayyeh hem*—only here for the invariable *'ayyam*—
serves to lend emphasis to the question. Some cannot see the
force of the second question, if it be considered as the prophet's.
They maintain it is the controversial reply of the people. Rabbi
David Kimchi in his valuable commentary on this prophecy says:
"Our Rabbis, of blessed memory have interpreted (in the Talm.
Bab. *Sanhedrin,* fol. 105, 1) the words, 'The prophets, where

are they,' as the answer of the people. They say that the congregation of Israel gave a controversial reply to the prophet. He
said to them, Return in true repentance, for your fathers sinned,
and where are they? The people answered him, And the prophets who did not sin, where are they? But they afterwards repented and made confession to him."[3] Some modern commentators, like Keil, have taken this view also. On the basis of the
strong disjunctive conjunction, *'akh* of the next verse, we see
no need to infer that the people answered the prophet by a question. Rather, the constructions are best cared for when the two
questions of verse 5 are placed in sharpest contrast to the ir-
refutable conclusion contained in verse 6. The weight of the
prophet's statements, then, is this: "Your fathers and the prophets are alike gone, but the testimony your fathers bore to the
truth of the prophets' warnings remains. You have not the same
warnings ringing in your ears that your fathers had; you have
not men like Jeremiah to move you to godliness; the prophets
did not live for ever. But you have what your fathers had not;
you have the awful truthfulness of God's words of warning
written in your fathers' fate."

The final word of the introduction is: "Nevertheless, my
words and my statutes, which I commanded my servants the
prophets, did they not overtake your fathers? and they returned
and said, As Jehovah of hosts purposed to do to us, according
to our ways and according to our deeds, so hath he done with
[to] us" (v. 6). The *debharay* and *huqqay* are the threatened
punishments and decrees of God uttered by the prophets (cf.
Zeph. 2:2; Psa. 2:7). God's Word is more lasting than any messenger of His who bears it and gives it utterance. The *take hold*
of the Authorized Version is quite colorless for *hissighu* which

---

[3]Translated by Rev. A. M'Caul (1837), p. 2.

conveys the thought of the words and the statutes of God as a dogged and relentless pursuer of the wicked. It is the same word used by Moses in Deuteronomy 28:15, 45 in speaking of the curses to come upon Israel in their disobedience. God's Word accomplishes all God desires and is successful in that whereunto it is sent, not only in the case of blessing (where Isaiah 55:10, 11 is almost exclusively applied by all too many), but in the matter of punishment also. The fulfillments of the threatenings were so patent that Israel had to admit after consideration that God's Word was true, even though it was to their own discomfiture. Proof that the fathers recognized the Lord's hand in their judgment can be found in Lamentations 2:17 (same construction with *zamam*—purposed—as here); Daniel 9:4 ff.; Ezra 9:6 ff.

By way of summary, we may note that Zechariah enumerates in his introductory address five great principles: (1) The condition of all God's blessings, verse 3. (2) The evil and peril of disobedience, verse 4. (3) The unchangeable character of God's Word, verse 6a. (4) God's governmental dealings with His people in accordance with their deeds, verse 6b ("according to our ways and according to our deeds"). (5) God's immutable purposes, verse 6b ("as Jehovah . . . determined . . . so did he with us").

Prophecy presupposes sin, failure, and God's judgment, but our God is not content to rest there. He causes the evil to be overruled for lasting good. We do well to bear in mind that Zechariah is the prophet, as Peter is the apostle, of hope.

PART TWO

CHAPTER I

THE PROPHET'S NIGHT VISIONS
(1:7-6:15)

I. The Vision of the Horses, 1:7-17

AFTER THE prophet's introductory admonition to his people, he turns immediately to a setting forth of a series of night-visions granted him some months after his first prophecy. "In the twenty-fourth day of the eleventh month, which is the month Shebat, in the second year of Darius, the word of Jehovah came to Zechariah the son of Berechiah, the son of Iddo, the prophet, saying" (v. 7). The date is more fully given here than in verse 1 which notes the call of Zechariah to the prophetic office. Here the day, three months after the first prophecy and five months after work on the temple had been resumed (Hag. 1:14, 15), is designated because of its significance and associations, evidently a day in which God had pleasure because of the obedience of His people.

But more important than the date are the visions that came to the prophet at that time. In verses 8-13 the vision is given; in verses 14-17 the explanation is presented. "I saw in the night and behold a man riding on a red horse, and he was standing among the myrtles which were in the deep place; and after him there were horses, red, sorrel, and white" (v. 8). The prophet saw his apocalyptic visions in an ecstatic condition, not in a dream, in which case we should expect *halamti* instead of *ra'ithi*. Such was the state of Peter when on the housetop of

25

the home of Simon the tanner at Joppa. (Cf. Acts 10:10; 11:5—
the word translated *trance* is the Greek *'ekstasis*). Chambers describes this phenomenon well, saying, "A man's usual state when
under the control of the senses and able to see only what his
own faculties discover, is one of spiritual sleep; but an ecstatic
condition, in which the senses and the entire lower life are
quiescent, and only pictures of divine objects are reflected in the
soul as in a pure and bright mirror, is one of spiritual waking."[1]
When the prophet informs us that he saw his vision in the night,
his intention is to convey that all these visions (1:7-6:15) were
seen in one night, in all probability to give a connected view of
the history of Israel.

The man on the red horse was an angel in the appearance
of a man. The other horses, to be sure, had riders also. The
horses speak of divine agencies in the government of the affairs
of the earth. In this case the special reference is to their operation among the nations of the earth apart from Israel. Who is
the rider on the red horse? Jerome says, "The Jews suppose the
man on the red horse to be the Angel Michael, who was to
avenge the iniquities and sins against Israel." Students of the
passage can be arranged on one of two principal sides: those who
maintain that he is an ordinary angel as the other riders, and
those who hold him to be the Angel of Jehovah. We take our
stand with the latter, finding clear proof and confirmation in
verse 11. There the man among the myrtles is definitely stated
to be the Angel of Jehovah. The other riders report to Him
their findings in a manner that reveals His authority over them
and His separate position from them.

---

[1] Lange's Commentary, Minor Prophets, *Book of Zechariah*, p. 25.
Compare, however, for a contrary position D. Riehm, *Messianic Prophecy*, pp. 14-31.

The place of His standing is important: among the myrtles which were in the deep place. The myrtle (*hadhas* from which the name of Esther, *hadhassah,* is derived) was a lovely, ornamental, and fragrant plant, native to Persia and Assyria. These trees were in the low place. There has been much discussion as to whether *metsulah* means a shady place or a deep place. The Vulgate (with many authorities agreeing) favors the latter meaning (as do we), translating it *in profundo.* Von Orelli is of the opinion that the word "applies to a locality in the immediate neighborhood of the temple, then known under this name, one of the ravines at the foot of the temple-hill."[2] Baron, in his work on the prophet, refers it to the great Gentile world-power at that time, namely, Persia. Some take the deep place or valley to refer to Babylon. No such specific designation need be assumed. The myrtle because of its fragrance and lowliness typifies and symbolizes Israel; the deep place speaks of her degradation. Is it not exceedingly interesting to note that although God had taken sovereignty from the hands of Israel and placed it in the hands of the Gentile powers, yet is the Angel of Jehovah not seen among the Gentile monarchies or nations, but in the midst of lowly Israel? This love of God for them is their portion even to this hour. (Cf. Lev. 26:44; Jer. 30:11.)

Can we attach any significance to the colors of the horses? Wright feels assured that "Any attempt . . . to assign any grounds for the employment of the special colours is in our opinion futile."[3] Yet in his footnote on the next page, he states that the position that the colors have no symbolical meaning whatever "is somewhat doubtful." Practically all commentators have seen significance in the colors. The colors are important, but can have no reference to the lands that the riders traversed (why, then,

---

[2] *The Twelve Minor Prophets,* p. 313.
[3] *Zechariah and His Prophecies,* p. 19.

just three colors?), nor to the succession of empires foretold by
Daniel (in that case four would be expected instead of three),
nor to the points of the compass (for the same reason as given
for the empires). The colors undoubtedly point to the work
which the riders had to accomplish. The first horses were
red, which speaks of blood, judgment, and vengeance (cf. Isa.
63:1, 2). The horse of the man among the myrtles is of this color,
because such is his attitude toward the nations of the earth. The
second horses are designated as *seruqim*. The interpretation of
this word is admittedly difficult, and the meaning has been dis-
puted from earliest times. Keil gives us the different renderings
of the versions.[4] The LXX has rendered it *psaroi kai poikiloi;*
the Itala and Vulgate, *varii;* the Peshito, *versicolores.* Possibly
what is meant is a mixture of the other two colors. The white
horses symbolize victory, triumph, and glory (cf. Rev. 19:11).
These providential agencies, then, portrayed the mission of vengeance and victory with reference to God's plans for His people,
Israel.

The prophet, however, did not readily comprehend the import of the vision. He says, "And I said, What are these, my
lord? And the angel that spake with me said, I will show thee
what these are" (v. 9). Zechariah inquired not who, but what
these horses were; that is, what do they mean? The question
is addressed to the angel who spake with him. He is not the
same as the Angel of Jehovah, for he is not given the honor
that the latter is accorded, nor is he addressed with the same title.
This angel is the *angelus interpres,* or interpreting angel.[5] He is
mentioned eleven times in this book; (cf. 1:9, 13, 14; 2:2, 7 [in
the Hebrew]; 4:1, 4, 5; 5:5, 10; 6:4). The office of the inter-

---

[4] *The Twelve Minor Prophets,* Vol. II, p. 231.

[5] For arguments why the interpreter is not the Angel of Jehovah, see
Hengstenberg, *Christology of the Old Testament,* Vol. III, pp. 274-275.

preting angel was to bring instructions to the prophet and to explain to him the meaning of the visions. The presence of this angel implies distance in the revelation of God's will to the prophet, seeing it must come through a third party. The fact that the angel has not been mentioned before he is addressed need not confuse us, for in visions persons are frequently introduced as acting or speaking before it is noted who they are. Pusey holds that *haddobher bi* "seems meant to convey the thought of an inward speaking, whereby the words should be borne directly into the soul, without the intervention of the ordinary outward organs."[6] For this speaking of God or an angel within a man we can be referred to Numbers 12:6, 8; Hosea 1:2; Habakkuk 2:1.

The question asked of the interpreting angel by the prophet is answered by the man among the myrtles: "And the man who was standing among the myrtles answered and said, These are they whom Jehovah has sent to walk to and fro in the earth" (v. 10). To these angelic riders governmental and supervisory powers are committed. *Hithhallekh* with its force of continuance and progression conveys the thought of exploring and reconnoitering. Just as Satan, the adversary, traverses the whole earth for evil, so God has His emissaries for His own purposes. (Cf. Job 2:2, same infinitive-construct form as the verse before us; I Pet. 5:8.)

The report of the angels follows immediately in answer to the unexpressed word of inquiry from the Angel of Jehovah: "And they answered the angel of Jehovah who stood among the myrtles, and they said, We have walked to and fro in the earth, and behold, all the earth sits and is at rest" (v. 11). This Angel of Jehovah is none other than the preincarnate Christ. The ablest presentation of this view, especially with reference to the rabbini-

---

[6] *The Minor Prophets*, Vol. II, p. 342.

cal Jewish interpretation and its refutation, is to be found in
M'Caul's translation of Kimchi's *Commentary on Zechariah* at
the end of the first chapter. Because of the excellent and pertinent character of the arguments, and because the book is now
out of print (dated 1837), we are much tempted to reproduce
the whole weighty argument. But other considerations make
this prohibitive. For the benefit of the reader, therefore, we give
as clear a summary of the material as we can. In the course of
his comments on Zechariah's first chapter, Kimchi (a noted rabbi
of France in the twelfth century, of an illustrious father who
with him was distinguished for studies in Hebrew grammar and
lexicography) takes the position that the angel in verses 8, 11,
and 12 of our chapter was one of the many angels to whom
the government of the world was entrusted.

M'Caul, who translates the commentary from Hebrew, knowing the non-Christian bias of the interpretations of Kimchi, takes
issue with this interpretation. We present his arguments. The
word *mal'akh* has the original meaning of messenger, without
reference to the character, position, or nature of the individual.
It is applied to men as well as heavenly beings (cf. Gen. 32:2,
4). Can the words *mal'akh Yhwh* be translated "The Angel
Jehovah,"   some Christians have attempted to do? The words
cannot be in apposition, because we should then be compelled
to translate it, "an angel, Jehovah." If the word for "angel" were
not in the construct then the article *h* would be surely required.
The Jews, on the other hand, seek to translate it, "an angel of
Jehovah." They argue that the word for "angel" does not have
the definite article. The rule is, however, clear that nouns in
the construct do not take the article with proper nouns, but
are already made definite, as *beth Yhwh,* "the house of Jehovah,"
and not "a house of Jehovah." The proper noun itself (Jehovah)
cannot and never does take the article. How, then, could the

expression be made definitely, "The Angel of Jehovah"? The article could not be placed before *mal'akh* because, as we have seen, it would make the meaning, "The Angel Jehovah." The word *Yhwh* would not allow the article either. "There remained one other course possible, and that was, never to use the expression in the plural of angels, but always in the singular, so as to indicate that one person, and one only, is intended." This has been *uniformly* done throughout the Old Testament. It might be objected that although there is no expression "the angels of Jehovah," there is the usage, "the angels of God." True, but there is a great difference between *'Elohim* and *Yhwh,* for the former admits of the article while the latter does not (cf. Gen. 31:11; Exod. 14:19).

Since there is but one heavenly being called "The Angel of Jehovah," we do well to inquire further wherein this peculiarity lies. The first characteristic of this person is, that He is called by the proper name of God, *Yhwh* (cf. Gen. 16:11, 13). Eminent rabbis pass these verses over in silence, while Abarbanel admits their difficulty. His explanation is, "The right answer here is, that all prophetic vision, whether mediate or immediate, is always attributed to God, blessed be He, for it is from Him and by His will, and on this account also the Messenger is sometimes called by the name of Him that sends him." (Cf. for other examples Judg. 6:11; Zech. 3:2.) The evasion—the messenger is called by the name of Him that sends him—is contrary to fact. In Daniel 8 and 9 an angel is sent to Daniel, but he is still called Gabriel. The angels in Zechariah 1:10 were not called by the name of their Sender. Both Jews and Christians have uniformly held that in the name *Yhwh* there is a peculiarity that differentiates it from all the other names of God (cf. Isa. 42:8; Hos. 12:6). Kimchi himself in commenting on the last passage says, "God of Hosts expresses that degree,

in which stand the angels, and the orbs with their stars, for in
the names *'El* and *'Elohim,* He [God] is associated with them;
but in this name He is associated with none but himself." Such
is the expressed opinion and position of the Talmud, Kosri,
and Maimonides. On this evidence M'Caul thus concludes this
phase of the question, "The author of the Kosri and Maimonides
were controversialists, and had the Christian controversy constantly in view, their testimony is, therefore, doubly valuable;
and when we combine the admissions of opponents with the
plain words of Scripture, there can be no doubt of these two
things, first, that the name Jehovah is the peculiar name of
God; and, secondly, that God has claimed it for himself, because it has reference to that substance and essence peculiar to
himself. Why, then, is it communicated to the angel of the
Lord? There can be but one answer: because He partakes of
that substance and essence which makes the communication of
the name suitable; or, in other words, because the angel of the
Lord is very God."

A second characteristic of the Scriptural portrayal of His
character is that He is presented as having the divine nature,
as being the God of Abraham, Isaac, and Jacob. For proof see
Genesis 31:13 where He is the object of worship. When the
law of Moses sets forth one as the God of Bethel and the object
of Jacob's worship, the only conclusion possible is that He is
very God, for the purpose of the law was to enforce the unity
of God (cf. Exod. 3:4-6 also). The conclusions, then, are
simple: that there is only one being called The Angel of Jehovah;
that his name is Jehovah, the incommunicable name of God;
that He is the one whom Jacob worshipped as God. The Angel
of Jehovah is God.[7]

---

[7] For entire discussion, see D. Kimchi, *Commentary on Zechariah,*
trans. by A. M'Caul, pp. 9-27.

In our passage under consideration in Zechariah we saw this Angel of Jehovah receiving the report of the angelic messengers. Their observation is concise and important. They all found the world at peace and at rest, unlike its usual condition of war and strife. *Shaqat* is the verb used repeatedly in the book of Judges to express the peaceful interims enjoyed by the land after its recurring subjections to foreign powers and the attendant revolts to throw off the yoke of the oppressors (cf. Judg. 3:11, 30; 5:31; 8:28). The word rarely, if ever, has a moral significance. The condition which the angels report is known to be that which prevailed in the second year of Darius' reign. It reveals the condition of Israel to be all the more distressing because of the contrast. Let her full plight come before us: the rest promised upon return from Babylon yet unfulfilled; Israel under the yoke of the Gentile powers; hindrances in building the temple; the holy city without walls; the desolation of Jerusalem; the promise of God for the shaking of the kingdoms of the world and yet their peaceful security (Neh. 1:3; 2:3; 7:4; 9:36; Hag. 2:7, 22).

Was God pleased, think you, with this state of affairs? Let the prophet speak God's mind: "Then the angel of Jehovah answered and said, O Jehovah of hosts, how long wilt thou not have mercy upon Jerusalem and the cities of Judah, against which thou hast been angry these seventy years?" (v. 12). The contrast between Israel and the nations of the earth is the occasion for the intercession now before us. Just as in the seventeenth of John we have afforded us an insight into the intercessory ministry of the Lord for His own now, so here we witness the intercessory ministry of our Lord in the Old Testament. Keil's words are eminently true, "The circumstance that the angel of Jehovah addresses an intercessory prayer to Jehovah on behalf of Judah, is no more a disproof of his essential

unity with Jehovah, than the intercessory prayer of Christ in
John 17 is a disproof of His divinity."[8] Wherever we meet
the cry, "How long?" it speaks of faith, expectation, and
wholehearted sympathy and longing. It was the cry of Isaiah
when God outlined to him the hardening effect of his ministry
upon Israel (Isa. 6:11). It was the expression of David's heart
in the first of the seven penitential psalms (Psa. 6:3). Calvin
often used these words in Latin, *Domine quousque?* when in
pain and suffering; it is said of him that the most exquisite
pain could elicit from him no other word. The Angel of Jehovah
is not speaking here as though the remnant had not returned
from Babylonian Captivity. They had, but their condition revealed the chastening hand of God that had been heavy upon
them (Jer. 25:11, 12; 29:10). While the nations were occupied
with their own selfish interests, God was concerned for the welfare of Jerusalem. The angel pleaded on the basis of God's promise to Jeremiah. So had Daniel (Dan. 9:1, 2). It is always blessed
to pray in conformity with God's thoughts for His people.

The prayer of intercession does not go unanswered, for we
are immediately told the outcome: "And Jehovah answered
the angel that spake with me with good words, comforting
words" (v. 13). The answer is given directly to the interpreting
angel instead of the Angel of Jehovah, because He had asked
it for the sake of the people to whom it was thus being transmitted. Others, however, believe the implication valid that it
was through the Angel of Jehovah to the interpreting angel.
The good words are those that promise good, and the comforting
words are those full of consolation (*nihummim,* a noun in
apposition, the plural expressing abstract ideas or qualities).
The good and comforting words, set before us in verses 14-17,
are threefold: (1) God still loves Jerusalem; (2) He is exceed-

---

[8] *Op. cit.,* Vol. II, p. 235.

ingly angry with the nations that afflicted Israel; (3) He has
purposes of glory, prosperity, and enlargement for Jerusalem.

These comforting words were not meant for the prophet
alone, so we read: "So the angel that spake with me said, Cry,
saying, Thus saith Jehovah of hosts, I am jealous for Jerusalem
and for Zion with a great jealousy" (v. 14). Here we have a
declaration of God's unfailing love for Israel. *Qinne'thi* is in
the perfect and conveys the force that God has been jealous for
His people even though He has not appeared to manifest it.
The intensity of that love and jealousy can be seen from the
root of the verb in the intensive (Piel) stem, meaning *to burn,
to glow,* as well as the emphasis added by the cognate accusative,
a great jealousy.

But the prophet gives the other side of the picture also:
"But with great anger am I angry at the nations at ease, because I was angry but a little, and they helped for evil" (v. 15).
There is a vivid contrast between this verse and the preceding
one, as much as to say that the anger of God against the oppressors of Israel is in direct proportion to His love for His people.
The prophet seeks to emphasize the anger, so he places the
words *great anger* at the beginning of the verse. That God's
wrath and indignation are lasting is seen from the usage of
qatsaph, the participle expressing the lasting and continuous
character of God's attitude. *Hashsha'anannim* expresses a
state of carnal, unfeeling, careless security. When used of persons, it always is in a bad sense (II Kings 19:28). Historically,
the city of Babylon itself had quickly recovered from the
devastations inflicted by Cyrus in the capture of the city. The
city was prosperous and flourishing, though subjected to the
Persian domination. God was angry for a little (while), but
the nations took their revenge. They helped with evil purpose
to exterminate them. God meant a moderate punishment, but

the Babylonians and others revelled in the sufferings of Israel
with delight in prolonging them. Babylon, like Assyria, was
the rod of God's wrath, but their own hearts designed evil
against Israel (Isa. 10:5, 7). Note it as an unfailing Scriptural
principle: God's relations to Israel are one thing and the relations
of the nations to Israel are another. God is never pleased
with the meddling of strangers in His relations with Israel
(Isa. 47:6). It is as though a father were chastening a child,
and a stranger began to punish with an iron rod. Some take
refuge in the plea that God has predicted these things beforehand. True, but the prediction of the sufferings of Christ and
of His betrayal at the hands of His own familiar friend mitigated
not one whit the crime of the Romans and Israel or that of
Judas Iscariot.

The passage continues with the promises of blessing for
Israel: "Therefore thus saith Jehovah, I will return to Jerusalem
with mercy; my house shall be built in it, saith Jehovah of
hosts; and a line shall be stretched over Jerusalem" (v. 16).
In this same vein he concludes: "Cry again, saying, Thus saith
Jehovah of hosts, My cities shall again overflow with good, and
Jehovah will again comfort Zion, and will again choose Jerusalem" (v. 17). *Lakhen* bears the thought that because God is
jealous for Israel and angry with the nations, the following
promises will be realized. The return of the presence of God
is predicted; the building of the temple in Jerusalem; the rebuilding of the city of Jerusalem; the prosperity of Israel's (here
called God's) cities; the comforting of Zion; the choosing of
Jerusalem. In verse 16 *rahamim* (only in the plural, and more
forceful and truer to the original when translated by the singular
in English, *mercy*) is the answer to the prayer of the Angel of
Jehovah in verse 12 (*therahem*, v. 12, being from the same root).
The stretching of the line over the city had meant its destruction

before (II Kings 21:13), but here it is the measuring line of the builders of the city. *Tephutsennah* usually denotes the scattering caused by an invading enemy; here it is the overflow that results from the pressure of abundant growth. The choosing of Jerusalem is not equivalent to the first choice of God in Abraham's or in David's time, but reference is made to the actual exhibition of this choice in the renewed favor of God upon them.

Where shall we seek for the fulfillment of these things? Wright takes the position that to refer any of this to days yet future, "is opposed to the whole drift of the vision."[9] This depends upon what we conceive to be the drift of the prophecy. If we see in the prophecy a message solely and only for that day, then there is justification for his position. But if God's words can comfort the then present generation and speak for Messianic times to come, as in multiplied numbers of passages, who shall say this is contrary to God's practice? We need not limit the Holy One of Israel. This is not to say that we find no fulfilment in that time. There were such: (1) the revolt of the Babylonians in the reign of Darius Hystaspes which was followed by severe reprisals; (2) the completion of the temple in the sixth year of Darius; and (3) Nehemiah's restoration of the walls. These phases of fufillment afforded comfort to the distressed remnant from Babylon. But this does not exhaust the prophecy; there awaits a fuller fulfillment. "Such double fulfillments of prophecy are not like alternative fulfillments. They are a more intricate and fuller, not an easier fulfillment of it."[10] These prophecies will be completely fulfilled in the return of Israel to her land in Messianic times, a return of which the restoration from Babylonian Captivity was a pledge and promise. Space would forbid the bringing forth of the many passages concerning the

9 *Op. cit.,* p. 26.
10 Pusey, *op. cit.,* p. 343.

Messianic reign which predict the presence of God in mercy in
Jerusalem (Ezek. 48:35); the building of His temple in it
(Ezek. 40-48); the rebuilding of Jerusalem (Jer. 31:38-40);
the prosperity of Judah's cities (Isa. 60:4-9; Zech. 9:17); the
comfort of Zion (Isa. 14:1). The composite picture is without
a doubt Messianic.

The distinctive features of comfort for Israel in this first
vision are: (1) the presence of the Angel of Jehovah in the midst
of degraded and depressed Israel; (2) His loving and yearning
intercession for them; (3) the promises of future blessings. We
may say, then, that the import of the vision is this: although
Israel is not yet in her promised position, God is mindful of her,
providing the means of His judgment on the persecuting
nations, and reserving glory and prosperity for Israel in the
benevolent and beneficent reign of the Messiah.

The series of visions carry us through God's dealings with
Israel from the time of their chastisement by God under the
Gentile powers until they are restored to their land with their
rebuilt city and temple under their Messiah King. The first
vision gives the general theme of the whole series; the others
add the details. How much there is here for meditation for the
believing and obedient heart! Truly, God's thoughts are not ours.
When the world was busy with its own affairs, God's eyes and
the heart of the Messiah were upon the lowly estate of Israel
and upon the temple in Jerusalem. Only the Spirit Himself
can empower us to think God's thoughts after Him. May that
be our ever-blessed experience.

II. THE VISION OF THE HORNS AND SMITHS, 2:1-4 [HEBREW]

Because the second vision of Zechariah is so closely linked
to that which precedes it, the LXX and Jerome add the second
vision to the first chapter. Although the Hebrew text does not

follow this division, it is to be found in the English versions.
Both the second and third visions aim at the consolation promised in 1:13; first, by setting forth the manner in which God
will execute His sore displeasure upon the nations who afflicted
Israel, second, by assuring of the prosperity and enlargement
foretold for Israel.

The prophet continues his series of visions: "And I lifted
up my eyes and I saw, and, behold, four horns" (v. 1). It
appears as though after each vision, the eyes of the prophet were
lowered to meditate upon the import of what he had been
shown. From this meditation he was aroused again and again
by the exhibition of another vision. Here Zechariah sees four
horns. In Scripture the horn is the symbol of power and also
of pride (Amos 6:13; Jer. 48:25; Dan. 8:20, 21). Various explanations have been given as to the identity of the four horns.
We note the two principal ones. Some have suggested that they
are symbolic of Israel's foes in all four points of the compass,
conveying the thought of the universality of the hatred against
the people of God. A large number of students of the passage
refer the horns to the four empires of Daniel 2 and 7. With this
position we agree. The number (four) and the symbol (horn)
surely point back to Daniel's prophecies. The Targum renders
"four horns," "four kingdoms," here as well as in verses 2 and 4.
After this same train of thought, Kimchi comments: "These
are the four monarchies, and they are the Babylonian monarchy,
the Persian monarchy, and the Grecian monarchy; and so the
Targum of Jonathan has it, 'the four monarchies.' "[11] He does
not name the fourth, but notes that each of the horns in its own
time did Israel evil.

There have been several objections to the view espoused
by us. First, it is claimed that the horns are contemporaneous,

---

[11] *Op. cit.*, p. 28.

whereas the position just taken would make them successive. The objection falls down completely when we consider that there were not four powers in open opposition to Judah in the time of Zechariah. Those with whom Judah had to deal at this period were subordinate to the Persian empire. That succession is meant here can be confirmed from the analogy of other prophecies. In visions and predictions events can be seen simultaneously which have their fulfillment in a certain succession. In Daniel 2 the entire image was revealed to Nebuchadnezzar; in Daniel 7 all four beasts are seen together by the prophet. But the empires referred to in both cases arose in succession. This perspective aspect of prophecy is well known by all students of the prophetic Scriptures. For a notable example compare Isaiah 61:1-3 with Luke 4:16-21. Second, it is objected to the view of the four kingdoms that all appear to come to an end by human instrumentality, while Daniel states that the fourth kingdom is brought to nought in another manner. If the vision in Daniel 8 is closely studied the transition there foretold from the Medo-Persian power to the Greco-Macedonian appears wholly dependent upon the work of the latter, but we have the assurance that "the Most High ruleth in the kingdom of men, and giveth it to whomsoever he will" (Dan. 4:32). The same is true here.

Third, Wright objects on the ground that "the vision appears mainly to refer to the past and not to the future."[12] He understands the horns to represent specifically the powers that scattered the northern and southern kingdoms of Israel and Judah, namely, Assyria, Egypt, Babylon, and Medo-Persia. If the argument is based on the form of the verb *zeru,* it cannot stand, because kind of action (*Aktionsart*) and not tense is implied in the Hebrew verbal inflection. The tense ever depends upon the

---

[12] *Op. cit.,* p. 27.

context. Furthermore, the prophetic Scriptures deal definitely
with Israel in her scattered condition during the times of the
Gentiles, though she has suffered much on other occasions. We
have seen even in the first of this series of Zechariah's prophetic
visions that we are carried from the time contemporary with
the prophet to the very consummation of Israel's history. Such
a span accounts for the facts in the second vision also. A fourth
objection to this view is that each of the horns destroyed its
predecessor, whereas the smiths are represented as distinct from
the horns. This is not an insurmountable difficulty, and can be
explained from the symbols employed in the vision.

The prophet is vitally interested in what he has seen and
asks: "And I said to the angel that was speaking to me, What
are these? And he said to me, These are the horns which have
scattered Judah, Israel, and Jerusalem" (v. 2). The verb used
to express the scattering is vivid, denoting to winnow, separate,
or scatter by means of the wind (cf. Isa. 41:16; Jer. 15:7; Ezek.
5:2, 10). The objects of this scourge were Judah, Israel, and
Jerusalem, namely, the southern kingdom, the northern, and the
capital in which both had an interest. No argument (such as
Keil's) can stand on the omission of *'eth,* because it is inserted
and omitted without particular significance. In Deuteronomy
12:6 there are nine direct objects, but only two have *'eth* while
the remaining seven do not. Evidently, the explanation of the
interpreting angel satisfied the desire of the prophet as to the
identity of the horns, so the second phase of the vision is brought
before us. "And Jehovah showed me four smiths" (v. 3). *Hara-
shim* designates a skilled workman in either wood, stone, or
metal. The LXX translates the word as *tektones,* whence the
Authorized Version obtains its "carpenters." From the nature
of the work accorded to them, "smiths" is the better rendering.
Wright, who holds all these events to be past, takes the smiths

to be Nebuchadnezzar, who subdued the power of Assyria;
Cyrus, who broke the might of Babylon; Cambyses, who sub-
jugated Egypt; Alexander, who conquered Persia. Kimchi records a curious rabbinical explanation.[13] Rabbi Simeon Chasida
identified them as the Messiah, the Son of David, the Son of
Joseph, Elijah, and the righteous priest.[14] The four smiths have
been dealt with in our identification of the four horns.

Zechariah does not comprehend the mission of the smiths,
so we read: "Then I said, What are these coming to do? And
he spoke, saying, These are the horns which scattered Judah, so
that a man did not lift up his head; but these have come to
frighten them, to cast down the horns of the nations who lift
up a horn against the land of Judah to scatter it" (v. 4). The
work of the smiths is to terrify and frighten the enemies of
Israel out of their confident rest (compare the *hashsha'anannim*
of 1:15) and trust in themselves. *Kephi* may have added to it
the relative *'asher, so that, according to the measure that,* or *in
such a manner that.* The words *'ish lo' nasa' ro'sho* portray the
utterly prostrate and forsaken condition of Israel after the infliction upon her of the severities of the oppressing nations. The
presumption and hostility of these nations are further brought out
by the statement that they lifted up a horn against the land to
scatter its inhabitants (cf. Psa. 75:5, 6, 11).

Several features are noteworthy in this vision: (1) God takes
account of every one that lifts his hand against Israel; (2) He

---

13 *Op. cit.,* p. 29.

14 The rabbis of Israel, noting the pasages of the Old Testament that
portrayed a suffering Messiah and a ruling Messiah, inferred that God
would send Messiah the Son of Joseph as a forerunner of Messiah the
Son of David, to suffer in order to prepare the way for the rule of the
latter. That the two prophetic aspects of the coming Messiah converge
in one Person is clear from both the Old and New Testaments (see
Zech. 12:10 and Acts 1:11.)

has complete knowledge of the dejected condition of His people
and the extent of their injury; and (3) He has already provided
the punishment for every foe of His chosen ones. As a definite
matter of history three of the empires or kingdoms symbolized
by the horns already knew of the visitation of God upon them.

III. The Vision of the Surveyor, 2:5-17 [Hebrew]

That the eight night-visions are inseparably connected is
clear from the use of the conjunction (*w*) introducing each one.
With the repetition of the same formula that was noted in 2:1
we read: "And I lifted up my eyes, and, behold, a man, and
in his hand a measuring line" (v. 5). Who is the man with the
measuring line? Some think he is a mere figure in the vision.
This is not in keeping with the general tenor of the visions
where each character has significance. Can it be said that the
man in 1:8 is also a mere figure for the vision? There we have
a similar introduction of an indefinite person. This man cannot
be the interpreting angel, because he is distinguished from the
latter in verse 7. He cannot be the prophet, because he is designated in verse 8 as *hanna'ar* and not "a man." By comparing
this verse with 1:8; 6:12; and Ezekiel 40:3 we come to the
probability that this man is the Angel of Jehovah, as a number
hold. The data are so insufficient that we cannot be dogmatic.
Zechariah loses no time in seeking the meaning of the mission
of the man, asking: "And I said, Whither art thou going? And
he said to me, To measure Jerusalem, to see what its breadth is
and length is" (v. 6). Just as in Ezekiel 40 and Revelation 11 the
measuring was the first step to the realization of blessing from
God, so here. In view of the increase, enlargement, and security
promised in 1:16, 17 this action is clearly comprehensible. *Jerusalem* may refer to the city as actually existing then or as completely restored and inhabited; perhaps the aim of the man was

to find out the then present size of the city·with a view to its future indefinite expansion.

The eyes of the prophet then rest upon another personage, "And, behold, the angel that spoke with me went out, and another angel went out to meet him" (v. 7). The interpreting angel went forth from the side of Zechariah to whom he is sent for instruction. He is met by another angel. It has been suggested by Chambers that the third angel is the Angel of Jehovah.[15] If this were so, he would be addressed by the usual title instead of an indefinite designation which of itself suggests that he was an inferior angel. The third angel went forth from the presence of the man with the measuring line to convey to the interpreting angel the message for the prophet. "And he said to him, Run, speak to this young man, saying, Jerusalem shall be inhabited as unwalled villages because of the abundance of man and beast in her midst" (v. 8). Here we have the burden of the message that was intended in the entire symbolism and action of the surveyor. The subject of *wayyo'mer* is grammatically and logically the third angel, who speaks to the interpreting angel. The latter is told to run, because the good news is to be proclaimed immediately. The prophet is not designated as *hanna'ar hallaz* because of inexperience or ignorance, as some have inferred, but on account of his youthful age. The statement is not meant to be derogatory. Older men are no more competent to fathom God's glorious purposes of blessing for Israel without a revelation from God Himself, than are younger men. Nor is the expression applicable to angels, for with them the human variations of age do not exist. They remain without increase, diminution, or advance in age, as they were created.

The glorious news is that Jerusalem will overflow her bounds because of her population, so that she will be inhabited like

---

[15] *Op. cit.,* p. 32.

unwalled villages. *Perazoth* comes from a verb meaning *to stretch out, to expand, to spread.* It refers to plains, open level country as contrasted with fortified and walled cities. A definition of the word is to be found in the explanation given in Ezekiel 38:11. For a similar promise see Isaiah 49:19, 20. Pusey concludes from the description that "Clearly then it is no earthly city."[16] Von Orelli in similar vein says, "Here, as in Isaiah 33:21, the idea abandons the image of a city conceivable to antiquity, and struggles after a more spiritual conception."[17] What baseless and unfounded hermeneutical alchemy is this which will take all the prophecies of judgment upon Israel at their face value, to be understood literally, but will transmute into indistinctness any blessing or promise of future glory for the same people? It is a sad state when men cannot see how kingdom conditions can exist alongside of spirituality. To many minds the introduction of literalness in kingdom promises does away with spirituality. What is so unspiritual about the personal, visible reign of the Messiah of Israel? Does not the same Word that predicts it also state clearly that from that Jerusalem, the seat of the government of the righteous King, will go forth the law and the Word of Jehovah (Isa. 2:1-4)? Wherein is the law lacking in spirituality? Paul declares the law to be holy, righteous, and good (Rom. 7:12). Again, we must maintain that literalness and a material kingdom with material conditions of prosperity *in no wise* exclude or militate against spirituality. Nor can we agree with Wright that "The prophecy was fulfilled by the restoration of the city of Jerusalem under the protection of God, even in troublous days"[18] (cf. Neh. 13:20, 21). The conditions here described have at no time been true in the

---

[16] *Op. cit.,* p. 348.

[17] *Op. cit.,* p. 322.

[18] *Op. cit.,* p. 36.

past since the time of Zechariah. The truth is rather with Kimchi who with assurance posits, "It is certain that this vision is of the future, referring to the days of the Messiah, as the visions of Ezekiel, in which he saw the angel measuring Jerusalem in its length and breadth."[19]

Lest Israel be inclined to doubt the security of such a dwelling, the prophet adds: "And I will be to her, saith Jehovah, a wall of fire round about, and I will be glory in her midst" (v. 9). *Wa'ani* is emphatic and is best translated *I Myself.* *Homath 'esh* may have in it a reference to the pillar of fire that went before Israel at night during their wilderness wanderings. God will not only sustain a relationship to threatening forces without, but He will be the Glory in the midst of His people (cf. Isa. 60:19). This is an announcement of the return of the glory of the Presence of Jehovah to Jerusalem seen by the prophet Ezekiel (Ezek. 43:2. See also Isaiah 4:5, 6). The message symbolized by the surveyor is thus twofold: (1) the character of the prosperity promised to Jerusalem, and (2) the manner of its preservation. In verse 9 the prophet sets before us (1) the protection of God, and (2) the presence of God. What good words, words of consolation are these for Israel!

In verses 10-17 of our chapter there is fuller explanation of verses 8 and 9 which give the meaning of the symbolical action of verses 5-7. The mind of the prophet is turned by the inditing Spirit of God from the far-off future to the then present need. He calls to his fellow-countrymen: "Ho, ho, flee from the land of the north, saith Jehovah; for as the four winds of the heaven I have dispersed you, saith Jehovah. Ho, Zion, deliver thyself, thou that dwellest with the daughter of Babylon" (vv. 10, 11). The particle *hoy* not only calls attention, but onomatopoetically conveys the thought of pain or compassion (cf.

---

[19] *Op. cit.,* p. 29.

Jer. 22:18; Amos 5:16.) This is a summons to the Israelites still
in Babylon to flee, before the wrath of God is poured out. Some,
because of senility, infirmity, or ties of one character or another,
had chosen to remain in the heathen capital rather than assay
the trying journey to the desolated home of their forefathers.
The prophecy had a primary, though only partial, reference to
the prophet's time. (Cf. Isa. 48:20; 52:11; Jer. 51:6, 9, 45.) It is
indeed difficult to comprehend upon what basis a fine student
of the Scriptures like Hengstenberg is proceeding when he can
state of this cry, "an appeal which was not intended to be put
in practice any more than the similar appeal in Jeremiah 51:6."[20]
No declaration of God is meant to be without effect; surely
not here when there was ample warrant for such an exhortation.
The land of the north is unquestionably Babylon, which, though
a southeastern power in relation to Palestine, is so called because
invasions and caravans coming from Babylon to Jerusalem came
from the north (cf. Jer. 1:13, 14).

The warnings to flee in verses 10 and 11 imply threatening
peril upon Babylon, which did come upon her two years after
this prophecy, in the fourth year of Darius. There has been
difference of opinion regarding the rendering of *perasti*. Keil
(taking the same position as the English versions) says, "For
apart from the fact that *paras* almost always means to spread
out, and has the meaning to disperse at the most in Psalm 68:15
and Ezekiel 17:21, this meaning is altogether unsuitable here."[21]
He feels that, if all lands were meant, then the charge would
be to flee from them all, not Babylon alone. He takes the verb
as prophetic perfect signifying the purpose of God to spread
Israel out to the four corners of the globe (cf. Isa. 27:6). If
this be true, then what connection is there between this spreading

---

20 *Op. cit.*, Vol. III, p. 246.
21 *Op. cit.*, Vol. II, p. 246.

out and the fleeing from Babylon? The difficulty here is that,
although *paras* is used of dispersion, "it is nowhere used of
diffusion, only of the spreading out of what remained coherent,
as hands, wings, a garment, tent, veil, cloud, letter, light."[22] The
scattering is not said to be to the four winds but as the four
winds, with a violence such as would result from the combined
action of all the winds of the heavens. They were enjoined to
flee from Babylon, because they had been so violently scattered
there. It was assuredly comforting to the exiled people to be
addressed still as *Zion*. The connection between verse 9 and
verses 10 and 11 is this: Jerusalem is yet to be restored and
enjoy the presence of God; come, share in the blessings and escape the judgments.

The protecting provision of God for His people is further
set forth: "For thus saith Jehovah of hosts, After glory he has
sent me to the nations spoiling you; for he that touches you,
touches the apple of his eye. For, behold, I will shake my hand
over them, and they shall be a spoil to their servants; and ye
shall know that Jehovah of hosts has sent me" (vv. 12, 13). The
moving agent here is the Angel of Jehovah, who is discernible
from the repeated thought of *sent me* (note the many occurrences
of these words in John's Gospel) and from the exhibition of
power stated in verse 13. There are two main views as to the
meaning of the words *'ahar kabhodh*. The first maintains that
it has reference to the glorious appearing of the Messiah to
Israel promised in verse 9. (So Kimchi, Dennett, Kelly, Hengstenberg, Chambers, and others.) It is doubtful whether the
appearing in glory of the Messiah would be designated by the
indefinite *kabhodh*. The second view holds that it points to
the vindication, display, and the procuring of the glory of God.
The Messiah is sent for the glorification of the Father. (So Von

---

[22] Pusey, *op. cit.*, p. 349, footnote.

Orelli, Baron, and others.) With the position just stated we do heartily agree. *'Ahar* is a preposition here and thus connected with the following word by a conjunctive accent (*munach*). When it is used adverbially before a noun, it is marked by a disjunctive. (Cf. Psa. 73:24 [Hebrew].) The interpretation with the first view is: the Messiah, after His glorious appearing, is sent to chastise the nations in executing God's judgments upon them. The second view conveys the thought: the Messiah is sent by the Father for the vindication of His glory on the nations that have spoiled Israel, for God's cause and glory are inseparably linked with the fortunes of His people. The humiliation and subjugation of Israel by the nations must be avenged by the One who is dishonored in their dejected condition.

How tender the affection of God is for Israel is to be seen in the words *babhath 'eno,* literally, the gate through which the light enters the eye, so the *pupil. Babhah* here is equivalent to the word *'ishon* in Deuteronomy 32:10 which means *little man,* and like our *pupil,* little boy. The pupil or apple of the eye is a proverbial figure for that which is most precious, most easily injured, hardest of repair, and most demanding of protection and care. This is a most fitting symbol for Israel, because, just as the light comes through the pupil, so the light of salvation has come through the Jews (Jn. 4:22). Note the provision for the protection of the pupil: (1) strong frontal bones (from a blow); (2) the brow and eyelash (against dust); (3) the lid (from painful glare); (4) the tear glands (for continuous cleansing). Some maintain that the original reading seems to have been *'eni.* Though several MSS. have this reading, the better supported reading is *'eno.* Those who contend for the first, claim that the alteration was made that the text might be referred to the apple of a man's eye; that is, whoever touches Israel, touches the apple of his own eye, doing himself irreparable damage.

In our opinion Deuteronomy 32:10 will allow no such interpretation, nor is it the more forceful here. True, that a man's
touching of the pupil of his own eye will bring him injury in a
most sensitive part, but how much more is this true if he
touch the apple of God's eye?

The complete reversal of position between masters and servants harks back to the prediction of Isaiah 14:2. When Israel's
oppressors have become their servants, then God's people will
know experientially the work and mission of the Messiah.
Israel seeks after signs and she will have them in abundance.
An interesting historical fulfillment of the prophecy of the
judgment of God upon Babylon, although only a partial one,
is the following. In the fourth year of Darius, the Babylonians,
after much plotting, revolted and shut themselves up in their
city, ready for a long siege. Zopyrus, Darius' friend and general,
cut off his own ears and nose, and by pretending that he had
been thus mutilated by Darius, gained entrance into the city
and the confidence of the besieged ones. By his craft the gates
were opened to the Persians, and when the city was mastered
thousands of Babylonian nobles were crucified. Surely, uneasy
should lie the head that plots evil against Israel, and woeful indeed will be the fate of such.

The prophecy of the glorification is seen as already fulfilled,
hence the words: "Sing and rejoice, O daughter of Zion, for,
behold, I come, and I will dwell in the midst of thee, saith
Jehovah" (v. 14). The rejoicing is to be over the presence of
the Lord and His glory among them (v. 9). A comparison
with 9:9 shows the Person is none other than Messiah Himself.
The coming here suggests His incarnation to be completed by
His return in glory (John 1:14 with Rev. 21:3). The emphasis
here is on the joy at His second coming as it is at His first
coming in 9:9. The immediate effect is thus stated. "And many

nations shall join themselves to Jehovah in that day, and shall be my people; and I will dwell in the midst of thee, and thou shalt know that Jehovah of hosts has sent me unto thee" (v. 15). The prophetic Scriptures are in harmony here as elsewhere: whenever Israel is in full possession of her glory, then the nations are joined (*nilwu* is the same word from which *Levi* comes) to the Lord. (Cf. Psa. 67:2, 3 [Hebrew]; 72:7; Isa. 2:1-4; 19:23-25; 60:1-3; Zech. 8:20-23.) The nations are unwittingly awaiting this very hour. Note that the *goyim rabbim* will be so unified as to become one *'am*.

This cleaving of the nations to Jehovah will not alter God's original choice of Israel, for the prophet continues: "And Jehovah shall inherit Judah, his portion, upon the holy land, and shall yet chose Jerusalem" (v. 16). God still acknowledges Israel as peculiarly His own. (Cf. Deut. 4:20; 9:26, 29; 32:9; Isa. 19:25; Ezek. 22:16.) The land is called *'adhmath haqqodhesh*, not because it is the land of promise, but in contrast to its former defilement. (This is the only occurrence of this phrase in the Bible.) *Baḥar 'odh* does not imply that God must choose Israel afresh, but that now, at long last, He will be able to manifest to the world the immutable character of His original choice and its practical outworking in renewed, restored, and resettled Israel. Wright's conclusion that "The prophecy was fulfilled in the blessings granted to the Jews in their own land, and in the honour placed upon that land by the advent and ministry of the Lord Jesus Christ,"[23] fails to grasp the potent truth that the first coming of Christ left much of Old Testament prophecy as to the promises and future of Israel unfulfilled. These depend upon their yet future acknowledgment of their Messiah. And they shall receive Him! Israel, in despair and dejection in the time of the prophet, may have asked, Why, then, in view of

---

[23] *Op. cit.*, p. 41.

all these glowing promises and pictures of future felicity and joy, is God so long silent? The prophet meets the implied longing and question, saying, "Be silent, all flesh, before Jehovah, for he is aroused from his holy habitation" (v. 17). The *has* of the Hebrew carries with it the sense of solemnity and awe, more so than the English *hush*. Mankind is called *flesh* to express its frailty and weakness in the sight of Almighty God (cf. Gen. 6:3; Isa. 31:3). Zechariah sees God coming in judgment for the carrying out of the program just outlined. "God has already set out from His heavenly abode."[24] Compare for the entire verse Habbakuk 2:20.

To summarize, the two visions of the second chapter are an elaboration of the three main features in 1:15-17: (1) the grievous displeasure of the Lord with the nations persecuting Israel, with the resulting punishment upon them; (2) the expansion and increase of Israel under the Lord's prospering; and (3) the tabernacling presence of God in their midst. Note the twofold mention in the chapter of judgment and glory; the first for the nations, and the second for Israel, thus: judgment upon the nations, 2:1-4; glory for Israel, 2:5-9; judgment upon the nations, 2:10-13; glory for Israel (with the nations), 2:14-17. The chapter reveals so vividly how little the nations of the earth realize how much of their blessing depends upon Israel. They do well to take heed lest they fall into the hands of the living God, which is a fearful thing.

---

[24] Von Orelli, *op. cit.*, p. 322.

CHAPTER II

IV. THE VISION OF JOSHUA THE HIGH PRIEST AND THE ANGEL OF JEHOVAH, 3:1-10

IN THE FIRST three visions of his prophecy Zechariah dwells on the themes of the deliverance of Israel from captivity and oppression, the consequent enlargement and expansion, and the subsequent prosperity and material blessing of the land. Now the prophet occupies himself under the direction of the sovereign Spirit of God with the matter of the internal cleansing and purification of Israel from sin. The fourth vision of the book reveals how Israel will be purged, cleansed, and reinstated into her priestly office and functions.

The chapter before us has a twofold division: (1) the symbolical act, verses 1-5; (2) the explanation and application, verses 6-10. The three foci around which the vision revolves are: (1) the immutability of God's choice of Israel; (2) His infliction of severest punishment upon them for their sins; and (3) the complete removal of their iniquity by God's servant, the Branch.

At the very outset we are introduced to a most interesting scene: "And he showed me Joshua the high priest standing before the angel of Jehovah, and Satan was standing at his right hand to be his adversary" (v. 1). Judging from the analogy of 2:3 [Hebrew], the probability is that the revealer of the vision to the prophet was God Himself. This function is nowhere assigned to the interpreting angel whose duty it is to explain and elucidate the visions. The Joshua mentioned here is the high priest of the restoration, the son of Jehozadak, who with Zerubbabel led the first group in the return from Babylonian

53

captivity. The phrase *'omedh liphne* properly conveys the thought of attendance upon a person, whether it be before man or God. With reference to judicial matters we find the expression in Numbers 27:2; 35:12; Deuteronomy 19:17; Joshua 20:6; I Kings 3:16. When used in connection with the priests it is practically a technical designation for priestly ministry. (Cf. Deut. 10:8; Judg. 20:28; II Chron. 29:11; Ezek. 44:15.)

Commentators on the passage differ as to whether the scene is a judicial or a priestly one. The question at issue is: Does Joshua stand before the Angel of Jehovah as a defendant in a lawsuit, or is he performing the proper functions of his high priestly office? The best solution of the matter seems to be that the priestly scene is changed into a judicial one in the following manner: the high priest is in the sanctuary (in the vision, to be sure, so no argument based on the incompleteness of the temple then in the process of construction can carry weight) before the Angel of Jehovah who is attended by His many angels, when Satan appears to lodge accusations against Joshua that the favor and grace of God might be hindered from flowing out toward His people. Pusey differs with this position, holding that "Although . . . the Angel speaks with authority, yet God's presence in him is not spoken of so distinctly, that the High Priest would be exhibited as standing before him, as in his office before God."[1] But this very passage refutes such a contention for we are given here further proofs of the deity of the Angel. In the first place, He is distinctly spoken of by the Spirit of God as Jehovah in verse 2. In the second place, He is seen forgiving sins (v. 4), a work that God has never delegated to mere man. Satan assumes the role of accuser as he did with Job (chapters 1 and 2 of the Book of Job) and does now with the children of God (Rev. 12:10). He stands at the

---

[1] *Op. cit.*, Vol. II., p. 353.

right hand of the high priest. Some take this as the position
of the accuser (cf. Psa. 109:6; Job 30:12). It is probably better
taken as the place of the protector and advocate (cf. Psa. 16:8;
109:31; 121:5; 142:5 [Hebrew]). The infinitive *lesitno* occurs
nowhere else in the Scriptures and constitutes an interesting case
of antanaclasis. It is of the same root as the word *Satan,* the
whole phrase probably best rendered, "the Adversary . . . to be
an adversary to him." The opposer opposes the high priest by
dwelling on the sins of the people of Israel that God might cast
them from His presence irrevocably and forever. (What a shame
that in every age there have been so many who have aligned
themselves with such a purpose!)

The picture is dark indeed, for how can the nation stand
in the light of the accusations of the Adversary? Thank God,
Israel has as Defender Jehovah Himself. (Cf. Isa. 50:8, 9.) So
we read: "And Jehovah said to Satan, Jehovah rebuke thee, O
Satan; yea, Jehovah who had chosen Jerusalem rebuke thee. Is
not this a brand snatched from the fire?" (v. 2). To the careful
student of the text it is evident that Joshua is not standing in
a personal and individual capacity, but rather in the place of
the representative of God's people. Three considerations lend
force here. First, the emphasis in the chapter is upon the fact
of the high priesthood of Joshua, the words *hakkohen haggadhol*
occurring twice in this short passage (vv. 1 and 8). Second, the
entreaty of the Angel in verse 2 is on the basis of God's choice
of Jerusalem, not Joshua. Third, the action of verse 4 is seen
to have its fulfillment in the removal of the iniquity of the
land, rather than the sin of but one individual. The situation
is both grave and solemn. If Joshua is vindicated, Israel is accepted; if he is condemned and cast off, they are rejected.
Chambers pointedly states: "Did the Lord cast off his people
entirely and recall his promised grace, the historical basis for

the Messiah to come would perish, and no room be left for his
appearance according to the ancient predictions. The issue, then,
was vital. It did not concern an individual merely . . . If the
confessed sins of Israel were sufficient to secure their final rejection from God at that stage of their history, the hopes of
the race were blasted, and the prospect of a blessing for all the
families of the earth, became a beautiful but empty dream."[2]
The outcome of the litigation, then, concerned not only Joshua,
but Israel as well, yea more, the entire redemptive plan and
purpose of God for the whole world.

The Angel of Jehovah, in espousing the cause of accused
Israel, calls down the rebuke of God upon Satan. *Yigh'ar* conveys the thought of actual suppression and the complete annihilation of the accusation, together with the silencing of the opposer. Pusey holds that "The rebuke of God must be with power"[3]
(Psa. 9:6 [Hebrew]; 76:7 [Hebrew]; 80:17 [Hebrew]; Isa. 17:13;
Mal. 2:3). Upon what basis is the rebuke of God directed toward
Satan and his diabolical indictments? We must guard ourselves
against Pelagianism. Joshua was not acquitted because he was
snatched from the fire through some merit of his own. The
ground of his acquittal was neither in his merit nor in the falsity
of Satan's accusations, but in God's own sovereign choice of the
nation in grace. The participle *habboher* vividly points to the
continuance and the maintenance of that choice. It is ever fresh
before God. (Cf. Jer. 31:36; Lev. 26:44.) Von Orelli translates:
"He has anew chosen Jerusalem."[4] Surely the emphasis of the
Scripture is not on the renewal of the choice of God, but rather
upon its lasting, continuing, and perpetual character. The elec-
tion of Israel by God was motivated by love alone. In Deuter-

---

[2] Lange, *op. cit.*, p. 39.
[3] *Op. cit.*, p. 354.
[4] *Op. cit.*, p. 324.

onomy 7:7, 8 Moses makes it clear that God chose Israel not because of their numbers, but because of His love for them and His oath to their fathers. In order for the grace of God to be true to its own character and the very nature of God, it can never be dependent upon nor implicated in the slightest degree with human merit. As another has said, "He chose you because He loved you; and He loved you because He loved you."[5]

The remaining clause of the second verse does not state the basis of the choice (to be sure, we have just shown the contrary), but points to one striking manifestation of the efficacy of it. For the figure of the brand plucked from the fire we can be referred to Amos 4:11. It is most meaningful here. It speaks of Israel snatched from Babylonian Captivity, for the wrath and fire of God (in Scripture a figure of the punishment visited by God upon sin) have not been permitted to do their complete work of destruction (see Isa. 48:10). Would Jehovah have delivered Israel from Babylon, if His ultimate purpose was to destroy her? Since God has done so much, not only is His love proved, but the continuance of it is assured and guaranteed. A piece of timber is rescued from fire only when its possessor sees further purposes in it. Similarly, God's plans for Israel did not close with the captivity of the southern kingdom and the deportation to Babylon. His love sought her out yet once more. Rightly has Israel been likened

---

[5] For an analogous rebuke of Satan see Jude 9. The incidents are not the same, though some have felt so. True, in both instances we have the mention of rebuke, the power of Satan by implication, the references to fire and the spotted garment (see Jude 23), but all else is different. The One who rebukes here is the Angel of Jehovah; in Jude it is Michael the archangel. They are not one and the same person. Then again, in the epistle the dispute concerns the body of Moses; in the prophecy it is relative to the sinful condition of Israel. Attempts to identify these two are both far-fetched and without analogy in Scripture.

to the burning bush that Moses saw in the desert, ever burning, ever aflame, and yet never consumed. And do you ask the secret of the mystery? It is because God Himself is in the midst of the burning bush. Such also was the truth of the Angel of Jehovah in the midst of the myrtles at the beginning of the night-visions vouchsafed to the prophet Zechariah on that memorable night.

But thus far the Spirit of God has not brought before us the actual condition of Joshua which called forth the opposition of Satan. To this He now directs our attention: "Now Joshua was clothed with filthy garments, and was standing before the angel" (v. 3). More clearly than any translation can convey, the periphrastic conjugation *hayah labhush* denotes the habitual condition of the high priest. This was no chance or unusual apparel for him; it was rather that with which he was customarily attired. The word *tso'im* is the strongest expression in the Hebrew language for filth of the most vile and loathsome character. Kimchi, oblivious of the evident anachronism involved, explains the filthy garments parabolically of Joshua's sons who married strange women (Ezra 10:18). Actually, these marriages took place some fifty years later.

Some expositors of the passage think these garments were those of a criminal. Proof is lacking that there was such a custom in Israel. Josephus, in narrating the trial of Herod before the Sanhedrin, relates how Herod silenced his accusers when he appeared before the body with his guard of men. Then Sameas, a righteous man, without fear arose and said: "O you that are assessors with me, and O thou that art our king, I neither have ever myself known such a case, nor do I suppose that any of you can name its parallel, that one is called to take his trial by us ever stood in such manner before us; but every one, whosoever he be, that comes to be tried by this sanhedrin, presents himself in a submissive manner, and like one that is in fear of himself, and that endeavors to move us to compassion, with his hair dishevelled, and in a black and mourning garment: but this admirable man Herod, who is accused of murder, and called to answer so heavy an accusation, stands here clothed in purple, and with the hair of his head finely trimmed, and with his armed men about him, that if we shall condemn him by our law, he may slay us, and by overbearing justice may himself escape death; yet do not I make this complaint against Herod himself: he is, to be sure, more concerned for himself than for the laws; but my complaint is against yourselves and your king, who give him a license so to do."[6] From this passage it is patent that in later times, at least, the accused was clothed in black mourning garments, not filthy ones. Keil (*et al.*) quotes Livy to show that the wearing of filthy garments on the part of the accused was a Roman custom. At any rate, it does not hold for Hebrew custom. Scriptures make plain that such garments represent the pollution and contamination of sin (Isa. 4:4; 64:5 [Heb.]; Prov. 30:12). As though to bring out the vast incongruity of the situation, it is added (a fact that has already been stated) that Joshua was standing before the Angel.

Such a condition could not long continue in the presence of the infinitely holy Angel of Jehovah, so we hear Him speak with the utmost of authority: "And he answered and spake to those standing before him, saying, Take away the filthy garments from him. And to him he said, Behold, I have caused thine iniquity to pass from thee, and I am about to clothe thee with festive garments" (v. 4). The command goes forth to the attending angels, for Joshua could do nothing to cleanse himself nor remedy his sinful condition. The meaning of the removal of the filthy garments is to be found in the words that immediately

---

[6] *Antiquities of the Jews*, 14. 9, 4.

follow, *he'ebharti me'alekha 'awonekha.* The act represents
symbolically justification, and not sanctification. That forensic
forgiveness is in view can be seen from verse 9. The Angel of
Jehovah justified him and the people of Israel in him. (Cf. II
Sam. 12:13; 24:10.) The infinitive absolute may stand here (as
in so many cases) for the finite verb, or may require the finite
verb *hilbashti* to convey the thought of the intensive, "clothing
I will assuredly clothe." The festal garments (this word used
only here and Isa. 3:22) speak of purity, glory, and joy, but their
chief significance is that they bespeak of the reinstatement of
the nation into their original calling (see Exod. 19:6; Isa. 61:6).
Joshua in filthy garments: "is it not a perfect picture of Israel
as it is yet today? A priest, but defiled and unclean."[7] Joshua
in festive garments: is it not a foregleam of her glory in her
reconsecration to the priestly office? But we need to be careful
that we see the import of all this for the contemporaries of the
prophet Zechariah.

Thus far the prophet has been a silent spectator, but now
he utters his heartfelt intercession: "And I said, Let them put
a clean mitre upon his head. So they put a clean mitre upon
his head, and clothed him with garments; and [while] the
angel of Jehovah was standing by" (v. 5). Perhaps Lowe has
inferred too much from this request and its answer in claiming:
"By the granting of his request, that a clean mitre be placed
on the head of Joshua, he is assured that the high priest is not
pardoned only personally, but also in his official capacity."[8] We
have already brought forth proof that Joshua is seen throughout
the chapter in his official and representative character. The
prayer of the prophet was not superfluous: he asked that the
work might be completed. God delights to have us ask Him

---

[7] Gaebelein, A. C., *op. cit.,* p. 37.
[8] *Op. cit.,* p. 5.

to do that which is in His heart to do. The mitre that was set
upon the head of Joshua was that worn by princely persons and
kings (Keil). (Cf. Job 29:14; Isa. 62:3.) The turban of the
high priest (for such it was, *tsaniph* coming from a root meaning
"to fold," "to wind") had upon it the golden plate bearing the
words "Holiness to Jehovah" (Exod. 28:36, 38). The presence
of the Angel graced the entire ceremony.

The transition from the symbolical act to the application is
short but pointed: "And the Angel of Jehovah testified to
Joshua, saying, Thus saith Jehovah of hosts, If thou wilt walk
in my ways, and if thou wilt keep my charge, then thou also
shalt judge my house, and shalt also keep my courts, and I
will give thee places to walk among these that stand by" (vss.
6, 7). The strong term *wayya'adh* bears out the importance and
the certainty of all that follows (cf. Gen. 43:3; Deut. 8:19;
32:46 [etymologically, "called God to witness"].) In the conditions that are set before Joshua and, through him, to all his
priestly colleagues, as well as the nation Israel, there is a double
emphasis on "walk" and "keep." Hebrew usage reveals that
bidhrakhay telekh has reference to the personal life and attitude
toward the Lord. (Cf. Gen. 17:1.) *Mishmarti thishmor* speaks
of the diligent and faithful keeping of official duties (cf. Lev.
18:30; 22:9). Judging the house of Jehovah (the temple) takes
into consideration the adjudication of matters of dispute in
connection with the sanctuary. (See Deut. 17:8-10.) Keeping
the courts of God implies guarding it from pollution and
idolatry. The third clause in the apodosis presents a difficulty,
because *mahlekhim* occurs nowhere else in the Old Testament.
Gesenius and Hengstenberg take it as the Chaldee form of
the hiphil participle for the ordinary *molikhim,* hence they
translate "guides" or "leaders." In that case the preposition
mibben would be expected. Hengstenberg explains the promise

as an assurance to the high priest that he would have the
ministry and guidance of angels as in verse 4. Kimchi thinks
the passage speaks of "his soul, when it should be separated
from his body." The Jewish Targum in similar vein (quoted
by Pusey) paraphrases: "In the resurrection of the dead I will
revive thee, and give thee feet walking among these seraphim."
We think it best to render the word "places to walk," that is,
ingress and egress, and the meaning of the whole would be
that Joshua would have ready and free access to God as high
priest, just as the angels do. This is indeed reinstatement into
the priesthood.

But God has much more in view, so the prophet continues:
"Hear now, O Joshua the high priest, thou and thy companions
that sit before thee, for they are men of wonder. For, behold, I
will bring forth my servant (the) Branch" (v. 8). The vision was
not to be exhausted in the conditions of that day, but the events of
the then present time foreshadow by way of type greater events in
the future. The call to hear denotes the importance of the
message that follows. Joshua and his fellow-priests are said to
be men of wonder, men of sign. The implication is not that
they are worthy of having a sign wrought for them by their
hands (Kimchi), nor that they are used to interpret prophetic
portents (Lowe), nor yet that they are able to interpret signs
(LXX), but that in themselves they foreshadow coming events
or persons. *Mopheth* means *wonder, astonishment,* as is clear
from the Hebrew usage (Psa. 71:7) and similar use in cognate
languages (Arabic). Its relation to *'oth* is analogous to that
which exists in Greek between *teras* and *semeion,* and in Latin
between *prodigium* and *signum* (Hengstenberg). They excite
wonder because they are types, foreshadowings of someone to
come. (Cf. Isa. 8:18; 20:3; Ezek. 12:6, 11; 24:24, 27.)

The coming Antitype is called My Servant, Zemach. These are two well-known names for the Messiah in the prophetic Scriptures. For Servant passages see Isaiah 42:1; 49:3, 5; 52:13; 53:11; Ezekiel 34:23, 24. For Branch passages compare Isaiah 4:2; Jeremiah 23:5; 33:15; Zechariah 6:12. In what way were Joshua and his associates types of the Messiah to come? It was not merely because they were in the position of mediators. Keil summarizes it well: "The miracle, which is to be seen in Joshua and his priests, consists rather in the fact that the priesthood of Israel is laden with guilt, but by the grace of God it has been absolved, and accepted by God again, as the deliverance from exile shows, and Joshua and his priests are therefore brands plucked by the omnipotence of grace from the fire of merited judgment. This miracle of grace which has been wrought for them, points beyond itself to an incomparably greater and better act of the sin-absolving grace of God, which is still in the future."[9]

Kimchi refers the Zemach to Zerubbabel. In all probability his intention was to obviate the difficulty of Zechariah 6:12 where He is both priest and king, and because our next verse (3:9) assigns expiation to Him. M'Caul, his translator, points out the untenableness of this position: (1) it is a departure from the received interpretation of the Jews. Kimchi admits: "But there are some who interpret 'The Branch' of the Messiah, the King." The Targum of Jonathan so interprets both 3:9 and 6:12. (2) It is at variance with the whole of the prophetic testimony (Isa. 4:2; Jer. 23:5). In these passages Kimchi admits reference is to the Messiah. (3) The view is untrue to the then existing conditions. Zerubbabel had long been on the scene of history; the Zemach was yet to come.[10]

[9] *Op. cit.*, p. 259.
[10] *Op. cit.*, pp. 37, 38, also footnotes.

What was the thought of the Spirit of God in designating the Messiah in this twofold manner? He is called My Servant, because He came into the world to do the will of the Father. The will of the Father was His perfect and holy delight always. It is through the service of the Messiah that God's world-wide redemptive plan is executed. The name Zemach (a proper noun in our text) conveys several truths. First, it brings out the lowliness and humiliation of the Messiah (Isa. 11:1). Second, it reveals His eminence (Isa. 53:2). He grows up before the Lord Himself. Third, it directs our attention to His humanity. He is connected with the earth, and more particularly the land of Palestine (Zech. 6:12). Fourth, it relates Him to the Davidic dynasty (Jer. 23:5, 6). Fifth, it focuses our thought upon the deity of the Branch (Isa. 4:2). Sixth, it conveys the truth of His fruitfulness in comparison with the barrenness of all others (Isa. 11:1; 53:10). Seventh, it speaks of his priestly work and character; for being touched with the feeling of our infirmities, He is a becoming and fit High Priest for sinful men (Zech. 6:12). How unspeakably full are the designations of God for His only-begotten and much-beloved Son! When God introduces His Son to our admiring and reverent gaze, we do well to prostrate ourselves at His feet and there abide.

The prophet has not yet revealed the work of the Antitype, so he lays this before us after this manner: "For, behold, the stone that I have set before Joshua; upon one stone are seven eyes. Behold, I will engrave the graving thereof, saith Jehovah of hosts, and I will remove the iniquity of that land in one day" (v. 9). This exceedingly beautiful and meaningful verse has found many interpretations at the hands of its expositors. The stone placed before Joshua for his consideration is said to be the plummet or headstone (Kimchi), restored Israel as the nucleus of the kingdom of God (Gaebelein), an altar (Von Orelli), the kingdom of God (Hengstenberg), the foundation stone of the temple, or the jewel of the high priest's breastplate. We see in the stone (with Wright, Baron, and many others) another well-known name for the Messiah. Early expositors were almost unanimous in assigning this name to the Messiah. (Cf. Isa. 28:16; Psa. 118:22; Dan. 2:35. Compare further Matt. 21:42; Acts 4:11; Eph. 2:20-22; I Pet. 2:2-7.) Pusey quotes an interesting word from the Zohar, an old Jewish book of mysticism: "The Shechinah is called the stone, through which the world subsisteth; of which it is said, 'A stone of seven eyes, and, the stone which the builders refused.' "[11]

Why is the Messiah called the Stone? It relates Him to Israel. To them He was the stumbling-stone and rock of offense (Isa. 8:14). But to those in Israel who trusted Him, He was a never-failing refuge (Isa. 28:16). The Stone relates Christ to the nations. He will be the Destroyer of the godless world-monarchies (Dan. 2:35). The Stone connects the Christ with the Church. He is her foundation and top-stone (Psa. 118:22; Eph. 2:20-22). The designation relates the Messiah to God. He is the Stone made without hands, the One who is called the Tabernacle which God pitched, not man (Dan. 2:34). The Stone speaks of the beauty of the Son of God (Zech. 3:9). The engravings (*mephatteah* used of engraving precious stones, as well as gold, carved work, and sculpture—Exod. 28:9; 28:36; II Chron. 2:13; Psa. 74:6) are those conducive to its beauty. The Church Fathers have written after this manner: "beautiful beyond all beauty must be those glorious scars, with which He allowed His whole body to be riven, that throughout the whole frame His love might be engraven" (quoted by Pusey). The Stone reveals Him to be the dependable Rock, Fortress, High Tower of the trusting soul. Compare the many passages in the

---

[11] *Op. cit.*, p. 357.

Psalms. The Stone relates Him to the Spirit of God, for the seven eyes are symbolic of manifold intelligence and omniscience (Isa. 11:2; Rev. 5:6).

The truth that is uppermost in the mind of the prophet (given to him of God) is the removal of the iniquity of the land in one day. Note that we have *umashti* and not *umash,* as though a third person were meant. No, it is the Angel of Jehovah speaking of His own future work of sin-purging and sin-cleansing. In this one word the entire vision is comprehended and its full import seen. *Ha'arets hahi'* is restricted by the context to Judah, but not limited in its ultimate outflow to all the world. The words *beyom 'ehadh* are more significant than they appear to be at first glance. They make the tremendous declaration that the removal of iniquity will be once for all. There will be no need of repetition as with the typical priesthood. Chambers has put it concisely: "It presents a contrast between the continually repeated sacrifices of the Levitical priesthood and the one final and effectual sacrifice of the Messiah."[12] This expression is always emphatic in Scripture usage. (See Gen. 27:45; I Sam. 2:34; I Kings 20:29; II Chron. 28:6.) It is analogous to *'ephapax in* Hebrews 7:27; 9:12; 10:10. What day is meant here? Rashi, one of the greatest of all Jewish commentators (12th century A. D.), confessed the mystery: "One day, I know not what that day is." Most Christian expositors claim it is the day of Calvary, but it must look beyond that to a day when Israel in a time of national atonement and repentance will have ratified for her in her national life actually, that which was wrought out potentially and provisionally at Calvary.

Immediately that Israel is seen cleansed and restored, the Scriptures always reveal the consequent quiet, peace, and prosperity which result from the work accomplished in and through

---

12 *Op. cit.,* p. 38.

them by the Messiah. Zechariah concludes the vision thus: "In that day, saith Jehovah of hosts, ye shall invite every man his neighbor under the vine and under the fig-tree" (v. 10). *Bayyom hahu'* relates the time of these conditions to the period of the cleansing of the land from iniquity. It is a phrase much used by Zechariah and has much prophetic significance. Every one calling his neighbor *'el tahath* is a pregnant construction for "to come and sit under." Such conditions of tranquility and fruitfulness of the land existed in the golden days of Solomon (I Kings 4:25) and were in themselves foreshadowings of the similar circumstances in the reign of the One greater than Solomon (Mic. 4:4).

As we look back over this important chapter, we note that its first part deals with the past sins of Israel as forgiven of God through the then ministering high priest; its second division looks forward to that coming day when the High Priest, unexcelled and unparalleled, will take away all the sins of Israel forever. The temple then being built was to have a cleansed and reinstated priesthood, only a foretaste, however, of the more wonderful priesthood of Israel yet to be made possible through the work of God's Servant, Zemach. We call attention to the fulness of the testimony of the Angel of Jehovah to Joshua (vv. 6-10):

1. He confirms the priestly position of Joshua (v. 7).
2. He predicts the coming of the Messiah (v. 8).
3. He foretells the work of the Messiah with its spiritual results for Israel (v. 9).
4. He pictures the attendant blessings of peace and prosperity for the nation (v. 10).

The revelation in verses 8 to 10 is remarkably complete. It gives us:

1. The Portents of the Coming One. Joshua and the priests.

2. The Person of the Coming One. My Servant, Zemach.

3. The Preparation of the Coming One. I engrave its graving.

4. The Performance of the Coming One. I will remove the iniquity of that land.

5. The Perfection of the Work of the Coming One. In one day—no renewal.

6. The Peace from the Work of the Coming One. Under the vine and under the fig tree.

7. The Prosperity from the Work of the Coming One. The same phrases.

We do well to turn from the men of wonder to the Man Christ Jesus who is the Wonderful, the Prince of Peace.[13]

---

[13] We cannot resist the temptation to bring out the analogy to the gospel story itself that we find here. We do so with hesitation lest the impression be given that this is the primary meaning. Delitzsch, writing in another connection, noted that "Interpretation is one; application is manifold." With this in mind, we submit the following. As with Joshua, the basis of God's dealings with any sinner is in His sovereign choice in grace. Of every individual in the world who has been brought to God, it can be truthfully said, "God hath chosen thee." That choice was before the foundation of the world (Eph. 1). But look at the sinner as he actually appears before God; it is with vile, filthy garments such as Joshua wore. Every righteousness of the sinner is only filthiness. And he is helpless to alter his condition. If left to himself and his own efforts, he would have to abide thus for all eternity. But thank God, Christ makes it possible for him to be clothed with new garments, even the robe of His own righteousness (Isa. 61:10; II Cor. 5:21). When so forgiven and cleansed of God, the sinner becomes immediately a priest before God with a priestly service and ministry, a part of the body of Christ who is Himself the great High Priest. Redeemed ones are truly men of wonder, for even the angels desire to look into these things (Eph. 3:10). A godly walk on the basis of redemption is the issue of the work of God; a godly and consistent testimony is an integral part of it as well. Behold, what God hath wrought!

V. THE VISION OF THE CANDLESTICK AND THE TWO OLIVE
TREES, 4:1-14.

The fifth vision of the book carries us forward from the
concluding point of the fourth in this manner: after Israel as
the priestly nation of God has been cleansed from all defilement
and has entered into the restoration of her priestly calling, then
she is prepared to fulfill God's original purpose in her as the
bearer of light and truth to all the surrounding nations in their
idolatry and paganism. In Deuteronomy 32:8 Moses sang:
"When the Most High gave to the nations their inheritance,
When he separated the children of men, He set the bounds
of the peoples according to the number of the children of
Israel." God's intention was that Israel might diffuse spiritual
light throughout the whole world by disseminating the truth
concerning the living and the true Creator of all men (cf.
Ezek. 5:5, 6).

While Israel is surely in view in the chapter, the foreground occupies itself with an individual, Zerubbabel, a scion
of the Davidic dynasty. Just as chapter three brings Joshua
and his work to the fore in order to encourage him, so this
chapter presents Zerubbabel as prominent that he might be
heartened for his arduous tasks. It must be remembered that
the Davidic descendant has been much hindered in his attempt
to build the temple of the Lord. Zechariah brings him the
message of hope and uplift so sorely needed. Zerubbabel is made
to understand that the work in the last analysis is dependent
upon God rather than upon any human agent or instrumentality.
Dods has well stated it in holding that "The preceding vision
was meant to reinstate the religious head of the nation; this is
meant to give Zerubbabel, the civil head, the assurance that he
also is God's anointed, endowed with power from God to do

God's work, as truly as ever any of his royal forefathers had been."[14]

This chapter allows of a simple, twofold division: (1) the vision proper, verses 1-5; (2) the interpretation of the symbolism, 6-14. It is interesting to note the emphasis on the number seven in this vision: seven lamps, seven pipes, and the seven eyes. The chapter itself consists of fourteen verses, a multiple of seven. But of the full significance of this number we shall speak more particularly and detailedly later.

The interpreting angel had evidently left the prophet at the conclusion of the preceding vision, so his return is stated thus: "And the angel that spake with me returned and awakened me, as a man that is awakened out of his sleep" (v. 1). We are not to understand the waking as ordinary, because the prophet was not asleep in the common sense of the word. The prophet had relapsed into his normal state of consciousness which was like the state of sleep compared to that in which visions and divine revelations are received. Keil has pointedly expressed it in this manner: "He has not only fallen back into the state of ordinary human consciousness, but his ordinary spiritual consciousness was so depressed that he resembled a man asleep, and had to be waked out of this sleep-like state by the mediating angel, in order to be qualified for further seeing"[15] (cf. Dan. 8:18; 10:9; Luke 9:32).

The fact of the condition of the seer is important but of greater significance is the vision which he saw in the ecstatic state, which he records: "And he said unto me, What seest thou? And I said, I see, and behold, a lampstand all of gold, and its bowl upon the top of it, and its seven lamps upon it; seven pipes to every one of the lamps which are upon the top of

---

14 *The Post-Exilian Prophets,* p. 79.
15 *Op. cit.,* Vol. II, p. 262.

it; and two olive trees by it, one on the right side of the bowl, and the other up on the left side of it" (vv. 2, 3). The second occurrence in verse 2 of the word *wayyo'mer* is clearly a copyist's error for *wa'omar,* the Qeri. The Qeri is found in many manuscripts and all the versions. The lampstand of the vision is the seven-branched lampstand of the tabernacle with three notable differences: (1) the bowl on top of it; (2) the seven pipes to each lamp; (3) the olive trees at the right hand and left of the lampstand (cf. Exod. 25:31-40). As to the number of pipes to the lamps there has been considerable difference of opinion. Von Orelli, Kimchi, and others hold that there were seven pipes in all. Keil, Chambers, Baron, and many others understand forty-nine in all. With this latter view we concur. There is no ambiguity in the original, as Wright would have it, for the expression *shibh'ah weshibh'ah* is to be taken distributively, seven pipes for each lamp. The usage is not without parallel as can be seen from II Samuel 21:20 and I Chronicles 20:6. The multiplied channels are purposely introduced to bring out the enlarged and abundant supply of the oil. The meaning of the olive trees is found in verses 12-14 of the chapter. Of what significance is the lampstand? What message was it meant to convey? The lampstand in the holy place of the tabernacle and of the temple later symbolized the combined testimony of Israel as a nation unto God in the power of the Holy Spirit in the midst of the unbelieving and pagan nations that surrounded them. Gaebelein quotes the Yalkut on Zechariah as saying, "The golden candlestick is Israel."[16] It has been well expressed by Wright that "The people of Israel stood to the nations of the world in a somewhat similar relation to that in which the tribe of Levi

---

[16] *Op. cit.,* p. 45.

stood to the whole family of Israel"[17] (see Isa. 60:1-3; 62:1, 2).
When Israel was set aside nationally for the duration of this
age of grace because of unbelief, then the Church, the Body of
Christ, the heavenly people of God, was committed with the
privilege of shining before the Lord and before all mankind in
the earth. Scriptures that bear on this truth are Matthew 5:14,
16; Luke 12:35; Ephesians 5:8, 9; Philippians 2:15; Revelation
1:20. But ultimately we see in the lampstand a symbol of the
Messiah of Israel, the Saviour and Light of the world. Isaiah
bore witness to this truth (49:5, 6), as did Zacharias and Simeon
later (Luke 1:78, 79; 2:32), and finally our blessed Lord Himself (John 8:12; 9:5). Kimchi fairly startles us at times with
his insight into such truths which culminate in the Messiah.
In commenting on the seven lamps he says: "like the candlestick in the law. And the middle one is a type of the Deity,
who forms the bond of union to unite contraries."[18]

But there is more in the vision for the eye that is illumi-
nated and will see. In the tabernacle and temple the light of the
lampstand was dependent upon the gifts and freewill offerings
of the people, as well as the priestly ministrations and care of
Aaron and his family (Exod. 27:20, 21; 30:7, 8). In the vision
there is no such need. The multiplied channels speak not only
of abundant, unceasing, spontaneous, free, and inexhaustible
supply, but of "perfect fullness of communications" (Dods).
No human hand is seen nor is it required.

The vision is not clear to Zechariah, so we read: "And I
answered and said to the angel that talked with me, saying,
What are these, my lord? Then the angel that talked with me
answered and said to me, Dost thou not know what these are?
And I said, No, my Lord" (vv. 4, 5). The question of the

---

17 *Op. cit.,* p. 91.
18 *Op. cit.,* p. 41.

prophet had reference not only to the matter of the two olive trees, but to all that was set forth in verses 2 and 3. The counter-query of the angel implies that to Zechariah, a pious Israelite, who was acquainted with the symbolism of the tabernacle and its furniture, the meaning of the vision should have been evident.

Since the prophet has confessed his ignorance of the inter-pretation of the vision, the interpreting angel, to whose office this function belongs, performs his appointed duty. We read: "Then he answered and spoke to me, saying, This is the word of Jehovah to Zerubbabel, saying, Not by might, nor by power, but by my Spirit, saith Jehovah of hosts. Who art thou, O great mountain? before Zerubbabel thou shalt become a plain; and he shall bring forth the top stone with shoutings of Grace, grace unto it" (vv. 6, 7). The *zeh* comprehends the entire vision, which was in reality a revealed prophecy for the comfort and encouragement of Zerubbabel. The civil head of the nation is assured that the prosecution and success of the work upon which he is laboring are dependent upon neither human strength nor external resources. The task before him requires more than mere human strength can afford. Just as the lampstand in the vision needed no human ministrations for its effectiveness, so the building of the temple ultimately rests upon the working of the Spirit of God. Meyer with spiritual insight points out that the wick of the lampstand, though needed for the light, has no large place in the production of the light. It has no lighting power in itself. It is a medium between the oil and the fire on its edge. So was Zerubbabel in the hands of God and under the sovereign influence of the Holy Spirit. The wick teaches us that "It accumulates nothing. It has no stores. From hour to hour it is always on the edge of bankruptcy, but always supplied."[19] Was not this divine revelation and encouragement calculated to meet

---

[19] *Zechariah the Prophet of Hope*, p. 58.

the very need, and a pressing one too, of the energetic son of Shealtiel?

What was the meaning of the oil in the vision? Hengstenberg has the support of all, surely, when he maintains that "Oil is one of the most clearly defined symbols in the Bible."[20] Everywhere in Scripture oil is seen as the type of the Holy Spirit. The oil of consecration for prophet, priest, and king was understood to symbolize the work and presence of the Holy Spirit. Why is oil given as a type of the Holy Spirit? The reason is not far to seek when we consider the functions and values of oil. First, oil lubricates, thus abolishing friction and promoting smoothness. The Holy Spirit it is who gives smoothness and abolishes wear in every service for God. Second, oil heals. In Biblical times wine and oil were applied to wounds. (Cf. Luke 10:34.) No one but the Spirit of God can heal the heart wounded by life's cares, sorrows, or unpleasantnesses. How the Church of the living Christ needs this ministry of the Holy Spirit today! Too many self-appointed physicians are going about to cauterize wounds with vitriolic treatment. We need to let the Holy Spirit have His undisputed sway. Third, oil lights. It is the Holy Spirit who illuminates the sacred page and the pathway of the believer. How unattainable is the meaning of Scripture when approached by our unaided reason, and how transparently lucid and clear when the Spirit Himself casts His blessed rays upon our impotent minds and hearts. (Cf John 16:12-15; I Cor. 2:9-12; I John 2:27.)

Fourth, oil warms. Whether it be the sad plight of the lost soul, or the need of a fellow-member in the Body of Christ, or the truth of God, our cold hearts are unresponsive and impregnable except the warming, glowing, pulsating power of the Spirit

---

[20] *Op. cit.*, p. 301.

of God penetrates and diffuses genial and welcome warmth.
Fifth, oil invigorates. It increases the energy of the body. Is it
not clear from the record of the book of Acts that the disciples
and apostles gave witness with power because they were Spirit-
filled, Spirit-led, and Spirit-possessed? The helplessness and
anemic impotence of the Church today are directly traceable and
attributable to the neglect or spurning of God's provision for
power in the Holy Spirit. Nowhere in the New Testament are
believers enjoined to ask for power. The energizing ministry of
the Spirit cares for all the power any believer will ever need.
Sixth, oil adorns. It was used in the feasts of Old Testament
times, and was never applied in times of sorrow and grief. (Cf.
II Sam. 12:20; Psa. 104:15; Isa. 61:3.) It was an adorning with
joy. The life lived under the control of the Spirit of God is
radiant with the joy of the Lord and fragrant with the perfume
of the presence of the Lord. Seventh, oil polishes. The Spirit
takes the rough edges from the character of the believer. The
fruit of the Spirit has none of the blemishes or blots of the old
nature. Small wonder, then, that God has used the figure of oil
as a type of the Holy Spirit and His manifold ministries. How
soul-satisfying is the contemplation of the relation of the Spirit
to the earthly life and ministry of our Lord. And all this can
be our portion too. In Psalm 133:2 we read of "the precious oil
upon the head, That ran down upon the beard, Even Aaron's
beard; That came down upon the skirt of his garments"; all this
is surely a prefiguring: the anointing of the Head is the portion
of all the members. Matchless grace of God!

But after the enunciation of the general principle, the very
key of the vision, in verse 6, we are carried forward to its immediate application in the life of Zerubbabel. The question of
verse 7 is really a defiant challenge since the outcome of the issue
is guaranteed. In the phrase *har haggadhol* the article is attached

to the adjective only, to give it the greater emphasis. Because
mountain usually symbolizes a kingdom or power, is no reason
that such must be its meaning always. The symbolism of the
Scriptures is not stereotyped. (Cf. Christ under the figure of a
lion, Rev. 5:5; Satan under the same figure, I Pet. 5:8.) The
mountain, then, stands neither for the Persian Empire (Hengstenberg, Kimchi, Keil, and others), nor for Sanballat and his
companions (Kimchi), nor for Anti-Christ and his power
(Gaebelein), but for all the obstacles and difficulties that stood
in the way of completion of the temple by the Davidic prince.
These hindrances will be removed by the working of the Spirit
of God. Zerubbabel will then bring forth the finishing stone, indicating the completion of the building, amid the shoutings of
the people, "Grace, grace [be] unto it." (Cf. Ezra 3:11.) The
people will call upon God's grace and favor to rest upon the
finished edifice. Thus the message of God to Zerubbabel through
the medium of the vision was intended to direct his gaze to the
only true source of power, the Spirit of God, and to encourage
him with the hope-inspiring promise of the successful completion
of his work.

Certain features of the vision have not yet been explained
and the force of the prophecy has not yet been exhausted, so the
divine communication proceeds to the prophet: "And the word
of Jehovah came to me, saying, The hands of Zerubbabel have
laid the foundation of this house, and his hands shall finish
it; and thou shalt know that Jehovah of hosts has sent me
to you" (vv. 8, 9). Wherein is this word an advance over verse
7 where the completion of the work is promised Zerubbabel?
Does the Spirit desire merely to repeat? No, the addition is to
be found in the last clause of verse 9. From the analogy of
2:13, 15 [Hebrew] it is evident that the prophetic finger is
being pointed at the coming Messiah. Just as chapter 3 had an

immediate application to Joshua, then went on to speak of the
Messiah, the Branch, the Stone, so this chapter has an immediate
reference to Zerubbabel and then beyond him to Christ. These
words of verse 9 "show that the promise was not exhausted
then, but that the work on which Zerubbabel was engaged is
regarded as a type and pledge of the sure fulfillment of that
which was set forth by the symbolism."[21] Just as the scion of
the Davidic house was to accomplish the completion of the
work on the restoration temple, so the One of whom Zerubbabel
was a type, David's greater Son, would begin and consummate
the work on the millennial temple (cf. 6:13). The building
in the days of the return from captivity was but a foreshadow-
ing of a far greater work in a future day.

But the Spirit of God has further encouragement for Zerubbabel through the words of the prophet. Zechariah asks: "For
who has despised the day of small things? for these seven shall
rejoice, and shall see the plummet in the hand of Zerubbabel;
these are the eyes of Jehovah which run to and fro through
the whole earth" (v. 10). Reference is made in *yom qetannoth*
to the day of the founding and continued building of the temple.
In the eyes of some of the contemporaries the work was insigni-
ficant and inconsequential (Ezra 3:12; Hag. 2:3). To such ones
God makes known that His pleasure is upon the work of Zerubbabel, and His omniscience, comprehending all the activities of
earth, is directed to the consummation of the building. How
easy it is for the unbelieving to see nothing in the very place
where God finds all His delight. Witness the Cross of Calvary.
Men may discount but God's favor and eyes were toward the
temple. Kelly says with fine perception: "the day when God
is morally testing souls is always a day of small things open

---

[21] D. Baron, *op. cit.*, p. 139.

to the scorn of him whose heart is not content to serve God."[22]
The seven eyes that rest with delight upon the plummet of
Zerubbabel are the same which in 3:9 were turned to the stone
placed before Joshua and his companions in the priesthood.

The number seven is so important in this chapter especially
that we advert to it here for a fuller word. Chambers gives us
a somewhat detailed treatment of this number and its significance. He points out the prominence of the numeral in both
Old and New Testaments, occurring not less than three hundred
and eighty-three times. From Genesis to Revelation the number
is to the fore. In Genesis there are the seven days of creation; the
sevenfold vengeance called down upon the slayer of Cain; the
sevens of clean beasts and fowls received into the ark; the dove
sent from the ark at intervals of seven days; Jacob serving seven
years for Leah and then a similar period for Rachel, his first
choice; the seven fat kine and seven lean, and the seven good
ears and seven thin of Pharaoh's dream; in Leviticus the sacrifices of seven victims often required by the Mosaic ritual; the
sprinkling of the blood seven times; the sanctity of the seventh
day, the seventh month, the seventh year, the seven weeks of
years. The historical books and prophetical books alike lay stress
on the numeral. When we come to the Revelation the recurrence
is still more prominent. There are seven churches, seven spirits,
seven lampstands, stars, seals, horns, eyes, trumpets, thunders,
seven angels, heads, crowns, plagues, bowls, mountains, kings,
and beatitudes.

Why is this number so important? Professor Hadley,
quoted by Chambers, gives five theories. "One is the Arithme-
tical, used by Philo the Jew, and based upon the peculiar
property of seven as compared with any other of the digits. A
second, the Chronological, is founded upon the early division

---

[22] *Lectures Introductory to the Minor Prophets,* p. 453.

of time into weeks. A third, the Symbolic, conceives seven to
be the union of two numbers, namely, three, which symbolizes
the divine, since the Godhead is a trinity, and four, which
symbolizes the cosmical, the created universe of space, this being
determined by the four cardinal points of the compass. The
seven then represents that reunion of the world with God, which
is the great aim and crowning consummation of all true religion. [In our opinion this theory has much to commend itself.
For instance, note how the seven churches of the Revelation
are divided into three and four with reference to the call to
heed and the promise to the overcomer.] A fourth is the Physio-
logical theory, tracing the pre-eminence of the seven to the fact
that there are seven parts of the body, namely, the head, chest,
and loins, with the four limbs; and seven openings of the head,
namely, the three pairs of eyes, ears, and nostrils, with the
mouth; and further, that the seventh, fourteenth, and twenty-first
days are critical periods in diseases. The fifth hypothesis is
based on Astronomical reasons. The nocturnal heaven offered to
the men of primitive times [?] a constant and impressive
spectacle. Here they could not be struck by the seven members
of the planetary system, as well as by the fact that the fixed stars
exhibited the same number in several of the most brilliant con-
stellations. . . . Upon the whole, in view of the antiquity of
the usage and the character of the early Hebrews, it seems most
natural to trace their sense of its sacredness and completeness
to its original associations with the times and means of religious
worship."[23] In our present context the number speaks of the
completeness of the divine oversight and pleasure in the labors
on the temple.

One feature of the vision has gone uninterpreted thus far,
namely, the two olive trees. Our attention is directed to it anew

---

[23] Lange, *op. cit.*, note on p. 38.

by the question of the prophet: "Then I answered, and said
to him, What are these two olive trees on the right side of the
lampstand and on the left side of it?" (v. 11). The angel has
not had time to answer when the prophet asks another question:
"And I answered the second time, and said to him, What are
the two olive branches which are by the side of the two golden
spouts, that empty the gold [golden oil] out of themselves? And
he answered me saying, Dost thou not know what these are?
And I said, No, my lord. Then he said, These are the two
anointed ones who stand by the Lord of the whole earth" (vv.
12-14). The second question has to do with the two olive
branches; in the original vision there is no mention of them.
They resembled ripe ears of grain, for such is the meaning of
shibbale. Pusey proves beyond a doubt that the olive branches
represent individuals. Says he, "Zechariah's expression, 'in the
hand of' or, if so be, 'by the hand' of the two pipes, shews that
these two were symbols of living agents, for it is nowhere used
except of a living agent, or of that which is personified as
such."[24] The reference is, of course, to the word *beyadh*. There
are two hundred and seventy-six cases besides this. In three (Job
8:4; Isa. 64:6; Prov. 18:21) other than a personal agent is mentioned, and in these the agent is personified. Practically all expositors interpret the last three verses thus: the two olive trees are
the priestly and kingly offices in Israel; the two olive branches
or twigs are their then incumbents, Joshua and Zerubbabel.
Theirs is a position of responsibility in service before the Lord
of all the earth. Ultimately, these two servants of God in their
official capacities adumbrate the Lord Jesus Christ, the Messiah
who is both King and Priest (cf. 6:13).

Let us continually note throughout the prophecy of Zechariah, and, indeed, throughout the entire revelation of God, how

---

[24] *Op. cit.*, Vol. II, p. 363.

the Spirit of God is ever zealous to point the believing heart and spirit beyond all human agencies to the Ultimate One. To recapitulate, the chief features of the message to Zerubbabel were: (1) the insufficiency and inadequacy of all human strength and resources; (2) the all-sufficiency of the power of the Spirit of God for the accomplishment of the work of God; (3) the unceasing, abundant, and inexhaustible supply of this power at his, Zerubbabel's disposal; (4) the assurance of the obliteration of all hindrances to the building; (5) the heartening hope of the completion of the work by the one commencing it; (6) the importance of the entire work of building as a prefiguring of the activity of the Messiah in a coming day; (7) the delight of God in the construction of the temple; (8) the positions of privilege of both Joshua and Zerubbabel as the media whereby the testimony of God is transmitted to the people; and (9) the typifying of the ministry of the Messiah in both the religious and civil offices.

Did we not say that the lampstand conveyed the thought of witness and testimony? Of what sort was it? Imperfection in testimony was first found in Israel, then in the Church (Rev. 2:5; 3:15, 16). Perfection of testimony is found only in Christ Jesus the Lord. He is the faithful Witness (Rev. 1:5), the faithful and true Witness (Rev. 3:14), the Faithful and True (Rev. 19:11). How becoming us to adore Him!

CHAPTER III

VI. THE VISION OF THE FLYING ROLL, 5:1-4.

THE LAST three visions of the prophet are of an entirely different nature than the preceding ones. The messages of the visions thus far have been of a decidedly consolatory character. There is to be enlargement for Israel; yes, more, the subjugation of all her enemies, the internal cleansing of the nation for priestly service, and the consequent ministry of illumination and witness to the rest of the world are all set forth. Before these prophecies can be fulfilled in the nation, there must be the righteous judgment of God upon all sinners and all transgression. This rightly presupposes what is elsewhere in Scripture stated positively: before the blessings of the first five visions will be actualized, there will intervene in the life of the nation a period of moral declension and apostasy. God must and will purge out all iniquity, though He has promised untold glory for the godly in Israel. Zechariah knows nothing (nor does any other writer of the Scriptures) of the mawkish theology that is so much in vogue in our day, that considers God as the God of love, over-looking every failure, shortcoming, and defection in man. True, twice over John the apostle in his First Epistle designates God as the God of love, but he sounds forth the warning of impending judgment upon all ungodliness in all the writings that the Spirit of God directed him to pen. If God can overlook sin lightly because of His love, then what need is there for Isaiah to state of Him that He is "the high and lofty One that inhabiteth eternity, whose name is Holy" (Isa. 57:15)? What object is accomplished in Habakkuk's great declaration: "Thou that art of purer eyes than to behold evil, and that canst not look on perverseness" (Hab. 1:13)? Why should the majestic Epistle to the Hebrews inject such notes as these: "It is a fearful thing to fall into the hands of the living God" or "our God is a consuming fire" (Heb. 10:31; 12:29)? Away with a half-baked theology! Let us magnify the love of God and at the same time maintain His irreproachable holiness.

The visions of the fifth chapter are closely related in thought and concept, so much so that some have taken the two as one (Keil, Lowe, and others). We prefer to treat the visions as distinct because, though connected in meaning, they are surely quite different in form and manifestation, as well as ultimate fulfillment. The two visions of this chapter and the one of the next are connected by their judgmental character and by the Hebrew word translated *going forth* (cf. 5:3, 6; 6:1). It is interesting to note that the verb *yatsa'* occurs in 5:1-6:8 no less than a dozen times. As for the interpretation of the concluding visions of the series, Ironside has well stated: "It is noticeable that, as we go on with the series, there is less and less given in the way of interpretation. It is as though the Lord would give enough in regard to the earlier visions to lay a solid foundation for the understanding of the later ones."[1]

As we come to this sixth vision, we hear Zechariah narrating: "And again I lifted up my eyes, and saw, and behold a flying roll" (v. 1). For the meaning of *shubh* as the adverb "again" we find other examples in Genesis 26:18; II Kings 1:11, 13; and Jeremiah 18:4. The object of the vision was a roll which is emblematic in Scripture of a pronouncement or message of great importance from God. (Cf. Ezek. 2:9, 10.) The significant features of the roll are: (1) its position, (2) its size, (3) its

---

[1] *Notes on the Minor Prophets*, p. 367.

message, and (4) its execution or fulfillment. The roll was unfolded—otherwise its measurement could not have been discerned—and flying to indicate the rapid and sudden approach
of the things declared therein. Its dimensions are given in verse
2: "And he said to me, What dost thou see? And I said, I
see a flying roll; its length is twenty cubits, and its breadth is
ten cubits." Immediately evident is the fact that these measure-
ments are exactly those of the tabernacle in the wilderness (Exod.
26:15-25) and those of the porch in Solomon's temple (I Kings
6:3). Various have been the explanations of this correspondence.
Hengstenberg expresses the opinion of many when he says, after
noting that the size can hardly be considered accidental, "By
giving to the flying roll, the symbol of the divine judgments
upon the covenant nation, the same dimensions as those of the
porch, the prophet appears to intimate that these judgments
were a direct result of the theocracy."[2] Chambers understands
the reference to be to the scope of the threatening judgment, that
is, the covenant people, while Keil, following Kliefoth, maintains that what is indicated is that the measure of judgment
will be meted out according to the measure of the holy place.
We conceive the thought of the prophet to be that the judgment
impending will be according to the measure of the holiness of
the house of the Lord and will begin there. (Cf. Ezek. 9:6;
Amos 3:2; I Pet. 4:17.)

The prophet now turns to the contents of the roll: "Then
he said to me, This is the curse that goes forth over the whole
land: for every one that steals shall be destroyed on the one side
according to it; and every one that swears shall be destroyed on
the other side according to it" (v. 3). The flying roll contains
a curse against thieves and perjurers. The correlatives *mizzeh*
. . . *mizzeh* remind us of the two tables of the law written on

---

[2] *Op. cit.*, Vol. III, p. 305.

both sides (Exod. 32:15; see also Exod. 17:12; 26:13; Num. 22:24; Ezek. 47:7). It is interesting to note that the middle commandment from each table is designated, but perhaps all that is meant is a sample or instance from the whole. God and man alike were set at nought by the ungodly. In this case *ha'arets* can only refer to the land of Israel, the whole of it. The reasons are to be found in the context: (1) because of the land of Judah only could it be affirmed that they swore in the name of Jehovah (v. 4); (2) because in verse 11 the land is distinctly contrasted with the land of Shinar; and (3) because the reference to the two tables of the law restricts the curse primarily to those under the law. In view of these facts it is difficult to see how the whole earth could be referred to here.

What, then, is the curse pronounced? In the broader sense it points to the curse which the law of Moses as such declared against any one who did not continue in the words of the law to do them (Deut. 27:26). Specifically, it touches upon the judgment due for the infraction of the two commandments singled out. In describing the force of the punishment according to the terms of the law, *naqah* is used in a new sense. In ordinary usage the verb has the sense of "to be clean, pure, innocent, not obligated"; here the force is that of "to destroy, extirpate." Lowe's observation has point; he says, "With regard to *niqqah* it must be observed that it is not elsewhere used (in the Niphal) of a person being destroyed, though it is found (Isa. 3:26) of a city being laid waste."[3] The thoroughgoing character of the punishment is set forth thus: "I will bring it forth, saith Jehovah of hosts, and it shall enter into the house of the thief, and into the house of him that swears falsely by my name; and it shall abide in the midst of his house, and shall consume it with its timber and its stones" (v. 4). This is the fulfillment of the

---

[3] *The Hebrew Student's Commentary on Zechariah*, p. 50.

curse. The language here reminds us of the destruction of the house of the leper in Israel (cf. Lev. 14:45). The leprosy of sin always carries desolation, extreme and final, in its wake.

To what period of Israel's history should this vision be referred? Dods supposes that allusion is being made to those who kept back money from the builders of the restoration temple, and then swore falsely that they had none to give. Kimchi thinks it is not clear to what time the prophecy applies, but considers it likely that the prophet was speaking to his own time, in which there were many guilty of numerous transgressions according to the record of the Book of Ezra. Fausset suggests that the theft and swearing had special reference to the withholding of the portions due from the people to the Levites (Neh. 13:10), and the holding back from the Lord of tithes and offerings (Mal. 3:8). Ironside, Dennett, Baron, and others find the setting of the prophecy in the last days when Israel will be returned and settled in the land in unbelief, a condition that is the precursor for the final culmination of Jewish and Gentile apostasy. We take the position that the immediate reference of the prophecy is to the time of the prophet without any need to specify that these sins were committed either with regard to the rebuilding of the temple or the offerings and tithes of the Lord. Surely these infractions were committed many times over by the contemporaries of the prophet in many of the phases of their life.

But, judging from the weight of the context, the fuller realization of the prophecy is in that time before the purging of the land from all sin and sinners, the period immediately preceding the setting up of the kingdom of the Son of David. Wright disallows this, according to his position on many phases of eschatology, saying: "But the idea that the expulsion of all sinners from the Holy Land at the commencement of the millennial era . . . is referred to finds no support in the language of this prophecy."[4] Keil in similar vein holds: "The vision refers to the remote future of the kingdom of God; and therefore 'the whole land' cannot be restricted to the extent and boundaries of Judea or Palestine, but reaches as far as the spiritual Israel or church of Christ is spread over the earth; but there is no allusion in our vision to the millennial kingdom and its establishment within the limits of the earthly Canaan."[5] According to the character of the former visions the prophet proceeds from the immediate present to the remote future (compare 3:1-5 with 3:9; 4:6 with 4:9; 6:10 with 6:13), and so here. It is sufficient to say, in refuting the contention of both Wright and Keil, that, granted that this passage does not speak of a cleansing preparatory to the kingdom of the Messiah, surely other passages teach it. First of all, we take the full force of this passage, but we must go on from this to compare Scripture with Scripture. There is a partial aspect to all prophecy which leads us not to expect all of any given truth in one prophetic revelation or passage. If it is sad to contemplate that such sins were actually present in Israel after the chastening of the Babylonian Captivity, it is all the more so to understand from the Word of God that such will be the condition after a world-wide exile and dispersion during this age of grace.

VII.   THE VISION OF THE WOMAN IN THE EPHAH, 5:5-11.

The seventh vision carries on the thought of the sixth in showing that the punishment on the sinners in Israel is not all, but that sin itself must be removed from the land, and that to the very place of its origin. There will be seen at this point a tracing of iniquity to its source. So we read: "Then the angel

---

[4] *Op. cit.*, footnote on p. 108.
[5] *Op. cit.*, Vol. II, p. 281.

that spoke with me went forth, and said to me: Lift up now
thine eyes, and see what is this that goes forth. And I said, What
is it? And he said, This is the ephah that goes forth. Then he
said, This is their appearance in all the land" (vv. 5, 6). The
going forth of the ephah probably refers to the movement of
the measure as it comes into view, rather than the fact of the
progress or development of iniquity. The ephah was the greatest
dry measure in use among the Hebrew people. What does its
use intend to convey to us? Here there have been conflicting
views. Kimchi takes the position, and one not generally accepted, that the vision refers to the past. Says he, "He showed
him the captivity of the ten tribes, who had long since been
led away captive, how that they were utterly lost in the captivity,
and did not now go forth, when the captivity of Judah and Benjamin went forth. He showed him an ephah, which is a measure,
to signify that God had measured out to them measure for
measure; for, according as they had done by continuing many
days in their wickedness, from the day that the kingdom was
divided until the day that they were led away captive; and as
they had not had one out of all their kings, who turned them
to good, but on the contrary, they all walked in an evil way;
according, I say, as they had continued long in evil, so they
shall be many days in captivity: this is measure for measure,
therefore the prophet saw an ephah, which is a measure."[6] In
keeping with this view he interprets the woman in the ephah
as the ten tribes, and the two women, who bear her away to the
land of Shinar, as Judah and Benjamin.

The objections to this position are several: (1) it is fatal
to his interpretation that he makes this vision speak of the
past when all of Zechariah's visions speak of the present or
future; (2) the ten tribes were not exiled to Babylon but to

---

[6] *Op. cit.*, p. 48.

Assyria; (3) the agents of her captivity were certainly not Judah and Benjamin. Baron (so also Wright, Meyer, Von Orelli, and others) believes the ephah stands for a godless commercialism. He admits that at one time he held the general interpretation of the passage; that is, that reference is here being made to the filling up of the full measure of Israel's sins before the time of banishment from the land in a coming day. He explains the reason for his change thus: the ephah is not seen as the place for the accumulation of the sins of the nation, but rather as itself going forth to pervade the nation with its influence. He thinks the ephah speaks of a new power exerted over Israel after the Babylonian Captivity, namely, that of commerce and trade, of which the ephah is the symbol. They were changed from an agricultural to a mercantile and commercial people. He feels that an ungodly commercialism is adapted to the production of the very sins set forth in verses 1-4. (Cf. Amos 8:5; Mic. 6:10.) The objections to this interpretation are two: (1) the author is probably reading modern conditions back into Zechariah's time; (2) wicked commercialism was not originated ("upon her own base" of verse 11) in Babylon, but wickedness in its most hideous and heinous form—idolatry—was. We understand the passage to speak of the heaping up of the full measure of Israel's sins prior to the time of God's separation of the wicked from the midst of the righteous remnant of the last days. Apart from the dispensational feature which we adhere to, this is the commonly accepted view of students of the passage. (Cf. Gen. 15:16; Matt. 23:32.)

But what is the meaning of the clause, "This is their appearance in all the land?" As many views have been advanced to explain this, as have been offered to account for the mention of the ephah. For the *'enam* in our text, the LXX (translating it, *'e 'adikia auton*), the Syriac Peshito, and the Arabic read *'awonam.* This change is based upon the scantiest of manuscript authority and appears to be an attempt to circumvent a difficulty. No, we cannot read it, "This is their iniquity in all the land," but "This is their appearance in all the land." Usage will bear out this translation of the word. (Cf. Lev. 13:55; Ezek. 1:4, 7, 16, 22, 27.) Von Orelli, preferring the reading of the LXX, discounts *appearance* as a translation, "because the ephah was not at all suited to give a sight of what was in it."[7] Keil not only refutes such a contention, but gives, I believe, the true sense of the words thus: "The point of comparison is rather to be found in the explanation given by Kliefoth: 'Just as in a bushel the separate grains are all collected together, so will the individual sinners over the whole earth [we differ in this, taking the reference to be to all of Palestine as in verse 3] be brought into a heap, when the curse of the end goes forth over the whole earth.' "[8]

But the prophet saw more still, so he records: "And, behold, a talent of lead was lifted up, and this is a woman sitting in the midst of the ephah. And he said, This is wickedness, and he cast her down into the midst of the ephah; and he cast the weight of lead upon its mouth" (vv. 7, 8). Within the ephah there is a woman who sits entrenched in her sins. Chambers takes "the woman as a personification of the ungodly Jewish nation."[9] She is rather a representation of all the sinners of the land. The figure of a woman in Scripture stands for a nation (Isa. 47:1-7; 62:1-5), a woman out of her rightful place of submission and humility (Matt. 13:33), or a system (Rev. 2:20; 17:5). The woman of the vision under consideration represents wickedness, as the interpreting angel specifically states,

---

[7] *Op. cit.,* p. 333.
[8] *Op. cit.,* p. 283.
[9] Lange, *op. cit.,* p. 48.

as it will be culminated in the last days. It will be organized both among Israel and the nations of the earth into a colossal confederacy, holding sway religiously over the earth. Nor is this wickedness dormant, for the great leaden weight must be cast upon the mouth of the ephah to keep it bound there (II Thess. 2:6-8).

What is to be done with the ephah and its occupant? The conclusion of the matter Zechariah narrates: "Then I lifted up my eyes, and saw, and behold, two women went forth, and the wind was in their wings; for they had wings like the wings of a stork; and they bore the ephah between earth and heaven. Then I said to the angel who spoke with me, Whither do they bear the ephah? And he said to me, To build for her a house in the land of Shinar; and when it has been established, she shall be set there upon her own base" (vv. 9-11). While the prophet viewed the ephah two women came forth and bore off the ephah in mid-air. That these women are representatives of God's agents for His purpose is clear from the fact that they have wings. They are like the stork's for he has broad pinions, and in his annual migrations covers great distances. The destination of the ephah's flight is said to be the land of Shinar. Here great difference of opinion prevails in interpretation. We shall set forth some of the studied views of expositors, then present our conclusions. The first mention of Shinar in the Bible is in Genesis 10:10. (It is found in all six other times: Gen. 11:2; 14:1, 9; Isa. 11:11; Dan. 1:2; and here.) In all instances where it occurs it is used as a definite geographical designation. Strictly speaking it covers more than Babylon, but is employed to denote that land.

Some expositors feel the passage speaks of a past event, the Babylonian Captivity, but this is untenable because all the rest of Zechariah's visions refer to the future, not the past. The force of the last verse of the chapter is to the effect, moreover, that a permanent settling of sin is in view. Wright contents himself with relegating the whole to the realm of the ideal. Hengstenberg concludes: "The future dwelling-place of the Jews, who were to be banished from their country, is called by the name of the land in which they were captives before, just as in chapter 10:11 their future oppressors are called by the names of Assyria and Egypt."[10] To such a conclusion we need only say that the references in 10:11 do not compel us to understand them as other than literal. Somewhat after the same manner, Chambers expresses himself on our problem: "This verse then simply foretells the punishment of wickedness by another exile,—like that to Babylon, and therefore called by its name, but far more prolonged . . . the vision was fulfilled centuries afterward, when the Jews as a whole, having rejected with scorn their Messiah, were given over to the stroke of vengeance."[11] This position fails to account for the words "upon her own base." Keil, too, takes the reference in a symbolic sense when he says: "The name is not to be taken geographically here as an epithet applied to Mesopotamia, but is a notional or real definition, which affirms that the ungodliness carried away out of the sphere of the people of God will have its permanent settlement in the sphere of the imperial power that is hostile to God. The double vision of this chapter, therefore, shows the separation of the wicked from the congregation of the Lord, and their banishment into and concentration within the ungodly kingdom of the world."[12]

This interpretation fails to account for the use of the name Babylon, nor does it explain the words "upon her own base."

---

[10] *Op. cit.*, p. 308.
[11] *Op. cit.*, p. 48.
[12] *Op. cit.*, p. 285.

The early chapters of Genesis reveal that religious and spiritual corruption and confusion originated in Shinar in rebellion against God. Throughout all the remaining books of the Old Testament Babylon is seen to be the object of the wrath of Almighty God. Prophet after prophet inveighs against her unmitigated wickness. Idolatry, of all sins most abhorrent to the true and living God, had its origin and full development in her. Now, the prophet Zechariah foretells that in the last days all wickedness, with idolatry particularly in mind (see Matt. 12:43-45), that will be existent in Israel at that time will go back forcibly to the place of its origin, Babylon, the great apostate religious system. Such is the meaning of being settled on her own base. When we come to the book of Revelation all this is clearly set forth in chapters 17 and 18. Not only the evil in Judaism, but that in Christendom as well, will wind up and culminate in that abominable system called mystical or mystery Babylon. The greatest sin in Israel, even wickedness itself, was idolatry. It will come to its settled abode at the very place of its inception (Rev. 18:24).

The two visions of our chapter thus bring before us God's twofold method of dealing with sin in His people. He pours out His wrath upon the transgressors who are impenitent, and then sees to the utter removal and banishment of sin from the land, that it may in truth be the holy land. Von Orelli has well compared the thought of the chapter to the Mosaic ritual. Says he, "The two cleansing acts of this chapter are complementary, like the two goats on the Day of Atonement, Leviticus 16, of which the first must give its blood as an expiation before the Lord, while the second carries away the guilt of the people, and the impurity springing from it, to the region of the impure desert-demon. The cleansing judgment, despite the terror, is a benefit to the land, which is thus purified and fitted to receive the blessing pictured in the former visions."[13] And the message of the chapter for the believer of this day may well be summarized in the words of the apostle, exhorting: "let us cleanse ourselves from all defilement of flesh and spirit, perfecting holiness in the fear of God" (II Cor. 7:1).

VIII. THE VISION OF THE FOUR CHARIOTS, 6:1-8.

There is a close relationship between this vision and the preceding ones of the fifth chapter. Just as the Lord will judge His nation for their unfaithfulness and disobedience, so He will visit the godless nations of the world who have arrayed themselves against Israel. Judgment, severe and irrevocable, will be the portion of both. Dods rightly states the object of the vision thus: "To convey the assurance that the reestablished order and peace of Israel, depicted in the foregoing visions, would not again be disturbed by the powers which had hitherto molested and oppressed God's people."[14] Similarity exists between the first and last visions of the series of night-visions. The eighth vision concludes the cycle of the series; in its use of symbolism like that of the first vision it denotes the accomplishment of the purposes outlined from the very outset. There, horses and riders were seen engaged in the work of reconnoitering; here, war chariots are the instruments of the divine judgment. That which was determined of God through the findings of His scouting agents in chapter one is fully executed in chapter six through the chariots.

The distinctive features of the last vision are given in four particulars: (1) the place of departure of the chariots (v. 1); (2) the color of the horses (vv. 2, 3); (3) the meaning of the symbol of the chariots (vv. 4, 5); and (4) the destinations

---

[13] *Op. cit.*, p. 335.
[14] *Op. cit.*, p. 85.

of the chariots (vv. 6-8). The prophet brings the vision before us thus: "And again I lifted up my eyes, and saw, and behold, four chariots came forth from between the two mountains; and the mountains were mountains of brass" (v. 1). What is the meaning of the four chariots? Many expositors see in this figure a reference to the four great empires of Daniel's prophecy (Pusey, Wright, Dennett, Kimchi, and others). Kelly states positively: "The four chariots are an unmistakable reference (*mutatis mutandis*) to the course of earthly power as already made known in detail by Daniel."[15] In keeping with the explicit word in verse 5 and in agreement with many other students of the passage, we understand the chariots to be symbols of power and great authority. (Cf. Psa. 68:18 [Hebrew]; Isa. 66:15; Hab. 3:8; Hag. 2:22.) The number four speaks of the universality of the judgment to be carried out by God's agencies which are further described in verse 5. The definite article in *heharim* indicates that the mountains were well known.

Since the chariots go forth to actual geographical designations, as we shall see later, just so the mountains from whence they proceed are to be taken as representing a specific geographical locality. The mountains, in all probability, are Mount Zion and Mount of Olives (so also Pusey, Keil, Baron, Gaebelein, Wright, Von Orelli, Dods, and many others). Between these two mountains in Palestine lies the Valley of Jehoshaphat which is related in Scripture to the judgment of the nations. (See Joel 4:2, 12, 16, [Hebrew]; Zech. 14:4.) The mountains are said to be of brass, not because of the height of the divine wisdom or the sublimity of His power (Pusey), nor because of the immovable firmness of the Lord's dwelling (Keil), but because of the divine righteousness in judgment (Psa. 36:7, [Hebrew]). Note the copious references to brass in the Pentateuch, especially with

---

[15] *Op. cit.*, p. 461.

regard to the tabernacle in the wilderness. God's aforeprepared agencies of His judgment will perform their task, God's strange work, with the utmost of righteousness.

But Zechariah would reveal more to us concerning these instruments of divine judgment by disclosing the colors of the horses attached to the chariots. So we read: "In the first chariot were red horses; and in the second chariot black horses; and in the third chariot white horses; and in the fourth chariot grizzled strong horses" (vv. 2, 3). The colors, here as in chapter one, are of importance, and signify the same truths. Thus, the red designates war and bloodshed; the black speaks of death and famine; the white denotes triumph and victory; and the grizzled indicates pestilence and plagues. Those who hold that the four chariots are the four great world empires have been driven to fantastic interpretations in their attempt to relate the colors to the specific kingdoms. For instance, Kimchi sees in the red horses the Babylonian Empire, in the black horses the Medo-Persian, in the white the Grecian, and in the grizzled the Roman. Pusey thinks "The symbol of the fourth empire, grizzled, strong, remarkably corresponds with the strength and mingled character of the fourth empire of Daniel."[16] To this end he tries in verses 6 to 8 to find historical events answering to each one of these actions and motions. As the vision unfolds itself the objections to such a view become more and more evident. (1) The destinations of the chariots as stated in the text do not at all conform to the geographical localities of all the four empires. (2) There is a lack of historical confirmation when the motions of the chariots are to be tallied with historical events. (3) The explanations are too far-fetched and fantastic (Wright shows this at great length, although he feels the four empires are

---

[16] *Op. cit.*, Vol. II, p. 369.

pictured by the chariots) that seek to connect the colors with specific kingdoms.

But there are difficulties in the passage for any view. These are: (1) in verse 3 the *beruddim* are identified with the *'amutst-sim* and in verses 7 and 8 they are clearly distinguished; (2) no mission of the *'adhummim* is given. Why are the grizzled joined with the strong in verse 3 and separated in verse 7, and why is no mission stated for the red horses? We shall mention a few of the explanations given. Lowe gives his opinion that the word "strong" in verse 3 is to be taken as a blunder of an early copyist. Such cuttings of the Gordian knot are not new in Biblical exegesis, and are to be avoided assiduously. Rashi, the scholarly and highly revered Jewish commentator, confesses he does not know the meaning of the word. Hengstenberg, after interpreting the *beruddim* as hail-like, says of the *'amutstsim*: "it can only signify *powerful*." (In this latter pronouncement Wright concurs.) Then, on the basis of verse 7, he refers this adjective to all the horses. But soon after he seems to contradict himself by holding that "The red horses of the first chariot are the strong ones."[17] Baron tries to solve the difficulty by maintaining that they are called speckled for their color and strong because of their special characteristic. Calvin and others advanced the view that *'amots* was a softened form of *hamots,* as in Isaiah 63:1, signifying bright red, but instances are lacking for a usage where ' and *h* are interchanged. In one point all seem to agree, and with this we must content ourselves, that verse 7 speaks of the accomplishment of the red horses of the first chariot.

In detailing for us the meaning of the symbol of the chariots, the prophet writes: "Then I answered and said to the angel that talked with me, What are these, my lord? And the angel

---

[17] *Op. cit.,* Vol. III, p. 310.

answered and said to me, These are the four winds of heaven
which go forth from standing before the Lord of all the earth"
(vv. 4, 5). The question of Zechariah does not imply that he
was ignorant that the vision presented chariots with horses, but
his query was directed toward the explanation of the symbol
of the chariots. He was asking what the chariots might represent.
The answer of the angel is so clear, that it scarcely leaves room
for us to see the four empires in the four chariots. The chariots
are said to be the four winds of heaven that stand in a place of
attendance and ministry before the Lord. Baron thinks that
the most natural explanation of *ruhoth* is "angelic beings."
Chambers shows how untenable this is when he marshals three
cogent arguments. (1) Says he, "I can find no instance in which
the plural is used to denote angelic beings. Certainly Psalm
104:4 is not one."[18] (2) The word *hashshamayim* in that case
would have no suitable meaning. (3) The Scripture reveals
nothing of four pre-eminent angels. The four winds speak of
divine judicial power exerted in judgment, carrying out the
purposes of God. Cf. Psalm 148:8; Jeremiah 49:36; Daniel 7:2;
Revelation 7:1. Keil summarizes well when he states: "the
meaning is not that the chariots represent the four winds, but the
less obvious figure of the chariots is explained through the more
obvious figure of the winds, which answers better to the reality."[19]

The chariots have missions and this is next set before us:
"*The chariot* in which the black horses were, went forth to
the land of the north; and the white went forth after them; and
the grizzled went forth toward the land of the south. And the
strong went forth, and sought to go that they might walk to and
fro in the earth; and he said, Go, walk to and fro in the earth.
So they walked to and fro in the earth. Then cried he to me, and

18 Lange, *op. cit.*, p. 50.
19 *Op. cit.*, Vol. II, p. 286.

spoke to me saying, Behold, they which went forth to the land
of the north have caused my wrath to rest in the land of the
north" (vv. 6-8). The land of the north, Babylon, and the
land of the south, Egypt, are singled out for the mission of the
chariots, because these two countries were the chief and invet-
erate enemies of the people of Israel in those days. Babylon
comes in for double mention in verse 6 and is particularized
still further in the last verse of the vision, where it is said that
God's wrath comes to rest, is quieted in Babylon. The sense
of *ruhi* is surely that of "my wrath" as can be substantiated
from such usages as Judges 8:3; Ezekiel 5:12; 16:42; 24:13;
Ecclesiastes 10:4; Proverbs 16:32. Keil denies that the word can
be so rendered, but gives no valid objection.

What was the application of these truths to the days of
the prophet? Ironside rightly states: "The special prophetic application of what Zechariah had beheld was at that moment
connected with the kingdom of Babylon on the north [Jer. 1:14,
15; 25:9] and Egypt on the south. Between these two powers
God would sustain His feeble flock, checkmating every effort to
destroy them till Messiah should Himself appear."[20] It would
appear from the fact that two teams go to the north that Babylon
would be doubly judged. Why, then, is Babylon again before
us in verse 8? First, it would serve to comfort and encourage
the returned remnant of Israel that had come from Babylon.
Second, the Babylonian world-empire, as a matter of history, had
already experienced the judgment of God in her overthrow
and downfall. Third, it is there that wickedness will again be
established and finally be extirpated. Cf. 5:11. In the end time
the coming of Christ again and the establishment of His glorious
kingdom in righteousness will be preceded by final judgment
on wicked Babylon.

---

[20] *Op. cit.,* p. 372.

IX. The Coronation of Joshua, 6:9-15.

The remarkable series of eight night-visions, going as it does from the time of Zechariah to the fullness of times in the history of Israel, is beautifully climaxed by the crowning of Joshua, a symbolical act of much significance. Here we have the end and consummation of all the prophetic Scriptures: the crowning of the Lord Jesus Christ. It is only after the dark night of world judgment and punishment is passed, that the glorious light of Christ's coronation day will follow. This is one of the sublimest passages in the Scriptures on the Person and work of the Messiah.

The close of the visions is indicated by the employment of the usual formula for direct prophetic utterance and revelation. So we read: "And the word of Jehovah came unto me, saying, Take of them of the captivity, of Heldai, of Tobijah, and of Jedaiah; and thou shalt come in that day and thou shalt enter into the house of Josiah, the son of Zephaniah, whither they have come from Babylon" (vv. 9, 10). From a cursory perusal of the passage it will be seen that five items are prominent: (1) the command to the prophet, Zechariah (vv. 9-11); (2) the truths symbolized (vv. 12, 13); (3) the memorial for the deputation (v. 14); (4) the participation of the Gentiles in blessing (v. 15a); and (5) the need of obedience in Israel (v. 15b). The setting and occasion for the symbolical act are given in verses 10 and 11. Evidently, three men had come as a deputation from the exiles in Babylon, bringing with them an offering of silver and gold for the temple then in the process of building. Many have occupied themselves at length to bring forth truths from the names of the men of the deputation (they are nowhere else mentioned in the Scriptures), but it seems that the matter of greater importance is the time indicated in the verse. The notation of time points to the day mentioned in 1:7, that is, the day preceding the night in which the visions were revealed.

The command to Zechariah was: "Yea, thou shalt take silver and gold, and make a crown, and place it upon the head of Joshua, the son of Jehozadak, the high priest" (v. 11). The prophet was enjoined to take the offerings of the deputation, and make of them a crown for the head of Joshua. Because *'ataroth* is a plural, Ewald (and this is, sad to say, indicative of his methods in Biblical exegesis) inserts *ubhero'sh Zerubbabhel* and in verse 12 changes *'elayw* into *'alehem*. His opinion is that one crown was made for Joshua and one for Zerubbabel, so the text must be altered to read so. This is neither translation, interpretation, nor exegesis, but eisegesis of a most capricious sort. Kimchi comes to the same conclusion as to the crowns, for he says, "as to the other crown, it was not necessary to mention what was to be done with it, for it is clear that it was to be upon the head of Zerubbabel, for he was in the place of king, and no king without a crown."[21] That these views are untenable can be seen from two considerations: (1) lexical and (2) contextual. Whenever the word *'ataroth* refers to crowns, it is used as a singular. Cf. Numbers 32:3, 34, 35; Joshua 16:5, 7; 18:13; I Chronicles 2:54. Jonathan in his Targum translates it "great crown"; the Syriac renders it "a crown." See also Job 31:36. There is but one head mentioned and in verse 14 the word "crown" is used with *tihyeh* which is singular. It is just such a composite crown as is indicated in Revelation 19:12, one magnificent crown made up of several circlets. Why we are so zealous in contending that no crown was placed upon the head of Zerubbabel, will become more clear as we consider the meaning of the symbolical act. But in passing we might say that to have crowned Zerubbabel, a scion of the Davidic dynasty, would have been misleading, for it might have been misunder-

---

[21] *Op. cit.*, p. 57.

stood as a restoration of the Davidic kingdom, which was not
the purpose of God at that time. (It is interesting to note that
this verse of our text is one of twenty-six in the Old Testament
that contain all the letters of the Hebrew alphabet.)

All that has thus far been presented to us has been by way
of type, prefiguring. Now we have the fulfillment in these
words: "And thou shalt speak unto him saying, Thus speaketh
Jehovah of hosts saying, Behold, a man whose name is Branch;
and he shall grow up out of his place and shall build the temple
of Jehovah. Even he shall build the temple of Jehovah; and he
shall bear glory and shall sit and rule upon his throne; and he
shall be a priest upon his throne; and a counsel of peace shall be
between them both" (vv. 12, 13). Baron has rightly said of this
prophecy: "This is one of the most remarkable and precious
Messianic prophecies, and there is no plainer prophetic utterance
in the whole Old Testament as to the Person of the promised
Redeemer, the offices He was to fill, and the mission He was
to accomplish."[22] The speaker in verse 12 is Zechariah and
the one addressed is Joshua in particular. No high priest of
the Old Testament ever needed to be told that the kingly and
priestly offices were kept apart in Israel. The regal office was
irrevocably lodged in the house of David (see II Sam. 7; Psa.
89), while the sacerdotal office was given to the tribe of Levi.
We have only to recall the awful visitation from God that
befell Uzziah when he essayed to offer incense, to realize that
God meant these offices and functions to be kept separate (II
Chron. 26). This being so, Zerubbabel had no right to perform
any priestly functions (and he did not), nor could Joshua, as a
priest, wear a crown, then sit and rule upon a throne. But this
is precisely what is pictured here of Joshua. Then it must be
in a typical sense, and such it is. Joshua is here a type of Christ

---

[22] *Op. cit.,* p. 190.

who is the true Melchizedek, both King and Priest. Cf. Hebrews
7:1-3 with Psalm 110:4. Joshua, being already high priest, had
the kingly dignity added to him in type; so with Christ: His
kingly office is grounded in His high priestly work for us, on
the Cross and then at the right hand of the Father.

Every word of these verses is worthy of note, so we look
more closely at the text. The proper name "Branch" we have
not only had before us in 3:8, but in the pre-exilic prophecies
of Isaiah and Jeremiah. (see chapter 3.) The words translated "Branch" and "he will grow up" are from the same
root, constituting a meaningful play on words: "the Sprout will
sprout out of his place." Wright notes that the LXX, Vulgate,
and Luther render *mittahtayw*: "It shall grow up under him,"
i.e., blessings shall spring up in His steps and follow Him. The
thought is rather the growth of the Messiah, the King-Priest,
from lowliness and obscurity to note and eminence from His
own nation and country. Chambers summarizes our position:
"Better is the view (Hengstenberg, Keil, etc.) that the Branch
will grow up from his place (cf. Exod. 10:23), i.e., from his
own land and nation, not an exotic, but a genuine root-shoot
from the native stock to which the promises have been made."[23]
In short, He will be from the seed of promise in the land of
promise. It is further credited to Him that He will build the
temple of Jehovah. This phase of His work is so important that
it is repeated in verse 13. Can this be the restoration temple?
Surely not, for the building of that temple had been promised
to Zerubbabel in 4:9. Those who do not differentiate between the
Church and Israel tell us that we are to take this temple as a
spiritual one, namely, the Church of Christ spoken of in the New
Testament. This is undoubtedly the millennial temple referred
to in Isaiah 2:2-4; 56:6, 7; Ezekiel 40-48; Micah 4:1-7.

---

[23] *Op. cit.*, p. 53.

In that millennial day He shall not only build the temple of Jehovah, but bear the glory. Pusey points out that "This word glory [*hodh*] is almost always used of the special glory of God, and then, although seldom, of the majesty of those, on whom God confers majesty as His representatives."[24] Cf. Psalm 96:6; 104:1; 111:3 and many others. Thus clothed with the divine glory, enhanced by His mediatorial offices, He will sit and rule on His throne. The first verb speaks of the dignity of the office, and the second speaks of the exercise of its authority. He sits! Priests never sat in their ministry. There was no seat in the tabernacle nor in the temple for the priests. Theirs was an unfinished work; His is a gloriously complete one. Cf. John 19:30; Hebrews 1:3; 8:1; 12:2. He rules! Governmental authority will be vested in Him. And He will rule on His own throne. He is on the Father's throne now (Rev. 3:21); He will yet sit on His own throne (Mt. 25:31). On His throne He will be a King-Priest. The repetition of the personal pronoun in verse 13 points to (1) the certainty of the fact, (2) the importance of the Person, and (3) the greatness of the tasks set forth.

Zechariah adds, in conclusion, that a counsel of peace shall be between them both. Most expositors take *ben shenehem* to refer to Jehovah and the Branch, Jesus and the Father. But what new thing is this? The counsel of peace has existed between the Father and the Son from all eternity. With Hengstenberg, Keil, Wright (although he favors the view just given also), and Von Orelli, we see the reference as made to the two offices or dignities residing in the Messiah, in such a way as never before and in such a manner as fully to realize the peace, the good, and the welfare of His people. We have the parallel to *'atsath shalom* (a counsel procuring peace) in Isaiah 53:5 where *mu'sar shelomenu* properly means the chastisement which issues

---

24 *Op. cit.*, p. 375.

or eventuates in our peace. Kelly brings out the full import of the prophetic announcement by saying: "He is now a priest after the order of Melchisedec; He will then exercise it in all its fullness of meaning (not as now Aaronically in the holiest, but) coming forth with refreshment for the conquerers over the hostile powers of the earth, blessing the most high God, the possessor of heaven and earth (manifestly so then), and blessing man, Himself the channel and security of all blessing for ever."[25]

Most Jewish expositors deny the Messianic character of our passage. Failing to realize that Joshua represented the Messiah in name as well as in office, and that the LXX's translation (*'anatole,* see Lk. 1:78) is not without significance, they have interpreted it of another. Kimchi, who is representative, holds that the Branch is Zerubbabel. M'Caul, his translator, effectively answers him by a sevenfold argument:

1. Kimchi makes *'ataroth* refer to two crowns when it may include any number. This is done in the interests of his interpretation.
2. There is nothing said about Zerubbabel and it cannot be read into the text.
3. Usage shows that the word *'ataroth* (as we have already indicated) refers to one crown composed of smaller crowns or diadems. Verse 14 uses the singular verb with it.
4. Kimchi claims *wehayah khohen 'al kis'o* should have *'al* translated as in verse 5, "before." "To what purpose should Zechariah tell Joshua that there should be a priest before the throne, when he himself was the high-priest?" If Joshua was neither to sit on a throne, nor to be a type of such a one, then why was he crowned at all?
5. *'Al* is not used in verse 13 with the same verb as in verse 5. This called for a different translation of the preposition.

---

[25] *Op. cit.,* p. 463.

Besides, previously in this very verse he has rendered it
"upon."

6. Abarbanel, another eminent Jewish commentator, refutes
   Kimchi's position by showing that no such advancement
   came to Zerubbabel in Jerusalem; no royal dignity was accorded him at that time or later. He never ruled in
   Jerusalem.

7. Ancient Jewish tradition and passages like Isaiah 4 and
   Jeremiah 23 point to the Messiah as the One indicated.
"In every chapter, without exception, from the first to the sixth,
we have symbolical prophecies, and in no case do the things
or persons employed as symbols, represent themselves, at some
future period of their history, but they are symbols of other
things and persons. The uniform nature, therefore, of all the
preceding visions, decides that the action here described is symbolical, and that it does not symbolize any thing referring to
Joshua, but to some one else."[26] For detailed proof of the Messianic character of 6:9-15 see Hengstenberg, *Christology of the
Old Testament,* Vol. III, pp. 325-327.

The fulness of this Messianic prophecy can better be seen
if we but marshal the distinctive features in order:

1. The humanity of the Branch.
2. The place of His birth.
3. The building of the millennial temple by Him.
4. His fitness to bear the glory of God.
5. His reign on the throne of David.
6. His priestly ministry.
7. The issue of His blessed ministry—peace.

How appropriate the designation Branch is for Him can be
seen from the remark of F. B. Meyer: "Through a branch the
fulness of the Root is carried to the fruit, which swells in ruddy

[26] *Op. cit.,* pp. 60-69.

beauty on its extremity, and presently falls into the hand of the wayfarer; so Jesus is the blessed channel of communication between the fulness of God, and the thirsty wastes of human need. We sit under his shadow with great delight, and his fruit is sweet to our taste."[27]

Zechariah concludes with a word that brings the deputation from Babylon before us with new and fuller meaning. Just as Joshua is a type, so the visitors from afar are symbolic of peoples of a future day. He writes: "And the crown shall be to Helem, and to Tobijah, and to Jedaiah, and to Hen the son of Zephaniah, for a memorial in the temple of Jehovah. And they that are afar off shall come and build in the temple of Jehovah; and ye shall know that Jehovah of hosts has sent me to you; and this shall come to pass, if ye will surely hearken to the voice of Jehovah your God" (vv. 14, 15). Now that the crown had served its chief purpose in the symbolical act, it is to be placed in the temple of Zerubbabel for a memorial to the devotedness of the embassy that had come the long trek from Babylon. Some suggest that *hen* be translated as an appellative noun, "favor, kindness, hospitality," but there is no need to take it as other than a name for Josiah. Just as Heldiah and Helem are the same, so Josiah and Hen refer to the son of Zephaniah. Kimchi quotes the Talmudic treatise Middoth as stating that chains were fixed in the beams of the porch so that the young priests went up and saw the crowns which were in the windows. Pusey thinks the tradition is not without historical basis, and well it might be. Those afar off that are to be builders in the coming temple of Jehovah are none other than the Gentiles. The ambassadors from far-off Babylon were types of the Gentiles who will come in a future day to help build with their wealth the house of the Lord. Cf. Isaiah 60:2, 6, 9.

---

[27] *Op. cit.*, p. 72.

It is the Messiah who will direct and supervise the building, but in His grace He will associate with Himself those from among the Gentiles also. All this will be patent proof that God has sent, not Zechariah primarily, but the Angel of Jehovah referred to in the suffix of *shelahani*. Cf. 2:13-15 (Heb.) and 4:9. Some take the last clause of the chapter as an aposiopesis (interruption in the text) or a lacuna. Kelly says of such an ending: "the Jews are left in this inexpressible solemnity on that hinge of personal responsibility, just indeed but ever fatal to the first man."[28] Examples of this usage are found in Genesis 31:42; 50:15; Psalm 27:13. The usage is permissible from the idiom of the language, but is not necessary. The thought is that their personal participation in the blessings promised will depend upon their obedience to God. By obedience only can the individual heart ever realize the promises of God. How the near and the far view are united in the passage is made clear by Dennett: "the remnant from Babylon would only be guarded, prospered, and brought into the enjoyment of present blessing in building the temple, even as the remnant in a future day, of whom they were the representatives, would only be permitted to see the fulfilment of these glorious predictions, if they diligently obeyed the voice of the Lord their God."[29]

In this manner have we been taken by the Spirit of God through the prophet from the time of the restoration under Joshua and Zerubbabel to the day of restoration in the land in the millennial era. Such is the broad and divinely meaningful scope of the night-visions of chapters one to six. As we view with faith and joy and adoration the blessed Saviour as King and Priest, let us realize anew that He has made us by His

---

[28] *Op. cit.*, p. 465.
[29] *Zechariah the Prophet*, p. 71.

grace kings and priests before God (I Pet. 2:5, 9; Rev. 1:5, 6), and that, having suffered here with Him in the day of His base rejection, we shall reign gloriously with Him (II Tim. 2:12). The believing heart can only pray that the day may be hastened.

PART THREE

CHAPTER I

THE QUESTION AND THE ANSWER
CONCERNING FASTING

(7:1-8:23)

I. The Question, 7:1-3.

IN THE FIRST section of the book (1:1-6) Zechariah occupied himself with an urgent exhortation to Israel to repent; in the second division (1:7-6:15) the prophet set forth a series of night-visions covering the period of Israel's national history from the then present hour till the climax of Messiah's coronation; and in the third portion of the prophecy, comprising both chapters seven and eight, the theme revolves around the subject of Israel's national fasts. In order to understand fully the basis of the question and the perplexity in the minds of the people, we need to review the historical setting of that day. It was the year 518 B.C. Two years had already elapsed since the time of the night-visions, and God was already bringing to fruition the promises relative to the building of the temple. Two years more were to pass before the completion of the temple (Ezra 5:16; 6:15), but the work was progressing now without hindrance. The royal decree of Darius had gone forth permitting the work to proceed without interruption in accordance with the former decree of Cyrus (Ezra 6). The people were aroused to the work and performed it with diligence (Hag. 1:14). Jerusalem itself was undergoing a transformation. Splendid private homes were being erected (Hag. 1:4). It was a time calculated to make

113

the people forgetful of all the hardships and captivity that
they had suffered. Such was the day in which the word of the
Lord came to Zechariah.

Perhaps a word should be said with regard to the last
eight chapters of the book. The reader is referred to the introduction of these studies for a treatment of these chapters
from the standpoint of authorship. From the seventh chapter
to the end of the prophecy, Zechariah leaves the language of
apocalyptic visions and writes in regular prophetic style. There
are those who would divide the last eight chapters to correspond
to the visions of the early chapters. To be sure, there are many
passages in both sections that bear upon related themes, but the
parceling out of portions in this fashion may turn out to be a
rather artificial procedure in the end. We do admit, for instance,
that a portion of chapter 7 is parallel to 1:1-6, but it would be
a fruitless task to attempt to seek out parallel passages for every
section of the first six chapters of the book. Besides, the messages of other prophets furnish us with just as important parallels
on the themes under consideration. In the treatment of the
remaining chapters of the book we shall see the importance of
the vast themes brought before us. The prophet is projected by
the Spirit of God into the far distant future to write of matters
that relate to Israel's latter days. We shall be viewing the introduction of the Messiah, His work among His people, His
rejection, the consequences of this sad decision, the final and
universal attack of world confederacies upon Jerusalem, the
mightly intervention of God to avert unspeakable catastrophe for
Israel, the establishment of the throne of Messiah, and the
recognition of the rightful reign of the Lord over all the world.
The student of Biblical prophecy finds himself referring again
and again to these vital chapters on the mighty events of the
end time.

We have already intimated that chapters 7 and 8 are related. They deal with the same theme and were delivered on the same occasion. Chapter 7 occupies itself first with the setting forth of the occasion for the revelation of God; afterwards the question of verses 1-3 is answered negatively in two sections. In chapter 8 the query is answered positively and that in two sections also.

Since we have dealt with the historical setting of the chapters, the chronological citation in verse 1 will not detain us. Here we read: "And it came to pass in the fourth year of Darius the king, that the word of Jehovah came to Zechariah in the fourth day of the ninth month, in Chislev" (v. 1). The division of the notation of time is not usual, but in no way obscures the sense. The month Chislev among the Hebrews today answers to our month December. At this time, the prophet tells us: "Now Bethel had sent Sharezer and Regem-melech, and their men, to entreat the face of Jehovah; to speak to the priests of the house of Jehovah of hosts, and to the prophets, saying, Shall I weep in the fifth month, separating myself, as I have done these so many years?" (vv. 2, 3). Much discussion has centered about the words *beth 'El*. Is the reference to the house of God (so Kimchi, Hengstenberg, and others) or is the city of Bethel meant? The latter view is held by Pusey, Keil, Wright, Baron, and others. With the latter view we must concur for a number of reasons. (1) There is no instance in the Old Testament where Bethel refers to the temple or house of God. According to Pusey *beth Yhwh* is used about 250 times, and *beth 'Elohim* or *beth ha' Elohim* about 50 times of the temple, but *beth 'El* not once. (2) Wright notes that all the versions on the text render the words of the well-known city. (3) As far as the Hebrew word order is concerned, Bethel is in the proper place of the subject. Therefore, the words cannot be translated "house of God."

It cannot be proved, moreover, that after the captivity Bethel became the religious center of the nation. Hence, Bethel would not have received a delegation inquiring concerning so important a national question. It was entirely possible for Bethel, the inhabitants of the city, to send a deputation to Jerusalem. According to Ezra and Nehemiah former inhabitants of Bethel returned with the remnant from Babylon. Cf. Ezra 2:28; Neh. 7:32; 11:31. The town seems to have been soon rebuilt. That it was Bethel who sent the deputation of inquiry is of more than passing importance. Wright pointedly states: "It is, therefore, interesting to observe that the lessons taught by the Babylonish and Assyrian captivities were not lost upon the men of Bethel. Notwithstanding the many sacred memories connected with their city, and the fact that it had been the seat of a remarkable temple erected to Jahaveh [the reader, to be sure, needs not to be told that this was brought about through the idolatrous worship instituted by Jeroboam, the son of Nebat] in the days of the Israelitish kingdom, to which the tribes of Israel had resorted in numbers, no attempt was made on their part to dispute the legitimate right of Jerusalem being regarded as the only place where the sacrifices and services enjoined by the precepts of the Mosaic law could be offered."[1] The men sent on this mission were probably born in Babylonia, for their names are of foreign origin.

The prophet states that the purpose of the embassy was to entreat the face of Jehovah. They came to inquire of the Lord with regard to a matter of spiritual moment at the time. The word *lehalloth* is indeed vivid, for it actually means "to stroke the face" or "caress"—an anthropomorphism for tender entreaty.

---

[1] *Op. cit.*, p. 168.

The picture is of one stroking the face of another to smooth away the wrinkles of displeasure (Dods). Pusey flatly denies the explanation of the idiom as we have given it, calling it "altogether imaginary" and maintaining that the word always means entreaty by earnest prayer. But, on the other hand, Gesenius in his lexicon and other commentators give the sense of the verb as we have first stated it. While verse 2 gives us the mission of the delegation in general terms, the following verse states explicitly the purpose of their coming. Specifically, it was to inquire whether they should continue to fast in the fifth month of the year as they had been doing for the seventy years of the exile.

Why did the exiles fast in the fifth month? In order properly to answer the question, we should couple with this fast those mentioned with it in 8:19 of our prophecy. They all commemorated disastrous events that eventuated in the Babylonian Captivity. In the fourth month (Tammuz), on the ninth day of the month, in the eleventh year of Zedekiah's reign, the city of Jerusalem opened to the invaders. Cf. Jer. 39:2; 52:6, 7. On the tenth day of the fifth month (Ab) the city and the temple were destroyed by fire in the nineteenth year of Nebuchadnezzar (Jer. 52:12, 13; II Kings 25:8, 9). The Kings' account gives the day as the seventh of the month; the seeming discrepancy disappears when we realize that the city, the temple, and the houses were in flames from the seventh to the tenth day. Apart from the fast of the Day of Atonement, that of the ninth of Ab is the most solemnly observed today among the Hebrews.

Kimchi gives the reasons Maimonides, probably the greatest Jewish philosopher of the Middle Ages and court physician to Sultan Saladin of the Third Crusade fame, has advanced for the keeping of the fast: "On the ninth of Av, five things

happened. 1st. The decree went forth in the wilderness that the
people should not enter the land. 2d. The first and second temple
were both destroyed on this day. 3d. The great city Bither was
taken [in the reign of the Emperor Hadrian], in which were
thousands of myriads of Israel; and they had a great king, whom
all Israel and the greatest of the wise men thought was the
King Messiah [the evident allusion is to Bar Cochba who was
hailed as Messiah by so great a scholar as Rabbi Akiba]: but
4th, he fell into the hands of the Gentiles, and they were all
put to death, and the affliction was great, even like the desolation
of the house of the sanctuary. 5th. On that day, devoted to
punishment, the wicked Turnus Rufus ploughed up the
sanctuary and the parts about, to fulfill that which was said,
'Zion shall be ploughed as a field.' "[2] As for the fast of the
seventh month (Tishri) it was held on the third day to mourn
the murder of Gedaliah, the governor whom Nebuchadnezzar
had set over the small remnant in the land after the final deportation. (Cf. II Kings 25:25, 26; Jer. 41:1.) On the tenth day of
the tenth month (Tebeth), Nebuchadnezzar began his siege of
Jerusalem in the ninth year of Zedekiah (II Kings 25:1; Jer. 39:1).
Such, then, were the occasions that had called forth fasting on
the part of Israel during the years of captivity. It is interesting
to notice that the deputation from Bethel knew to whom to
come. They addressed themselves to the priests and the prophets.
The latter, doubtless, were Haggai and Zechariah; the former
had of old been designated as the teachers of the people in
matters pertaining to the law of God. (See Deut. 33:8-10; Hag.
2:11; Mal. 2:5-7). The thought in *hinnazer* is that of abstinence
from both food and pleasures. It is clear from the expression
"so many years" that they were already wearied of the fasting,
that they viewed the time spent in fasting through the years

---

[2] *Op. cit.*, footnote to p. 71, quoted from *Yad Hachasakah*.

as of "incalculably long duration" (Keil), and that they supposed they were surely now past these exercises.

What occasioned their questioning after this manner in the first place? When the people of Israel saw the work on the temple progressing under the prospering of God, when the city of Jerusalem itself was showing signs of new life, when the communal life of the nation was regaining its normal aspects, when the signs of the devastation and destruction wrought by Nebuchadnezzar were fast disappearing, it seemed to the people quite incongruous to continue the keeping of the fasts that brought to remembrance the former desolations. Why continue to fast and weep when the cause of it no longer existed? It appeared to them that in the prospering of the nation, the Lord was manifesting His desire to reverse their long-endured disasters. It were well for us to keep in mind that in the law of Moses there was commanded but one day of fasting upon Israel, the Day of Atonement, and that by implication only (Cf. Lev. 16:29—"ye shall afflict your souls."). It is true that at other times God may have called for fasts in the nation (see Joel 1:13, 14), but these were never meant to be perpetuated as set or annual fasts. The fasts, then, in the fourth, fifth, seventh, and tenth months were of the people's own making. Although God had not commanded these fasts, the people, nevertheless, seem eager to know whether this is the time to leave off the observance of them.

II.   The Rebuke, 7:4-7.

From verse 4 to the end of this chapter we have the negative part of the prophet's answer to the deputation's question. So we read: "Then came the word of Jehovah of hosts to me, saying, Speak to all the people of the land and to the priests, saying, When ye fasted and mourned in the fifth and in the seventh month these seventy years, did ye really fast unto me, even to me? And when ye eat, and when ye drink, are not ye the ones

who eat, and are not ye the ones who drink?" (vv. 4-6). The
Lord answered the inquiry of the people by a direct revelation
to the prophet who was to transmit the message to all the people
and the priests. Although Bethel alone sent the deputation the
Lord knew the question was in the minds of all the people,
hence the answer to all. But the nature of the reply was far
different from what they expected. If the Bethelites had antici-
pated any commendation for long years of meticulous fasting,
they were sadly disappointed. Rebuke was their portion instead.
The Lord, by one fell swoop, cut away the sham and externalism
in their fasting. It was not that they did not go through the
ceremonies, for they actually fasted and even beat upon their
breasts as *saphodh* explicitly states. (Cf. Gen. 50:10; Isa. 32:12
(especially); Joel 1:13; Zech. 12:10-12.) But since genuine self-
humbling and self-judgment were lacking, the Lord was not
really taken into account, and therefore, it was not fasting to
Him.

Moreover, they were probably fasting because of the punishment that had befallen them, rather than out of sorrow that
God's righteousness and holiness had been offended in the sins
that brought about their calamities. The prophet says more than
that God was not glorified by their fasting; in their eating and
drinking He had no part. Kimchi summarizes the argument
well: "When ye fast it is because of your sins, and when ye eat
and drink it is for your own profit: the whole matter is for yourselves; but what have I in all this, for neither in the fasting nor
the eating is there anything for my glory?"[3] For the believer
of this age Paul makes the principle clear in 1 Corinthians 10:31.
It is so easy to have self alone in view and put God out of the
reckoning altogether. Such was the sad condition of Israel of

---

[3] *Op. cit.*, p. 72.

that day and of myriads of others from whatever nation since
that time.

And it was not as though Israel had not known better, for
Zechariah reminds them: *"Do ye not know* the words which
Jehovah cried by the hand of the former prophets, when Jerusalem was inhabited and at rest, and the cities about her, and
the south and the lowland were inhabited?" (v. 7). The verse
is admittedly elliptical, a verb such as "know" or "hear" being
required to complete the thought. Not only does the prophet
point out the futility of heartless fasting, but would turn their
minds to the words that had been preached to God's people by
the pre-exilic prophets, especially Isaiah and Jeremiah. He is
saying in effect that had the warnings of the prophets of God
been heeded when the land was tranquil and secure, then there
would not have been a captivity, and fasting would not have
been necessary. The localities designated are meant to comprise
the whole land. Just as God desired obedience above all at that
time, so now, in the day of Zechariah, He seeks for the same
attitude of heart. In the preaching of the former prophets the
people could easily ascertain that path which was pleasing to
God. (See I Sam. 15:22, 23; Isa. 58:3-8; Jer. 14:12.) Dennett
has written a pertinent word that we must all face. Says he,
"If therefore we would discover the causes of the broken and
captive condition of the church, we must go back to Pentecost,
even as the Jews were here commanded, to go back to the time
of Jerusalem's prosperity, and when we have done this we may,
by comparing the present with the past, easily learn the means
of restoration and blessing."[4] Indeed, it would have been far
better for Israel to have heeded the words of the prophets than
ever to have fasted.

[4] *Zechariah the Prophet*, p. 77.

CHAPTER II

III. THE WARNING FROM THE PAST, 7:8-14.

In the last portion of the chapter we find an epitome of God's former message to His people, then the manner in which the truth had been received, and lastly the resultant judgments upon people and land alike. The first truth is found in verses 8-10 where the prophet says: "And the word of Jehovah came to Zechariah, saying, Thus spake Jehovah of hosts, saying, Judge true judgment, and show kindness and mercy every man to his brother; and oppress not the widow, nor the orphan, the sojourner, nor the poor; and let none of you think evil against his brother in your heart." Instead of formal, lifeless fasting God delights in practical righteousness, as He made known through the prophets (cf. Jer. 7:4-7). These things were not new in Israel for the substance of the messages of the prophets was well known. Wherever God ordained rites and ceremonies in the law, there were still moral implications of the same that had to be met.

The classic passage on this very truth, it seems to us, is to be found in Isaiah 58:3-9: "Wherefore have we fasted, and thou seest not? wherefore have we afflicted our soul, and thou takest no knowledge? Behold, in the day of your fast ye find your own pleasure, and oppress all your laborers. Behold, ye fast for strife and contention, and to smite with the fist of wickedness: ye fast not this day so as to make your voice to be heard on high. Is such the fast that I have chosen? the day for a man to afflict his soul? Is it to bow down his head as a rush, and to spread sackcloth and ashes under him? wilt thou call this a fast, and

122

an acceptable day to Jehovah? Is not this the fast that I have
chosen: to loose the bonds of wickedness, to undo the bands of
the yoke, and to let the oppressed go free, and that ye break
every yoke? Is it not to deal thy bread to the hungry, and that
thou bring the poor that are cast out to thy house? when thou
seest the naked, that thou cover him; and that thou hide not
thyself from thine own flesh? Then shall thy light break forth
as the morning, and thy healing shall spring forth speedily;
and thy righteousness shall go before thee; the glory of Jehovah
shall be thy rearward. Then shalt thou call, and Jehovah will
answer; thou shalt cry, and he will say, Here I am." The
latitudinarian in theology on reading this exclaims: "It is as
we have always said, 'It is not what you believe that counts;
it is what you do.'" But such shortsightedness forgets that such
practice can only come from the realm of faith. On the other
hand, the conservative who indolently and smugly cries: "It is
what you believe that counts, and not what you do," forgets that
the root of the tree is ultimately revealed in the fruit. Chambers
has beautifully put it: "Morality is certainly not piety, but the
piety which does not include morality is a mere delusion. It mocks
God and insults man."[1]

Such was the burden of the messages of the prophets. They
reiteratedly besought the people to manifest their faith in the
living God by exhibiting it in their daily contacts with men
about them. The widow, the orphan, the stranger, and the poor,
without human defenders, are seen throughout the Scriptures as
the special objects of the loving and jealous care of God (cf. Isa.
1:11-17; Hos. 6:6; Mic. 6:6-8). Any infringement of their rights,
though not rectified by man, nevertheless incurs the wrath of
God Himself. Men charge the Scriptures with being impractical.

[1] Lange's Commentary, Minor Prophets, *Book of Zechariah,* p. 58.

Could such exhortations as these given to the messengers of
God be more practical than they are?

Israel, then, in pre-exilic days had the revelation of truth
from God upon their ways. How did they receive it? Again,
Zechariah summarizes for us: "But they refused to hear, and
turned a stubborn shoulder, and made their ears heavy, that they
might not hear. And their heart they made as an adamant stone,
that they might not hear the law and the words which Jehovah
of hosts had sent by his Spirit at the hand of the former prophets;
therefore there was great wrath from Jehovah of hosts (vv. 11,
12). In these words the prophet with short strokes but with
telling force declares the rebellious character of Israel when the
message came to them. A variety of expressions is used to convey the thought of obstinate disobedience: the rebellious shoulder,
the heavy ears, and the adamant heart. The picture that under-
lies the figure of the rebellious shoulder is that of an ox that
is refractory and refuses to allow the yoke to be placed upon its
neck (cf. Neh. 9:29; Hos. 4:16). Israel would brook no re-
straint in her ways. She would have freedom to do her own will.
The heavy or dull ears speak of a lack of submissiveness that
would not hear nor heed the charges of God. The adamant
heart, as though by a climax, portrays the manner in which they
steeled their hearts against the words of God to make them impregnable and impenetrable (cf. Ezek. 11:19). They would
hear neither the law nor the prophets, and so wrath remained
for them (1:2). In verse 12 we have a clear setting forth of the
two factors in all the inspired writings: the Spirit and His human
instruments (II Pet. 1:21).

In outlining the dire consequences suffered because of disobedience, the prophet would bring it more vividly before them,
so he uses direct speech: "And it came to pass that, as he cried,
and they did not hear, so they shall cry, and I will not hear,

saith Jehovah of hosts; but I will scatter them as with a whirl-
wind among all the nations whom they have not known. Therefore the land became desolate after them, so that no one passed
through nor returned: for they made the pleasant land desolate"
(vv. 13, 14). The last verses of the chapter elaborate on the
thought of the wrath of God mentioned in verse 12. Since God
had remonstrated with them repeatedly and they would not
hear, they were to cry out for help, and God would not heed.
Jeremiah had warned them of such a plight before the destruction of the land (Jer. 11:11, 14; 14:11, 12). Pusey quotes another
as saying, "It shall be too late to cry for mercy, when it is the
time of justice." God threatened them with a scattering among
the peoples (and it is well to note that, although a nucleus did
return from the Assyrian and Babylonian captivities, many remained dispersed among the nations) and the complete desolation of the land of Palestine, called the pleasant land. They were
to be cast among the nations that did not know them, and so
(as Keil suggests) would not be moved with pity or compassion
for them. Though the desolation of the land was brought about
through the judgment of God, ultimately it is viewed here as
having been so brought to ruin because of the fathers.

In many ways this chapter reminds us of 1:1-6, for, here
as there, the prophet aims to dissuade the returned exiles from
following in the disastrous disobedience of their fathers. However sincere the people were in desiring to know about the continuance or cessation of the fasts related to the captivity, there
were issues more vital and pressing for them to consider. Had
they stopped to think that perhaps they had God no more in
mind when they fasted than when they went about their
customary pursuits? Did it never occur to them that perhaps
they were making the form an end in itself, and that the
reality for which it stood no longer existed? More than that:

did they ever recall to mind the words which were ever upon
the lips of the prophets when the land knew no invasion nor
desolation by the enemy? Were not those principles just as
applicable to the returned exiles as to their forefathers? Was
not the whole past ablaze with fiery warning that the path
of disobedience is a fruitless and sad one?

Zechariah says, in a word, that God wants much more
than formal fasting. If they would know what that is, they
have only to turn to the oft repeated messages of the servants
of God given with deepest of sincerity and with hearts breaking
for the impending destruction that finally came upon the people
in the captivity. True piety is the will of God in all ages and
history bears this out. But, you say, Zechariah has never really
answered their question. We need not fear; he will in due
time. In the meantime, does the wise child of God now need to
have the application of all this pointed out to him? If he claims
the position of bondservant (as did Christ the Lord, Phil. 2:7),
he will know the true worth of submission and yieldedness.

IV. The Restoration of God's Favor, 8:1-17.

The prelude and background to this chapter are to be
found in the previous chapter where the urgent and perplexing
question of the people was met with rebuke and sad warnings
from the past history of Israel. In the seventh chapter of his
prophecy Zechariah contented himself, through the directing
Spirit of God, with revealing the spiritual emptiness of the
nation's fastings and ceremonies and the basic and actuating
cause of all their woes. The problem of the nation has been
treated only from the negative standpoint. But God has the
positive answer to their query and this we find in the chapter
before us. Zechariah now points with the unerring finger of
prophecy to the glorious future God has in store for His people,
Israel, and the exact manner in which He will utimately

remove all their fasts. As in other passages of the prophetic Scriptures, many in number, here we find the chastisement and judgment of God upon sin and unbelief followed by words of consolation and hope. The heart of God, overflowing with love, will not allow Israel to think that He is intent on judgment alone, for judgment is His strange work. Love, mercy, and grace are the work in which He delights.

Our chapter lends itself easily to division. There are two broad divisions: (1) the passage from verse 1 to 17, and (2) the portion from verse 18 to 23. Each section in turn falls into several parts, each beginning with the words: "Thus saith Jehovah of hosts." (Compare verses 2, 3, 4, 6, 7, 9, 14, 19, 20, and 23.) The name *Jehovah* occurs in the chapter some twenty-two times, the purpose being to lend assurance and fixedness to all that is predicted. If chapter seven was designed to awaken the consciences of the people, then this chapter purposed to pour into the hearts of the godly the soothing balm of God's consolations and compassions. Dennett has well observed: "The subject of this chapter, in contrast with chapter 7, reveals the whole truth of God's ways with Jerusalem and the house of Judah, and indeed with man."[2]

Without lengthy preface the prophet comes directly to his prediction of the future for Israel, saying: "And the word of Jehovah of hosts came, saying, Thus saith Jehovah of hosts: I am jealous for Zion with great jealousy, and I am jealous for her with great wrath. Thus saith Jehovah: I will return to Zion, and will dwell in the midst of Jerusalem; and Jerusalem shall be called the city of truth, and the mountain of Jehovah of hosts, the holy mountain" (vv. 1-3). A comparison of these verses with 1:14, 15 will readily show that Zechariah is depicting a millennial scene with conditions as they will obtain at that

[2] *Op. cit.*, p. 83.

time. (Compare Isa. 1:21, 26; Zeph. 3:13.) When the Scriptures
speak of the jealousy of God there is meant no implication of
envy, but rather the boundless zeal of the Lord which loves
holiness, hates sin, brings judgment upon sinners, and inter-
poses on behalf of His godly ones. The Hebrew has preserved
for us a vivid anthropomorphism in *qinne'thi* which speaks
of the redness of the face that accompanies strong emotion
(Dods). The jealousy for Zion is to be understood as one for
her benefit and vindication, while the jealousy with great wrath
speaks of God's attitude and purpose toward the nations that
have afflicted and oppressed down-trodden Israel.

The careful student of the Old Testament will note that
the prophets are one in predicting that the selfsame intervention
of God in human affairs that will result in Israel's deliverance
will ultimately eventuate in the utter discomfiture of the godless
nations harassing her. The vehement affection of the Lord
set forth in verse 2 is manifested toward Israel in the manner
described in the following verse. It is the presence of God that
insures all the blessings mentioned. If He be present, all the
rest will come to pass. The glory of God resident in the tabernacle and then in the temple, had departed from the nation,
as declared by Ezekiel. (Compare 8:3, 4; 10:4, 18; 11:22, 23;
see also Zech. 2:14-17.) The dwelling of God again in Jerusalem
will give to the cleansed city a name in which she may well
boast. The Hebrew idiom does not necessitate that the city
actually be called by this name, but that she will be worthy
of it, and that it will adequately express her true characteristic.
Compare the names of the coming Messiah in Isaiah 9:5, none
of which the Lord Jesus Christ actually bore, though every one
truly described Him and His character. When Jerusalem is
once holy and truth dwells in her, then the mountain of
Jehovah, Moriah, will indeed be the holy mount.

Keil notes in this respect that "Jerusalem did not acquire this character in the period after captivity, in which, though not defiled by gross idolatry, as in the times before the captivity, it was polluted by other moral abominations, no less than it had been before."[3] Such a position is surely more to the point than the view of Dennett. He takes the return of the presence of God to Zion as having been fulfilled in the return from Babylonian Captivity, quoting Jeremiah 29:10 which, to us, has no substantiating value in this instance, for it has reference to the return of the people of Israel to the land, rather than the return of God to Jerusalem. Rather strangely, also, he takes the actual dwelling of God among His people to be in Messianic times.

We feel the unity of the prophecy will not allow such a long interval of centuries to enter in between the words "I will return to Zion" and "I will dwell in the midst of Jerusalem." The two are linked in the verse as cause and effect, and transpire in the same Messianic era. Wright, according to his manifest desire to find for the entire prophecy only a historical fulfillment, is certain that our passage has no reference whatsoever to Messianic days nor can any evidence be adduced in support of such an opinion. For him all is fulfilled in the time of the prophet. Says he, "There was unquestionably an earnest spirit abroad among the Jewish people in the days of the prophets; and though those days of revival were succeeded by days of religious declension, the prophecy of Zechariah must be regarded as having been fulfilled when even the laws concerning Sabbath observance were rigidly carried out under the governorship of Nehemiah (Neh. 13)."[4] Indeed, he maintains that all the promises of chapters seven and eight have been fulfilled in the

---

[3] *The Twelve Minor Prophets,* Vol. II, p. 312.
[4] *Op. cit.,* p. 180.

time between Zerubbabel and Christ. Such a course is possible, it seems to us, only when the promises are diluted and made to convey so much less than they literally import.

The theme upon which the prophet has dwelt in the early verses of the chapter he continues in the following verses, declaring: "Thus saith Jehovah of hosts: Old men and old women shall yet dwell in the streets of Jerusalem, every man with his staff in his hand for abundance of age. And the streets of the city shall be full of boys and girls playing in the streets thereof" (vv. 4-5). The scene before us is a millennial one depicting peace and prosperity. Long life and an abundant progeny were well-known blessings of the Old Testament theocracy. (Compare Exod. 20:12; Deut. 4:40; 5:16, 30; 7:13, 14; 11:9; 32:7; Ps. 128:3-5; Isa. 65:20-22.) The classes specified—the old men, old women, boys and girls—are the most defenseless of all the population, yet these will dwell securely in the midst of the city of Jerusalem. The population would not be slain in battle nor carried captive. In times of war neither the young nor the old were spared; thus there must have been a long peace for men to live out their days. Kelly says: "Under Messiah men will go on living and last out the whole millennial reign."[5] We would limit this statement to the godly only, for the rebellious and the wicked will be cut off, even at one hundred years of age (Isa. 65:20).

Pusey has given us a word of real beauty on this thought. Says he, "The tottering limbs of the very old, and the elastic perpetual motion of childhood are like far distant chords of the diapason of the Creator's love."[6] There are those who find the God of the Old Testament to be arbitrary, harsh, even cruel at times. We do not know Him as such. Here Zechariah reveals

---

[5] *Lectures Introductory to the Minor Prophets,* p. 467.
[6] *Minor Prophets,* Vol. II, p. 385.

Him as finding delight in the laughter of children. (The piel of the verb *mesaḥaqim* expresses the truth of the repeated laughter, so common to childhood.) Happy, indeed, is the people whose God is our Lord. Out of the entire realm of human experience God has taken these pictures to express the delightful tranquility and peace of the millennial era. Someone has pointed out the verbal similarity to this prophecy in First Maccabees 14:9, where the peaceful prosperity of Judea under the rule of Simon, is described in this manner: "The ancient men sat all in the streets, communing together of good things, and the young men put on glorious and warlike apparel." Needless to say, this passage does not approximate the beauty, force, and simplicity of the Biblical prophecy.

Before the prophet continues the delineation of Israel's blessedness in the days to come, he reminds the nation both of the greatness of the things predicted and the certain foundation upon which they rest, in these words: "Thus saith Jehovah of hosts: If it be marvellous in the eyes of the remnant of this people in those days, should it also be marvelous in my eyes? saith Jehovah of hosts" (v. 6). The *gam* of this verse is clearly meant for *hagham,* making the sentence interrogative rather than declarative. Otherwise, God is placed upon the same plane of astonishment as Israel. The fulfillment of these grand promises may indeed astonish and amaze Israel in the time of realization, but with God nothing is impossible. Thus the promises are altogether certain. For the same sentence structure see I Samuel 22:7; for the thought, see Genesis 18:14; Jeremiah 32:27; Mark 10:27; Luke 1:37. The Authorized Version has unfortunately translated *bayyamim hahem* as "in these days." The prophet's intention is not to point out the amazement of his contemporaries, or of the remnant in his day, but the wonder in the hearts of those living in the day of fulfillment, the remnant of the millennial generation.

Zechariah passes from the question of the Lord to further portrayal of the restoration of God's favor: "Thus saith Jehovah of hosts: Behold, I will save my people from the east, and from the west; and I will bring them, and they shall dwell in the midst of Jerusalem; and they shall be my people, and I will be their God, in truth and in righteousness" (vv. 7, 8). Baron has well said: "This is one of the greatest and most comprehensive promises in reference to Israel's restoration and conversion to be found in the prophetic Scriptures."[7] The directions of east and west stand here representatively for all the earth; it is a world-wide regathering. (Compare Ps. 50:1; 113:3; Isa. 43:5, 6; Mal. 1:11; Matt. 8:11, 12.) In that day Israel will be settled in Jerusalem; they will in truth be the people of God with all covenant privileges in effect. (See Hos. 2:19-22.)

The return spoken of here cannot be the restoration from Babylonian Captivity, because "From the 'west' they could not then have been brought back, since very few of the Jewish nation had as yet wandered westward. It was only at the second stage of Israel's dispersion, which was brought about by the destruction of Jerusalem and the Temple by the Romans, that Israel became in the fullest sense a Diaspora—scattered over all the face of the earth—the majority always found in lands more or less to the west of Palestine."[8] Wright maintains that "The promise that all Israel shall dwell in Jerusalem is peculiar. . . . Such prophetic statements as that which occurs here (chap. 8:8) are not, of course, to be taken as literal."[9] Literal promises to Israel like these are peculiar only when the force of similar prophecies in

---

[7] *Op. cit.*, p. 237.
[8] Baron, *op. cit.*, p. 238.
[9] *Op. cit.*, p. 184.

the Word has been vitiated and dissipated by spiritualizing
methods of interpretation. It seems as though the more inescap-
able and inevitable the fact, the more positive is the denial of it.

From the contemplation of the far distant future, the eyes
of the prophet rest on the conditions of his day. He exhorts his
people: "Thus saith Jehovah of hosts: Let your hands be strong,
ye that hear in these days these words from the mouth of the
prophets who were in the day that the house of Jehovah of
hosts was founded, even the temple, that it might be built.
For before those days there was no hire for man, nor any hire
for beast; neither was there any peace to him that went out or
came in, because of the enemy; for I set all men every one
against his neighbor" (vv. 9-10). The Scriptures never reveal
the future events of prophecy for mere curiosity's sake, but for
the practical effect that they may have upon the lives of the
readers. The practical bearing of the facts in verses 1 to 8 upon
the contemporaries of the prophet is now before us in verses
9-17, the application of the view of future things to the work
of the present. The returned remnant is urged by the prophet
to be strong, not only for the building of the temple, but for
all acts of righteousness (cf. v. 16).

The prophets alluded to are the restoration prophets, Haggai
and Zechariah, who ministered at the time of the first founding
of the temple. The peculiar expression "that it might be built"
is well explained by Keil: "As a more precise definition of
yom yussadh the word *lehibbanoth* is added, to show that the
time referred to is that in which the laying of the foundation of
the temple in the time of Cyrus became an eventful fact through
the continuation of the building."[10] (Compare Hag. 1:14; 2:15-
18; Ezra 5:1, 2 with Ezra 3:10.) There were two beginnings,
two foundings, of the temple. The latter would issue in the

---

[10] *Op. cit.*, p. 315.

completion of the structure. Note the contrast between "these days" of verse 9 and "those days" of verse 10. The burden of the prophet's words to them is that there has been improvement already in their condition from the time that they had applied themselves again to the building of the temple. Before the days in which work on the temple had been resumed, the fields of the land produced so little that neither man nor beast was remunerated for the labor spent. Far from the labor being lucrative, it amounted to practically nothing. God knows full well how to touch our temporalities in order to turn our gazes and hearts to worthwhile spiritualities. Compare Haggai 1:6, 9-11; 2:15-19.

Not only did labor bring no return, but there was the oppression of the enemy as well. The books of Ezra and Nehemiah reveal the hostility of the Samaritans, the Arabians, the Ammonites, and the Ashdodites against the people who were rebuilding the temple, and later against those who labored on the walls of Jerusalem. Compare Ezra 4 and Nehemiah 4. "Over and above the difficulties which were created by reason of the hostility of the border nations and of those Gentiles who dwelt in the land (Ezra 4), Hitzig observes that the expedition of Cambyses to Egypt occurred during this period, and, though it is not referred to in the book of Ezra, the march of the Persian troops through the land southwards must have caused no little affliction to the colonists under their distressing circumstances."[11] In addition to these hardships internecine strife prevailed in the midst of the nation. It has been supposed that reference is made here to the excessive usury practiced at the time which caused some to sell all their possessions, including children, but the *usus loquendi* of the verb *shalah b* requires us to understand it of personal attacks on the part of individuals,

---

11 Wright, *op. cit.*, p. 185.

for in other instances it is used of the hostile attacks of nation against nation (Keil). Compare II Kings 24:2. Bitter is the experience of the nation (or individual) which slights or neglects to do the will of God, whether the visitation be an external or an internal one.

Such were the conditions in the time before their obedience to God in the resumption of the temple work, "But now I will not be unto the remnant of this people as in the former days, saith Jehovah of hosts. For the seed of peace, the vine, shall yield its fruit, and the ground shall yield its increase, and the heavens shall give their dew; and I will cause the remnant of this people to inherit all these things. And it shall come to pass that, as ye were a curse among the nations, O house of Judah and house of Israel, so will I save you, and ye shall be a blessing. Fear not; let your hands be strong" (vv. 11-13). God now announces through the prophet that since the nation has turned from its former ways, He will deal with them in blessing. These blessings are divided, as were the afflictions of the nation, into the temporal or external and the spiritual or internal. Whereas formerly there was no peace at home or abroad, there will be such now.

The words *zera' hashshalom* have been variously translated. The Authorized Version renders them: "the seed *shall be* prosperous," while the American Standard Version translates: "*there shall be* the seed of peace." Kimchi translates it in his commentary: "Your seed shall be peace and a blessing, so that they will call it 'a seed of peace.'"[12] Chambers quotes the Targum of Jonathan and the Syriac Peshito as giving the meaning: "the seed shall be secure." These are contrary to the canons of Hebrew grammar. His own view fares no better, for he renders it (as the Vulgate and Pressel): "there shall be a

---

[12] *Op. cit.*, p. 77.

seed of peace" as embodying a general statement of the land's productiveness, which is amplified in the following clauses of the same verse. Keil, Lowe, Baron, Wright, and others give the sense, "the seed of peace, namely, the vine," and in this we concur. It is not only grammatically permissible, but is true to conditions of war and peace. Keil quotes Koehler as stating that "the vine can only flourish in peaceful times, and not when the land is laid waste by enemies."[13] The temporal benefits listed are those promised in the law for the obedience of the people. (Compare Lev. 26:4; Deut. 33:28; Ps. 67:7; Jer. 2:21.) Note the constant reference through the chapter to the remnant of this people (vv. 6, 11, and 12), signifying that the blessings will accrue only to the godly in Israel.

Just as the nation's physical condition will be altered, so will her spiritual status be changed. The meaning of verse 13 is not that Israel was a curse to the nations in her dispersion (the word is *baggoyim*, "among the nations" and not *"laggoyim,"* "to the nations"). The thought conveyed is that "the Lord promised, that as Israel had been a curse among the nations— that is, as other nations, when imprecating curses upon their foes, were wont to wish them the fate of Israel—so it would come to pass in time to come that Israel's lot should be so remarkable for its happiness that those who prayed for blessings on their friends would wish that they might be as Israel."[14] As they were used in the formula for cursing, so they will be referred to in the formula for blessing. (Compare Isa. 65:15; Jer. 24:9; 29:22.) It is evident to the careful student of the passage that, although Zechariah has returned to the sphere of the then present hour in verse 9, he advances as he unfolds the prophetic revelation to the time of the age of Israel's realized

---

[13] *Op. cit.*, p. 316.
[14] Wright, *op. cit.*, p. 187.

blessings, the millennium. Only so can we understand the full force of the words before us. The section from verse 9 is now closed with the same words of exhortation that are found at the heading of the division.

If the nation still lacks assurance with regard to these foregoing predictions, the prophet appends that word: "For thus saith Jehovah of hosts: As I purposed to do evil unto you, when your fathers provoked me to wrath, saith Jehovah of hosts, and I repented not; so again have I purposed in these days to do good unto Jerusalem and the house of Judah: fear ye not. These are the things that ye shall do: Speak ye every man the truth with his neighbor; judge truth and the judgment of peace in your gates; and let none of you devise evil in your hearts against his neighbor; and love no false oath: for all these are things which I hate, saith Jehovah" (vv. 14-17). With exactly the same definiteness and certainty that the threatenings of judgment from God found their fulfillment in the nation's history, so the purposes of blessing will not fail of their materialization as well. Learn from this how steadfast are the promises of God, especially in view of the truth that He does not willingly afflict the sons of men. After this fashion, as Chambers so pertinently points out, "the very sorrows of the past became pledges for the hopes of the future."[15] In the injunctions of verses 15 and 16 we have words similar to those in chapter 7, verses 9 and 10. He still desires truth in the inward parts. "Practical righteousness and true morality are the same in all dispensations."[16] If we catch the force of the words *love* and *hate* in verse 17, we shall understand the definition some one has given of religion. He said it "consists in conformity to God's nature, that we should love what God loves and hate what God hates."

---

[15] Lange, *op. cit.*, p. 64.
[16] Ironside, *Notes on the Minor Prophets,* p. 378.

In concluding this passage, it is most interesting to note that there is here no warning against idolatry, so prominent and flagrant in the time of the pre-exilic prophets. The reason is clear: the nation had been cleansed of it in Babylon.

This portion on the restoration of God's blessing to His people concludes, as it must, with the requirements for blessing. We do well to learn thoroughly this lesson for our own lives and the well-being of our own spirits. Meyer has expressed the truth so well that we quote his words in closing: "This is God's way still. He chastens sorely. If we profane his name and pollute his temple; if we strike hands in ungodly alliances, and go after strange gods; if we dye our hands in the vats of the world's vanity—we are sent, as Israel was, into captivity, and our seventy years are fulfilled. But when we have profited by his stern discipline, and returned to Him with all our heart and soul, we are restored to our former position; God's hand wipes the tears from our eyes, and He bids us turn from our bitter repinings over an irretrievable past, to accept the unalloyed mercy which remembers our sins no more. . . . He set himself to assure his people, in effect, that in the future, when they could view his dealings in their true perspective, they would discover that their darkest days had been the source and origin of their gladdest ones."[17]

By way of summary let us recapitulate the prophet's declaration upon the vexing problem of his people. In answer to their question he had first turned their gaze to the actual character of their fastings, and indeed all their acts. God was not in them. The basic cause of all their woes was their disobedience to the clear words of God's messengers, with the resultant judgment upon the land. But there is a sequel to all this, for God has set before the nation a period of peace, blessings, prosperity, and

---

[17] *Zechariah the Prophet of Hope*, pp. 83, 85.

joy, in which no mention of fastings is to be found. The bearing of this upon present life and conduct is pointed out. Thus, by implication the prophet has answered the question positively. In the remainder of the chapter he answers it fully and directly, and of this we shall treat later.

CHAPTER III

V. The Abrogation of the Fasts, 8:18-23.

NOW THAT Zechariah has turned the gaze of his contemporaries in Israel to the vital and all-important matter of their proper heart attitude and life conduct toward the Lord and their coreligionists, he simply and distinctly answers the question first posited to him by the deputation from Bethel. They had plainly asked, "Shall I weep in the fifth month, separating myself, as I have done these so many years?" The very use of the singular reveals how united was the nation in asking and how pointedly the matter affected all alike. The prophet now answers: "And the word of Jehovah of hosts came unto me, saying, Thus saith Jehovah of hosts, The fast of the fourth *month,* and the fast of the fifth, and the fast of the seventh, and the fast of the tenth, shall become to the house of Judah joy and gladness, and good feasts; but love ye truth and peace" (vv. 18, 19). The question of the embassy had included only the fasts of the fifth and the seventh months, but God's remedy and promise relate to all the fasts. Through the mouth of Zechariah God promises that He will restore the years that the canker-worm hath eaten. Well had Amos warned the nation in the days before the Captivity when they were bent upon sin: "And I will turn your feasts into mourning, and all your songs into lamentation; and I will bring sackcloth upon all loins, and baldness upon every head; and I will make it as the mourning for an only son, and the end of it as a bitter day" (Amos 8:10).

Isaiah was projected into the far distant future by the spirit of prophecy to reveal that the work of the Messiah would

140

be directed to comforting the mourners of Zion, to give them
a garland instead of ashes, the oil of gladness instead of mourning, the garment of praise for the spirit of heaviness, to make
the people of Jerusalem a rejoicing, so that the voice of weeping
and the voice of distress would not be heard in her any more.
(Cf. Isa. 61:2, 3, 7; 65:18, 19.) Zechariah and Isaiah speak of
the same time and their witness agrees. The answer ends with
an exhortation to love truth and peace. The objects *ha'emeth
wehashshalom* are placed first for emphasis, and in the proper
order: there must ever be the maintenance of the truth of God
first before there can be the issue of peace to the people of God.
The admonition is directed to the contemporaries of the prophet.

As a matter of history, what was the outcome of these
facts? Were they done away with in the time of Zechariah?
Was that the intent of the prophecy? Students of the prophecy
differ on the question. Some have supposed that the answer
of the Lord was taken to mean that the fast days were to be
retained, but celebrated as festival days. Wright is inclined to
follow the Jewish tradition, for, says he, "It is asserted . . .
that, according to Jewish tradition, the result of this answer of
the Lord was that the four special fast days were forthwith
abolished, as that was judged to be the course most in accordance
with the spirit of the Divine oracle. The fasts were, however,
reintroduced after the destruction of the second temple."[1] At
first sight this ancient tradition seems to fit the situation well,
but upon further consideration it must be held untenable.

Keil's position is much more cogent and reliable. He explains: "The promise, that the Lord would change the fast-
days in the future into days of rejoicing and cheerful feasts,
if Israel only loved truth and peace (verse 19), when taken in
connection with what is said in chapter 7:5, 6 concerning fasting,

---

[1] *Op. cit.*, p. 191.

left the decision of the question, whether the fast-days were to
be given up or to be still observed, in the hands of the people.
We have no historical information as to the course adopted by
the inhabitants of Judah in consequence of the divine answer.
All that we know is, that even to the present day the Jews
observe the four disastrous days as days of national mourning.
The Talmudic tradition in *Rosh-hashana* (f. 18, a, b), that the
four fast-days were abolished in consequence of the answer
of Jehovah, and were not restored again till after the destruction
of the second temple, is not only very improbable, but is no
doubt erroneous, inasmuch as, although the restoration of the
days for commemorating the destruction of Jerusalem and the
burning of the temple could easily be explained, on the suppo-
sition that the second destruction occurred at the same time
as the first, it is not so easy to explain the restoration of the fast-
days in commemoration of events for which there was no link
of connection whatever in the destruction of Jerusalem by the
Romans. [The truth of this so important statement will be
readily admitted by all.] In all probability, the matter stands
rather thus: that after the receipt of this verbal answer, the
people did not venture formally to abolish the fast-days before
the appearance of the promised salvation, but let them remain,
even if they were not always strictly observed; and that at a
later period the Jews, who rejected the Messiah, began again to
observe them with greater stringency after the second destruction
of Jerusalem, and continue to do so to the present time, not
because 'the prophecy of the glory intended for Israel (vss. 18-23)
is still unfulfilled' (Koehler), but because 'blindness in part is
happened to Israel,' so that it has not discerned the fulfilment,
which commenced with the appearance of Christ upon earth."[2]

But we cannot follow Keil in his conclusion. Rather is the

---

[2] *Op. cit.*, Vol. II, p. 319.

truth with the view taken by Koehler, and disallowed by Keil. Our reasons are these: (1) the entire chapter revolves within the sphere of the future, the time of the ultimate accomplishment of Israel's hopes and promises. Should these two verses be made an exception? True, the exhortations are in the realm of the present, but the promises are placed in Messianic times. (2) Then, too, with these hopes as with scores of others in the prophecies of the Old Testament, the godly ever looked to the consummation of all things for the fulfilment of all their national hopes. Such an interpretation does justice also to the portion of the chapter that follows.

The concluding section of the eighth chapter and of this division of the book concerned with the question on fasting continues in the same millennial era. The prophet predicts, "Thus saith Jehovah of hosts, *It shall* yet *come to pass,* that peoples shall come, and the inhabitants of many cities; and the inhabitants of one *city* shall go to another, saying, Let us go speedily to entreat the favor of Jehovah, and to seek Jehovah of hosts: I will go also. Even many peoples and strong nations shall come to seek Jehovah of hosts in Jerusalem, and to entreat the favor of Jehovah. Thus saith Jehovah of hosts, In those days *it shall come to pass,* that ten men of all the languages of the nations shall lay hold, yea, they shall lay hold of the skirt of him that is a Jew, saying, We will go with you, for we have heard that God is with you" (vv. 20-23). There is brought before us in these short verses a scene of surpassing importance. It reminds us of the two great pre-exilic prophecies in Isaiah 2:2-4 and Micah 4:1-5. See also this prophecy 2:14-16 (Hebrew); 14:16-19. The passage depicts for us that world conversion of which so many erroneously speak as taking place in this Church age. Israel restored in millennial glory will be the means of blessing to all the world. London, Berlin, Paris,

Washington, and all other capitals of the world will go to Jerusalem to learn of the Lord and to seek His all-glorious favor. This will be a true confluence of nations. The citations in Isaiah and Micah, as well as here, bring out forcefully the voluntary and uncoerced character of the action of the nations. As Ironside has well pointed out, there will be the fulfilment of Psalm 122 on a world-wide scale.

The prophet is informing us that, although formerly even Israel was kept from the joyful feasts of the Lord's house, now all nations will enjoy them also. Now, this is not being done by the preaching of the gospel today. It is not a matter of the power of the gospel (for then hell would be divested of its every victim), but of the purpose of the gospel. (Cf. Acts 15; Eph. 2.) Dennett discerningly relates this portion of the answer to the deputation from Bethel with the original query after this manner: "Bethel—one small city—had sent men to pray before the Lord (7:2); and this incident is taken up to shadow out the time when the house of God should be the house of prayer for all people (see Isa. 56:7; also Isa. 2:1-3; Ps. 65:2; and Zech. 14:16); when such embassies as that which had been sent from Bethel should proceed from many cities to the house of the Lord in Jerusalem, for in that day all nations will own the Messiah as their King and be His servants."[3] Mark how glorious was the promise and how ill the circumstances of the day were suited to bring about the fulfilment of the prediction of the prophet. Says Pusey, "Yet where was the shew of their fulfillment? The Jews themselves, a handful: the temple unfinished; its completion depending, in human sight, upon the will of their heathen masters, the rival worship at Samaria standing and inviting to coalition. Appearances and experience were against God. God says virtually, that it was, in human

----

[3] *Op. cit.*, p. 98.

sight, contrary to all expectations. But 'weakness is aye Heaven's might.' "[4]

The last verse of our chapter, indeed an amazing one, indicates the manner or agency by which the prediction of verses 20-22 will be fulfilled. First, we must notice the time element: it is *in those days,* specifically, the days mentioned in the verses immediately preceding this. Second, the number ten is to be understood, as in other cases, as representative of all. (Cf. Gen. 10:20, 31; 31:7; Lev. 26:26.) Third, the laying hold of the skirt signifies the attitude of one who claims to be listened to or to be protected. See I Samuel 15:27; Isaiah 4:1. But how are we to interpret the words *'ish yehudhi?* Needless to say, there has been no paucity or exiguity of interpretations. Pusey, Hengstenberg, Wright, and others understand the entire passage (vv. 20-23) of the world-wide expansion of the kingdom of God set forth symbolically. Jerome interpreted the words before us of Christ or the Apostles, and placed the whole scene in the gospel dispensation. The Jews saw here a reference to the Messiah. Pusey and others quote the Pesikta Rabbathi, in Yalkut Shimoni: "All nations shall come, falling before the Messiah and the Israelites, saying, Grant, that we may be Thy servants and of Israel."

Dods similarly interprets the verse, saying, "The western world has found its God in Judea. It is God as manifested in the history of the Jews, and especially in the Nazarene, that has been and is acknowledged and worshipped by Christendom "[5] (cf. John 4:22). Lowe, Meyer, and Baron hold that the reference is to the Jew as a nation with each individual Jew being sought after. Lowe tells us: "Verse 23 must not be taken as a direct prophecy of the coming of our Lord, for the expression

---

[4] *Op. cit.,* Vol. II, p. 390.
[5] *The Post-Exilian Prophets,* p. 97.

'a man a Jew' is used in the singular merely for the sake of
contrast with 'ten men from all languages of the nations,' and
in reality denotes not an individual Jew, but the whole Jewish
nation (Isa. 45:14)."⁶ Meyer also gives the proper interpretation,
we believe, when he writes, "And in all the so-called Christian
ages, while persecuting the chosen people, the foremost nations
of the world have taken hold of their skirts, going with them
to their sacred shrines, using their conceptions of God, appropri-
ating their sacred writings, and venerating their lawgivers,
prophets, and saints, with a reverence equal to their own . . .
There is also a time, yet future, but probably not far away [and
to this time we believe the prophet is specifically and primarily
referring—that is, the Messianic era], when the Jewish people
shall be brought to own the claims of Jesus, and shall look on
Him with repentance, faith, and love; and then they will be
still more sought after by the nations of the world as the
representatives and teachers of the only true religion."⁷ The
prophecy teaches, then, that Israel will be the means of drawing
the nations of the earth to the Lord in the time of the Messiah's
reign of righteousness upon earth. We have no objection to
referring the passage, in a secondary sense, to the Lord Jesus
Christ, for it is in a sense true of Him, but we must keep the
primary thought of the prophet before us.

By way of summary, now, we can see the purpose of the
Spirit through the prophet in answer to the question concerning
fasting. It was a twofold objective: a present and a future one.
For the time then present the Spirit pointed out the sham in
the fastings, the need for reality and sincerity, the vivid warning
from the past sins of the forefathers, and the imperative demand
for righteousness in all the relationships of life. With reference

---

⁶ *Hebrew Student's Commentary on Zechariah*, p. 78.
⁷ *Op. cit.*, p. 86.

to the future Zechariah was directed to point to a day of glorious promise for Israel when the Lord would dwell in her midst, when prosperity and peace would characterize her land, when her dispersed ones would be gathered back to their homeland, and, yes, when her fasts would be turned into feasts, the glory of the Lord being so manifest in Israel that all the nations would be drawn to Him through His people. How much the blessed God can place in an answer to a question on fasting. Do not these two chapters (7 and 8) speak eloquently to us who read them today of that reality and sincerity which God must demand of us, as well as of the glory that yet awaits the earth when the blessed Lord Jesus Christ rules upon the earth with His Bride, the Church, and His vicegerents, the people of the land, Israel?

PART FOUR

CHAPTER I

THE FUTURE OF THE WORLD POWERS, ISRAEL, AND THE KINGDOM OF MESSIAH

9-14

THE LAST six chapters of this prophecy constitute an incomparable treasury of prophetic truth. The careful student of the prophetic Scriptures finds himself repeatedly referring to this section of Zechariah for the presentation of God's plan for the days ahead. Conservative and liberal scholars alike have noted the marked differences both in style and subject matter between this portion of the book and the first eight chapters. The liberal solution to the phenomenon, gained from long practice on the problem of the Pentateuch, Isaiah, and Daniel, is multiple authorship.[1] Differences in style and subject matter are explicable upon the grounds that the prophet wrote these concluding chapters at a later period in his life, and that the vision of Zechariah is focused upon events far beyond his age. Wright, who cannot be said to give this position its full weight, nevertheless holds that "It need not surprise us that prophecies uttered under such peculiar circumstances (the harassing of Judea by the Persian hosts before the conquests of Alexander the Great), and in all probability many years after those recorded in the earlier chapters of Zechariah, should, even if supposed to be written by the same author, be composed in a somewhat different style from that of his earlier productions."[2]

---

[1] For a brief summary of this position as well as the conservative approach, see Chapter I.

[2] *Op. cit.,* p. 200.

The prophecies of the last chapters are couched in two burdens: the first burden covers chapters 9-11, while the second burden includes chapters 12-14. In most general terms the title to this division given above indicates the contents of the remainder of the prophecy now before us. Events of nothing less than cosmic importance are brought to the discerning heart as one views the coming colossal conflict between world powers and Israel with the grand consummation in the inauguration of the Messianic kingdom. Baron summarizes the teaching of the two final burdens thus: "In the first (chaps. 9-11), the judgment through which Gentile world-power over Israel is finally destroyed, and Israel is endowed with strength to overcome all their enemies, forms the fundamental thought and centre of gravity of the prophetic description. In the second (chaps. 12-14), the judgment through which Israel itself is sifted and purged in the final great conflict with the nations, and transformed into the holy nation of Jehovah, forms the leading topic."[3] The various delineations of the Lord Jesus Christ throughout the present portion are strong meat for the meditation of the reverent and devout believer. Zechariah presents the Lord in His first and second coming to Israel.

I. The First Burden, 9-11.

1. Judgment on the Land of Hadrach, 9:1-8.

Most expositors of conservative outlook interpret these verses as the course of the victories of Alexander the Great after the Battle of Issus (so Kelly, Meyer, Ironside, Pusey, Baron, Hengstenberg, Chambers, and others). We have in this section of Zechariah's prophecy a remarkable pre-writing of history. At the time of the writing of this prophecy Israel was no longer troubled by those who opposed the reconstruction of the temple and the

---

[3] *Op. cit.*, p. 285.

walls of Jerusalem; now they were pressed by such powers as Tyre, Ashkelon, Gaza, and Ekron. The prophet depicts the invasion that would sweep away the hostile neighbors. Pusey summarizes for us thus: "The foreground of this prophecy is the course of the victories of Alexander, which circled round the holy land without hurting it, and ended in the overthrow of the Persian empire. The surrender of Damascus followed first, immediately on his great victory at the Issus; then Sidon yielded itself and received its ruler from the conqueror; Tyre he utterly destroyed; Gaza, we know, perished; he passed harmless by Jerusalem. Samaria, on his return from Egypt, he chastised."[4] The section before us has a double application: it sets forth the past judgment upon the kingdoms surrounding Israel as well as the future punishment that awaits the enemies of God's people which will be living in lands contiguous to Palestine. The message of Zechariah was intended to hearten and encourage the people of Israel with the thought of God's special and sufficient protection of them in spite of the harassings of the hostile powers about them.

The prophet introduces his prediction thus: "The burden of the word of Jehovah upon the land of Hadrach, and Damascus *shall be* its resting place, for the eye of man and of all the tribes of Israel is toward Jehovah; and Hamath also, which borders on it: Tyre and Sidon, because she is very wise" (vv. 1, 2). More than a little discussion has been carried on with reference to the first word of our text: *burden, massa'*. Unquestionably the common rendering of the word is *burden*, which is employed in prophecies of judgment and woe. Some prefer to take it as *oracle* or *prophecy* (Lowe), usually of a threatening character. (Cf. Jer. 23:33-40 for a classic passage, also Isa. 13:1; 15:1; 17:1; 19:1; 21:1, 11, 13; 22:1, and others.) Lowe notes that it is only

---

[4] *Op. cit.*, p. 394.

in Zechariah (9:1 and 12:1) and Malachi (1:1) that *massa'* is
followed by *dhebhar*.[5] Chambers points out that it is never
joined with the name of God or any other individual but the
subject of the prophecy.[6]

Hengstenberg has the fullest and, to us, the most satisfactory
discussion of this important word. He prefers the translation
burden to either *prophecy* or *utterance,* for the following reasons:
(1) it is almost always employed in the prophetic books in predictions of a threatening or admonitory character. Besides the
references given above see the prophecies of Nahum and Habakkuk also. (2) There is no place where *massa'* is derived from
nasa' in the sense of "to utter." The verb has no such significance.
It means "to lift." (3) The passage, Jeremiah 23:33 ff., which
is supposed to prove that *massa'* means *prophecy* actually signifies
the opposite. It is well known that Jeremiah's prophecies were
mainly of a burdensome and mournful nature. His hearers
mocked him by playing on this word, because it did signify
burden to them. (4) If the word under consideration refers only
to *utterance,* it is unusual that it is not used with the genitive of
the speaker (except Zech. 9:1; 12:1; Mal. 1:1). If the force of
the word were *utterance,* it should be used of utterance in general.
(5) The meaning *utterance* would be unsuitable in certain con-
texts. Note Isaiah 15:1 where the reason is assigned for the
title of "the burden of Moab." In our passage (9:1) the rendering *utterance* gives us a meaningless tautology. (6) The parallelism of *massa'* with *menuḥah* is preserved by the translation
burden. The burdensome message of the Lord is directed against
Hadrach and comes to rest finally on Damascus.[7]

---

[5] *Hebrew Student's Commentary on Zechariah,* p. 78.

[6] Lange's Commentary, Minor Prophets, *Book of Zechariah,* p. 67.

[7] See *Christology of the Old Testament,* Vol. III, pp. 339-43, for a
fuller treament.

Expositors of this prophecy are divided as to the identity of the land of Hadrach. Some take the word *Hadhrakh* as a symbolical name. Keil holds that such is its meaning and finds it originated with Zechariah himself. It represents a land inimical to the covenant nation and so must mean Medo-Persia, which is sharp-soft or strong-weak because of its divided character.[8] Kimchi also adheres to a symbolical interpretation. Says he, "We find in the words of our rabbis, of blessed memory, that 'R. Benaiah says, that *Hadhrakh,* Hadrach, is the Messiah, who is sharp, *hadh,* to the Gentiles, and tender, *rakh,* to Israel.' "[9] Hengstenberg concludes from the fact that Hadrach was often confused with Adraa that Hadrach is not a proper name at all. He asks how it could have escaped notice for so many years if it were in the well-known region about Damascus. He takes Hadrach as "a figurative appellation," just as Jerusalem is called "Ariel" ("lion of God") in Isaiah 29:1. The prophet used the term to signify the Persian Empire, which was at the height of its power in Zechariah's day.[10] Chambers concurs in this interpretation because, he says, "No such name as Hadrach is now or ever has been known."[11]

We prefer to take the name as indicating a specific city, because it is now certain, as Pusey has pointed out as well as others, that such a city did exist in the vicinity of Damascus and Hamath. The exact location is not known. Professor Rawlinson first found it upon the geographical tablets of the Assyrian inscriptions. He notes: "From the position on the lists, I should be inclined to identify it with Homs or Edessa which was certainly a very ancient capital (being the Kedesh of the

---

8 *The Twelve Minor Prophets,* Vol. II, pp. 322-325.
9 *Commentary on Zechariah,* p. 82.
10 *Op. cit.,* pp. 330-339.
11 *Op. cit.,* p. 67.

Egyptian records), and which would not otherwise be represented in the Assyrian inscriptions."[12] Dods thinks the name applied to a territory as well as a town. Our chief objections to the symbolical interpretation, apart from the force of archaeological findings, are: (1) when the name is to be understood symbolically the context always makes it clear. (See Ezek. 23:4; Jer. 25:26 with 51:41 for good examples; so Wright also.) (2) All other eight names in these verses (9:1-8) are surely literal geographical localities, and there is no necessity that calls for an exception here.

Thus, the judgment which first lighted (or from the viewpoint of Zechariah, was yet to light) upon Hadrach would ultimately rest upon Damascus from whence it would spread to all the surrounding district. History bears out well the accuracy of the words spoken by the prophet through the Spirit. Before Zechariah goes on to manifest how the punishment would overflow the specified lands he notes the dread and consternation which would be engendered in the hearts of "man" (the nations apart from Israel) and "all the tribes of Israel." Some translate the words *ki laYhwh 'en 'adham* as "Jehovah has an eye upon man," in the sense that God providentially rules over all the earth. In that case the Massoretic pointing of *'en* as a construct and the absence of a preposition after it seem difficult to explain. The picture is surely one of terror at the visitation of God upon the then great world-powers. (So Baron, Wright, and others also.) Hamath near Damascus will share in its judgment. This is the principal city of Upper Syria, on the Orontes. It was Antiochus Epiphanes who named it Epiphania. Tyre with the lesser city of Sidon will also know the wrath of God for she assumed

---

[12] *The Minor Prophets,* Vol. II, p. 394. For Rawlinson's quotation see footnote of the page.

a worldly-wise, over-confident attitude toward God. See Ezekiel 28:1 ff.

What this worldly wisdom consisted of is made clear when the prophet writes: "And Tyre built herself a stronghold, and heaped up silver as dust, and fine gold as the mire of the street. Behold, the Lord will dispossess her, and he will smite her power [wealth] in the sea; and she shall be devoured by fire" (vv. 3, 4). In the words *tsor* and *matsor* we have a telling play on words which is difficult, if not impossible, to reproduce in English. Tyre's mistake has been that of many a strong city before her and many since: she thought wealth would answer all purposes. In her day she was the greatest commercial and naval city in the world (Wright). She was considered impregnable because she was situated on a rock removed from the mainland by a strait about a half a mile broad (Dods). Alexander had warned her that the island in which she trusted would yet be found to be a continent. The Assyrians under Shalmaneser had laid siege against her for five years; the Chaldeans under Nebuchadnezzar for thirteen years—all without success. But Alexander made good his words by defeating her after seven months.

Zechariah, like a true student of history and as the instrument of the unerring Holy Spirit, sees no secondary causes or agent. He knows that it is God who will dispossess her of the wealth which she has amassed, the strongholds and fortifications she has built, and the supposedly invincible position she has maintained for years . It is Alexander who builds the vast mole to the island to take the city, but ultimately it is the Lord who brings Tyre low in the sea. Wright has well said that "the prophecy of Zechariah had been fulfilled to the letter. The city lost its insular position; for the mole of Alexander was never removed, and covered over and strengthened by deposits of sand and other matter, it remains even to this day, a monument to the execution of the Divine wrath upon the proud, luxurious, and idolatrous city."[13] Blessed be our God for He knoweth how to bring low the proud and to exalt the humble (cf. Phil. 2:5-11)! It is a fearful thing to fall into the hands of the living God, for our God is a consuming fire (Heb. 10:31; 12:29). Wisdom, riches, and strength are of no avail against the judgment of God.

The judgment of God, as Zechariah graphically pictures it, will fall not only upon Hadrach, Damascus, Hamath, Tyre, and Sidon, but also upon the chief cities of Philistia. Says the prophet, "Ashkelon shall see it, and fear; Gaza also, and she shall tremble exceedingly; and Ekron, for her expectation shall be put to shame; and a king shall perish from Gaza, and Ashkelon shall not be inhabited. And a bastard shall dwell in Ashdod, and I will cut off the pride of the Philistines" (vv. 5, 6). Zechariah portrays the march of Alexander along the Mediterranean Sea from Phoenicia to Philistia. The destruction of the great commercial city of Tyre instills terror into the lesser cities of Philistia. If this powerful city could not withstand the conquest of Alexander, their expectation could only be turned into disappointment. A similar fate assuredly awaited them. And so it was. All the principal Philistine cities experienced the rod of the invader. Just as in Amos 1:6-8, Zephaniah 2:4, and Jeremiah 25:20, Gath is omitted. Compare Joshua 13:3.

It has been suggested (Chambers) that the prophet omitted Gath because of its political insignificance after the campaign of Uzziah (II Chron. 26:6). It was the custom of kings of the East to allow royalty to remain in conquered countries as tributary, assuming for themselves the title of "king of kings" (cf. Ezek. 26:7). But conquered Gaza will not be granted this privilege; she will be divested of her native dynasty. Hengstenberg suggests that "the disappearance of the king from the city de-

---

13 *Op. cit.*, p. 213.

notes the utter ruin and extinction of the city itself."[14] A like chastisement was meted out to Ashkelon, for she was left without inhabitant. In Ashdod a bastard people was to dwell. The word *mamzer* has been variously rendered. It occurs but twice in the Old Testament—Deuteronomy 23:3 (Hebrew) and the passage before us. The LXX does not translate the passages uniformly. In Deuteronomy the translation is *'ek pornes,* while in Zechariah it is rendered as *'allogeneis.*[15]

The etymology is obscure. Gesenius treats the word as from the root *mazar,* "to be corrupt, polluted," with the primary meaning of "bastard" and the metaphorical sense as "foreigner."[16] (So also A. B. Davidson in *Hebrew and Chaldee Concordance.*) Hengstenberg translates it generally as "rabble"; Von Orelli, of one born out of wedlock; Kimchi, the same as *zar,* "a stranger"; Chambers, as mongrel, whereas he translates it "bastard" in the Deuteronomy passage; Pusey, of one illegitimately born, whether out of wedlock, in prohibited marriage, or in adultery; the Mishnah, of the issue of adultery or incest (see Davidson). Modern Hebrew usage confines it to one illegitimately born, and such is the rendering of the Authorized and American Standard Versions also. Ashdod will lose its native population. Alexander's conquests furthered the breaking up of small nationalities, and this was the death knell of Philistine pride. With its power laid low, its chief cities destroyed, and its nationality done away with, the pride of Philistia will suffer an incurable blow.

But there is hope in the future for Philistia, for the prophet outlines it thus: "And I will remove his blood from his mouth

---

[14] *Op. cit.,* Vol. III, p. 348.

[15] Swete, H. B., *The Old Testament in Greek,* Vol. I, p. 389, footnote and Vol. III, p. 85.

[16] *Hebrew and English Lexicon, in loco.*

and his abominations from between his teeth; and he also shall
be left to our God; and he shall be as a chieftain in Judah, and
Ekron as a Jebusite" (v. 7). The idolatry of Philistia will at
last be taken away. Mercy will follow upon judgment. The
picture is of one eating the sacrificial animals at an idolatrous
feast. The conversion of the Philistine to the God of Israel lies
beyond the time of Alexander (see Keil, Baron, and others);
in fact, in the sphere of that time indicated by verses 9 and 10
of this chapter. The Philistine in that coming day will be elevated to the honor of a chiliarch. Of the word *'alluph* it should
be noted that "In the earlier books it is applied only to the tribe-
princes of Edom, but it is transferred by Zechariah to the tribal
heads of Judah."[17] Compare Exodus 15:15. And Ekron (to
individualize) shall become as the Jebusite. Reference is made
to the remnant of the tribes of Canaan who were incorporated
into the commonwealth of Israel in the time of David and
Solomon. See Araunah in II Samuel 24:18, also I Kings 9:20,
21. Philistia will become a part of the people of God and will
share in the blessings of Israel.

Before Zechariah closes this portion of the prophecy he declares God's provident care over His own people Israel. He
promises, "And I will encamp about my house because of the
army, that none pass through nor return; and no oppressor shall
pass through them any more; for now have I seen with my
eyes" (v. 8). Since the context is so manifestly dealing with
the Alexandrian conquests,[18] the prophet's reference must be to
the protection afforded God's house, that is, His people, during
the time of the campaigns of Alexander in the region of Jeru-

---

[17] Lange's Commentary, *op. cit.*, p. 68.
[18] The expression *me'obher ummishshabh* is found but twice in the Old
Testament, here and 7:14, an incidental indication of the similarity of
both parts of Zechariah. *Cf.* Exodus 32:27 and Ezekiel 35:7 for similar
but not identical constructions.

salem.   Interesting indeed is the account given us by Josephus
of the sparing of the city of Jerusalem and her people by Alexander.[19] He narrates how, during the siege of Tyre, Alexander
sent to the Jewish high-priest for help and provisions for the
army. This the high-priest refused to do, professing his fealty
to Darius. At this reply Alexander became furious and threatened the high priest with dire consequences. After the conquest
of Gaza Alexander set out for Jerusalem; Jaddua, the high-priest,
on hearing of it, feared the wrath of the Macedonians and besought the people to turn to God. Says Josephus, "He therefore ordained that the people should make supplications, and
should join with him in offering sacrifices to God, whom he
besought to protect that nation, and to deliver them from the
perils that were coming upon them; whereupon God warned
him in a dream, which came upon him after he had offered
sacrifice, that he should take courage, and adorn the city, and
open the gates; that the rest appear in white garments, but
that he and the priests should meet the king in the habits proper
to their order, without the dread of any ill consequences, which
the providence of God would prevent. Upon which, when he
rose from his sleep, he greatly rejoiced; and declared to all the
warning he had received from God. According to which dream
he acted entirely, and so waited for the coming of the king.

"And when he understood that he was not far from the
city, he went out in procession, with the priests and the multitude
of the citizens. The procession was venerable, and the manner
of it different from that of other nations . . . and when the Phoenicians and the Chaldeans that followed him, thought they
should have liberty to plunder the city, and torment the high-
priest to death, which the king's displeasure fairly promised

---

[19] Flavius Josephus, *The Antiquities of the Jews* (trans. by William
Whiston), XI, 8, 3-5.

them, the very reverse of it happened; for Alexander, when he saw the multitude at a distance, in white garments, while the priests stood clothed with fine linen, and the high-priest in purple and scarlet clothing, with his mitre on his head having the golden plate on which the name of God was engraved, he approached by himself, and adored that name, and first saluted the high-priest. The Jews also did all together, with one voice, salute Alexander, and encompass him about: whereupon the kings of Syria and the rest were surprised at what Alexander had done, and supposed him disordered in his mind. However, Parmenio alone went up to him, and asked him how it came to pass, that when all others adored him, he should adore the high-priest of the Jews? To whom he replied, 'I did not adore him, but that God who hath honored him with that high-priesthood; for I saw this very person in a dream, in this very habit, when I was at Dios, in Macedonia, who, when I was considering with myself how I might obtain the dominion of Asia, exhorted me to make no delay, but boldly to pass over the sea thither, for that he would conduct my army, and would give me the dominion over the Persians; whence it is, that having seen no other in that habit, and now seeing this person in it, and remembering that vision and the exhortation which I had in my dream, I believe that I bring this army under the divine conduct, and shall therewith conquer Darius, and destroy the power of the Persians, and that all things will succeed according to what is in my own mind.' " The account closes with Alexander's entrance into the city of Jerusalem, his sacrifices to God in the temple, the explanation to him by the high-priest of Daniel's prophecies foretelling of his empire, and his granting of favors in religious matters to the Jews of Palestine, Babylon, and Media.

Great as was the deliverance of God's people during the

campaigns of Alexander, there is a still grander pledge of protection from all oppression and oppressors, for God has seen with His eyes their long affliction. The protection afforded them from Alexander was but the pledge of a greater deliverance which is elaborated on in the following verses. The promise of the cessation of all oppression forms the transition to the Messianic prophecy of verses 9 and 10.

In the verses which have been before us Zechariah has given us the conquests which brought to an end the power of Persia in Palestine and adjacent lands. Mighty as was the hand of Alexander, the omnipotence of God kept him from harming His land and people. In a far distant day, when God's complete liberation of Israel will be manifest, it will be clear that God has had His watchful eye upon the house of Israel, so that their enemies have not been able to prevail against them.

2. Israel's King of Peace, 9:9, 10.

When the prophet lifted his eyes from the time a few centuries before him to a day of complete freedom from persecution, the prophetic law of suggestion carried him to the hour of Messiah's deliverance not only for Israel but for all the nations of the earth. The prophets were so filled with expectations of the Messiah that they turned, by the operation of the directing Spirit, from every deliverance, no matter how small, to the last and greatest of all. From an earthly conqueror of great ruthlessness Zechariah gazes upon the coming King of the earth. The prophecy of Israel's King of peace is inserted between two martial scenes. Though the nations of earth in this sad hour of world carnage and destruction, turning in every direction for a long-promised peace, believe it not, nevertheless in these two verses of this much-neglected prophecy is God's plan for permanent and lasting peace. We have pictured for us: (1) the Agent of peace, (2) the method of peace, and (3) the kingdom of peace.

Such is the Biblical and logical order of peace for the entire world.

The prophet issues the command to rejoice in the coming Deliverer. "Rejoice greatly, O daughter of Zion; shout, O daughter of Jerusalem: behold, thy king cometh unto thee; he is just, and having salvation; lowly, and riding upon an ass, upon a colt the foal of an ass" (v. 9). The reception to be accorded the King, His qualifications, and the manner of His coming are all here. When Alexander approached a land in his conquests, his coming was attended with fear and great dread. But the coming of this One is not met with fear, but is cause for great rejoicing. He is called "thy king," the King promised to and long awaited by Israel. (Compare Isa. 9:6, 7; Luke 1:32, 33.) The word *lakh* may signify not only to Israel, but for them as well, that is, for their benefit and their good. His advent is not for His own profit or self-aggrandizement as with earthly monarchs and rulers. Just as the high-priest in Israel wore the names of the tribes on his breast, so this King, the High-priest of God, carries on His heart the interests of His people in love.

He is further characterized as "just" or righteous. This is truly the prime prerequisite in a true ruler and the foundation principle for true and enduring peace. With Him there is no unrighteousness whatsoever. If such be the basic requirement for peace, and it is, is it not immediately evident why man-made plans are and have ever been a failure? The righteousness of God's Messiah is everywhere attested to in Scripture. Compare Isaiah 11:3-5; Jeremiah 23:5; Psalm 45:7, 8 (Hebrew). Peace must be grounded and founded in justice and righteousness; this credential the King Messiah will have in evidence. A second quality of the Agent of peace is "having salvation." The niphal participle has commonly been taken to be equivalent to *moshia'*. The LXX (*sozon*) and other versions, both Jewish and Christian, render the verb actively. Grammatically, the niphal may be a reflexive, but in this verb under consideration it occurs only as a passive in the Old Testament (Pusey and Hengstenberg). Some do take it as a passive in the sense of "saved," delivered from His sufferings by His glorification. We prefer to take it as a passive, but with the sense of "endued, endowed, or clothed with salvation" (so also Pusey, Keil, Hengstenberg). Compare Deuteronomy 33:29; Psalm 33:16. God has laid help upon One that is mighty (Ps. 89:20, Hebrew). The world's peace depends upon a Saviour and His salvation.

The third credential of the King is lowliness. The thought in '*ani* is not so much meekness as it is suffering, lowly of outward appearance with lowliness of soul. Pusey explains: "The Hebrew word expresses the condition of one, who is bowed down, brought low through oppression, affliction, desolation, poverty, persecution, bereavement; but only if, at the same time, he had in him the fruit of all these, in lowliness of mind, submission to God, piety."[20] In contradistinction to the haughty and proud of earth's monarchs, He comes lowly and riding upon an ass. The thought of lowliness is further brought out by the manner of His travel. He comes without pomp or earthly splendor. Hengstenberg has pointed out that "from the time of Solomon downwards, we do not meet with a single example of a king, or in fact of any very distinguished personage, riding upon an ass."[21] The One who had not where to lay His head in order that we might rest our heads upon the bosom of the Father from whence He came, did not conceal His lowliness nor His poverty. Pride was as foreign to Him as it is common to the world's kings.

Between verses 9 and 10 of our chapter have come all the

---

[20] *Op. cit.*, Vol. II, p. 403.
[21] *Op. cit.*, p. 360.

centuries of the Christian era. Looking ahead the prophet describes the work of the King of peace: "And I will cut off the
chariot from Ephraim, and the horse from Jerusalem; and the
battle bow shall be cut off; and he shall speak peace to the
nations; and his rule shall be from sea to sea, and from the
River to the ends of the earth" (v. 10). Having laid the foundation for peace in the blood of His Cross, He now puts into
effect peace for all the world. He destroys all instruments of
war from His people and by so much from all the nations.
Compare Isaiah 9:4-6 for the same order or method of peace as
is given here. No defenses for carnal reliance will be left. All
symbols of earthly might and oppression will be brought to
nought. This will be done, not by the meek Lamb of God, but
by the wrath of the Lamb, the Lion roaring out of Zion. Compare Joel 4:16 (Hebrew). Hengstenberg and Keil take this
prophecy to mean the political extinction of Israel (the former
holding that it is accomplished by the Romans; the latter, by
the changing of the nation from a political character into a
spiritual kingdom), but such is not the intention of the prediction. The verse, by its mention of Ephraim and Jerusalem,
points ahead to a reunited nation.[22]

But there is a constructive phase to His method of peace, as
well as a destructive aspect. He speaks peace to the nations:
in three short words in the original we have the blessed act
told forth. This does not mean that He will speak peaceably
or teach peace, but by an authoritative word He will command
it. Then will be accomplished by His word what men have
sought to bring about by the use of arms and munitions. True,

---

[22] The mention of Ephraim does not prove a pre-exilic date for this
prophecy, because Zechariah uses the common designations of the two
parts of the land which were still in use after the exile. Note the mention of Israel in 8:13 which is admitted to be post-exilic in origin.

He speaks peace to individual hearts now (Eph. 2:17), but
in that day He will speak peace to the nations. Note that peace
is not the result of peace conferences, nor of the preaching of
social gospelizers, but of the direct, immediate activity of the
glorified Son of God, the Prince of Peace. Therefore, is He the
Desire of all nations, though they know it not.

Finally, the limits of the kingdom of peace are set forth.
It will be a rule from sea to sea and from the River to the ends of
the earth. Alexander the Great thought he had conquered all
the world, but a glance at a map of the then-known world will
reveal how far astray he was. God has reserved universal dominion for one and for Him alone. Some try to restrict the
geographical designations to the land of Palestine: from the Nile
to the Euphrates and from the latter to the Mediterranean.
Compare Genesis 15:18. But this is impossible, as Hengstenberg
and others have ably shown. (1) *'Aphse 'arets* nowhere refers to
the land of Palestine but the whole earth. (2) Since the second
designation is the broadest possible, the first cannot be circum-
scribed to the land of Israel. (3) Psalm 72 shows the extent
intended. Note verses 8 to 11 of that psalm in particular. (4)
The articles are omitted throughout the clauses, leaving them
indefinite. Compare Psalm 2:8. No matter how alluring the
plan of an isolated peace may sound, it will never work. There
can never be peace of a lasting nature on one continent while
it is absent from another. The nations of the earth and their
rulers who can give permanent peace to no one land, cannot,
of course, give it to all lands. He who can give it to all the
earth will be able to give it to any land. It is not peace at any
price, but peace at infinite price—the life of the Messiah. It is
not peace for one, but for all. May that hour be hastened.

Hengstenberg and M'Caul (the latter in his observations
on the commentary of Kimchi) show clearly how the Messianic

interpretation of this passage was the oldest among the Jews. The Zohar (first century A.D.) and Saadiah Gaon so interpreted it. "The Talmud shows us that this interpretation continued in later ages, 'Rabbi Joshua, the son of Levi objects, that it is written in one place, "Behold, one like the Son of Man came with the clouds of heaven:" but in another place it is written, "Lowly, and riding upon an ass." The solution is, if they be righteous, he shall come with the clouds of heaven. If they be not righteous, he shall come lowly and riding upon an ass.' "[23] In the twelfth century Aben Ezra quoted Rabbi Moses as referring the prophecy to Nehemiah, quoting Nehemiah 6:7. Aben Ezra refutes this opinion by designation of Judas the son of the Hasmonean as the one meant by the prophecy. Abarbanel refutes both views with vehemence. Except for these two writers all Jews assigned this passage to the Messiah. It was also the general opinion in the Church until the rise of deism and rationalism.

We summarize Hengstenberg's four arguments in proof that the passage has reference to the historical Christ.[24] First, there is the testimony of the New Testament, especially of our Lord Himself (Matt. 21:4, 5; John 12:12-16). Second, the tradition of the Jews, though insufficient in itself, is valuable in conjunction with other proofs. Third, the parallel passages are clear in this direction (Ps. 72; Micah 5:9 ff., Hebrew). Fourth, the elements of the prophecy itself are unmistakable. They can only refer to the Lord Jesus Christ who is the only King of Israel, *kat' 'exochen*. For this King and His rule Israel and all the earth groan this hour. But that predicted hour of fulfillment hastens nearer and is a source of joy to the heart set upon God and His Word.

---

[23] D. Kimchi, *op. cit.*, p. 93.
[24] *Op. cit.*, pp. 371-377.

3. The King's Mission in Relation to Israel, 9:11-17.

Zechariah turns from the blessings of peace for the world under the reign of the Messiah to address Zion once more, and to reveal what His coming will mean for her. To her he says, "As for thee also, because of the blood of thy covenant I have sent forth thy prisoners from the pit wherein is no water" (v. 11). The last verses of this chapter give in greater detail the benefits of Israel in the appearing of her Messiah. Most expositors refer the war-like period noted in these verses to a time nearer than the one just outlined in verses 9 and 10; that is, they refer the events to the Maccabean age. While in full agreement with this position we should like to add that the passage, as in so many others in the prophetic writings, goes from a nearer future to a far distant future. In short, the prophet has not only the time of the Maccabees in mind, but the time of the end things for Israel. Ironside has stated it well: "Again we have to notice a secondary application of a part of this prophecy. Verses 13 to 16 seem to refer in measure to the Maccabean contest with Antiochus Epiphanes, type of the Antichrist of the last days. . . . But undoubtedly the fuller interpretation is that which refers these words to the conflicts of the great tribulation."[25]

The words *gam 'at,* addressed to Zion who was mentioned in verse 9, are emphatic by their position at the head of the sentence, a *nominativus pendens.* The force of the expression is: "Even though you are in such a forlorn condition, seemingly lost, yet I have mercy in store for you."[26] The blood of the covenant referred to is to be taken as the blood of the Mosaic covenant of Exodus 24:8 (so Pusey, Baron, Chambers, Wright, and others). Dennett (*in loco*) prefers to understand the covenant as the new covenant of Matthew 26:28. This would necessi-

---

[25] *Notes on the Minor Prophets,* p. 394.
[26] T. W. Chambers, in Lange's Commentary, *op. cit.,* p. 74.

tate taking the verb *shillaḥti* as a prophetic perfect and explaining the verse as of a future event. Such is not necessary, because (as we shall see later) the prophet is speaking of events of his own day. Indeed, Dennett himself understands the pit to refer to those in captivity at that time. The view of Kimchi, though interesting, can scarcely be valid here. He holds, "As it is said of the King, the Messiah, that he shall be saved by his righteousness, so it is said, As for thee, thou shalt be saved by the blood of thy covenant, and that is the blood of circumcision, which Israel in captivity has adhered to more tenaciously than to all the commandments."[27]

The questions arise: In what way can the Mosaic covenant be made the basis of any of God's dealings in mercy with Israel? Did they not repeatedly break the provisions of this covenant? These questions are well answered by Baron: "But though Israel proved themselves unfaithful, and this particular covenant itself was 'broken,' 'the blood of the covenant,' on which emphasis is laid in this prophecy, was a sign and pledge of the faithfulness of God (though all men prove liars), and typically set forth the provision which God has made by which eventually His disobedient and rebellious people would be brought back within the sphere of blessing."[28] Probably the best meaning for the passage is obtained when understood as a statement from God to Israel that He has, on the basis of covenant relationship, sent forth her prisoners, the entire nation being involved, from the pit of captivity. Dry cisterns were often employed as places of imprisonment (cf. Genesis 37:24). The figure is used for general distress and misery. Those who refused to return to the land of Palestine under Cyrus' benevolent decree were in reality still prisoners, bound in exile.

---

[27] *Op. cit.*, p. 89.
[28] *Op. cit.*, p. 318.

To such the prophet issues the invitation: "Return you to the stronghold, O prisoners of hope; even today I declare that I will render double to thee" (v. 12). The verse is in beautiful contrast to the one immediately preceding it. The call is to return to the land of Zion, not to safety and prosperity in general, nor to the Lord Himself in particular. Pusey (*in loco*) interprets the stronghold as a *hapaxlegomenon* of God Himself, citing Joel 4:16 (Heb.) and Nahum 1:7. This view, though it does no violence to the context since their return to the land would have to be preceded in a measure by their turning to the Lord, is not demanded by the context. From the pit of captivity they are urged to return to the stronghold of Zion, the city of God. The prisoners are designated here by a special name, "prisoners of hope." The word *hattiqwah* (so Baron) is found with the definite article but this one place in the Hebrew Old Testament. Pusey, in commenting on the usage, says, "not... any hope, or generally, *hope,* but *the* special hope of Israel, *the hope* which sustained them in all those years of patient expectations."[29] Those who were imprisoned in captivity in Babylon, but who have such a bright hope and prospect before them, are enjoined to come back to the land of their hopes.

The call has a promise attached to it that, even in that day with its unpromising circumstances, God would in response to their faith render them double. What is meant by the Scriptural use of the thought of "double?" It is employed both of blessing and of punishment. The idea probably goes back to the double portion of the first-born son (cf. Deut. 21:15-17). In the case of Joseph the double portion came to Ephraim and Manasseh (I Chron. 5:1, 2) when Reuben was set aside because of his sin. The Scriptures reveal that Israel is the first-born among the nations of the earth (Exod. 4:22). When in sin

---

[29] *Op. cit.*, Vol. II, p. 408.

and disobedience he receives "double" punishment. (Cf. Isa.
40:2; Jer. 16:18.) In the future, when returned to the land in
blessing and conversion, Israel will receive double of good from
the hand of the Lord. See Isaiah 61:7 and Baron, *in loco.*
(The idea is also to be found outside of God's dealing with
Israel, referring to a large and good measure as in Job 42:10.)

The remaining verses of the chapter start from the time
of the Maccabean Wars, as we have already noted, and go
on to the consummation of all things for Israel in the kingdom
era. The passage portrays for us the means whereby the blessing
will come to Israel. The world-powers antagonistic to God and
His people Israel must be brought to nought. Thus our portion
bears striking resemblances to chapters 12 and 14 of our prophecy. The Greeks, the more immediate power of the near
future of that day, stand for the power inimical to the people
of the Lord, but they are not thereby to be taken as other than
literal. In their conflict with Israel in Maccabean times the
Greeks display the manner in which 'Israel's foes of the future
will be annihilated, to trouble God's people no more. In graphic
manner Zechariah depicts for us the scene of battle: "For I
have bent Judah for me, I have filled the bow with Ephraim;
and I will stir up thy sons, O Zion, against thy sons, O Greece,
and I will make thee as the sword of a mighty man" (v. 13).
Judah is the bow, Ephraim is the arrow, and Zion is the sword.
God uses these three against His enemies. The *ki* which introduces this verse gives the logical basis for the hope mentioned
in verse 12: God is able to subdue all His enemies and theirs
in order to bring about the realization of that hope. The verbs
are prophetic perfects.

Dennett, in commenting on the presence of the Greeks
here, says, "They are named for the reason already given that
the invasion of the holy land by Alexander is in the foreground

of the prophecy as the shadow of the attacks which will be
made upon Israel on the eve of, and especially after, the appearing of their Messiah."[30] The picture in *dharakhti* (literally,
"tread") is that of stretching the bow by placing the foot on
it to steady it. The bow is filled by putting the arrow on it.
God uses both to shoot at the enemy. It is God who stirs up
the sons of Zion against the sons of Greece. Strange views
have been taken of this prophecy because of the mention of
the Greeks. There are those who maintain for this prediction
a pre-exilic date. To them this passage means that the prophet
was predicting the rebellion against their masters of those Jews
who had been sold as slaves to the Greeks by the Phoenicians
and Edomites (Wright). (Cf. Joel 4:6 [Heb.] and Amos 1:6-9.)
It is generally agreed that *Yawan* means Greece (the Ionians).
It is true that there was early intercourse with the Greek people
by the Israelites through the Phoenicians in the north and
the Philistines on the south. But such is no sufficient ground
for the contention of a pre-exilic date for the prophecy.

On the other hand, some contend for a date much later
than Zechariah, in the time of the Grecian supremacy. The
mention of Greece, we maintain, is prophetic, and comes from
Zechariah's post-exilic standpoint. Pusey shows the remarkable
character of the prophecy thus: "There was not a little cloud,
like a man's hand, when Zechariah thus absolutely foretold the
conflict and its issue. Yet here we have a definite prophecy later
than Daniel, fitting in with his temporal prophecy, expanding
part of it, reaching on beyond the time of Antiochus, and fore-
announcing the help of God in two definite ways of protection:
(1) *without war,* against the army of Alexander; (2) *in the war*

---

[30] *Zechariah the Prophet*, p. 112.

of the Maccabees; and these, two of the most critical periods in their history after the captivity."[31]

The Lord's defence of His people is given in poetic description under the figure of a tempest. "And Jehovah shall be seen [appear] over them; and his arrow shall go forth as the lightning; and the Lord Jehovah will blow the trumpet, and will go in whirlwinds of the south. Jehovah of hosts will defend them; and they shall devour, and tread down the sling-stones; and they shall drink, and make a noise as through wine; and they shall be filled like bowls, like the corners of the altar" (vv. 14, 15). To protect His people God reveals Himself as their Champion and Defender. He has all the accouterment necessary: He has the arrow, sharp as lightning, and the trumpet to order and lead the march. His coming is no dropping down of the dew upon the mown grass, but is as violent and destructive as the whirlwinds of the south of Palestine which come from the desert southeast of the land, where there is no break to the storm. (Cf. Isa. 21:1 with Hos. 13:15.)

The Lord's defence of His people is so real and empowering on their behalf, that they are viewed as rapacious lions tearing the foe to pieces, eating their flesh, and drinking their blood. (Cf. Numbers 23:24.) Not a very delightsome picture, we are told, but opposition to God never issues in delight but in dire and dread calamity. The figures are all priestly and suggest a holy war and victory (so Chambers). The enemy is likened to sling-stones which, when shot wide of the mark, are both harmless and useless. See I Samuel 25:29 for a similar picture. The noise they make over the enemy expresses their exhiliration; their being filled like the sacrificial altar bowls conveys the idea of overflowing with excitement.

---

[31] *Op. cit.*, p. 409, a quotation from his work on Daniel.

The scene closes with a vision of peace and prosperity for the people of God. Zechariah foretells: "And Jehovah their God will save them in that day as the flock of his people; for *they shall be as* the stones of a crown, glittering over his land. For how great is his goodness, and how great is his beauty! Grain shall make the young men flourish, and new wine the virgins" (vv. 16, 17). The result of the victory will be not only physical deliverance for Israel, but spiritual salvation as well. This is clear from the words "as the flock of his people." In contrast to the worthless sling-stones of the previous verse, the people of God are seen as stones of a crown, precious, esteemed, and cherished. The participle *mithnosesoth* has been rendered "to lift up," in accordance with the meaning given in lexicons, but Keil (*in loco*) holds that the rendering is without foundation and unsuitable here. We prefer to translate it "glitter, sparkle, gleam," as do Wright, Keil, and others. The LXX uses the word *kuliontai* which means to "roll, roll along," and suits neither the context nor the usage of the word. Undoubtedly, "The reference is to precious gems set in a crown and flashing from the brow of a conqueror as he stalks over the land."[32] The land is His land, the land of Jehovah.

The prophet concludes with an exclamation over the goodness and beauty of the Lord. The pronouns in *tubho* and *yophyo* have been referred to Israel (Dods, Wright, Keil, and others), because it is thought that the ascription of beauty to the Lord would be strange. But the beauty of the Messiah is extolled in Psalm 45. Besides, all the pronouns in this context which are third masculine singular refer directly to the Lord. We take the pronouns as extolling these virtues in the Lord (so also Baron, Pusey, Lange, and others). The corn and the new wine, blessings

---

[32] T. W. Chambers, *op. cit.*, p. 74.

of abundance in conformity with the promises for obedience to the Lord, are rhetorically divided between the two groups mentioned. Wright feels that the prosperity in and after the Maccabean period meets the requirements of the text, but the picture is a familiar one of the benefits flowing from the millennial reign of the Messiah. Someone has well said: "From Him all things sweet derive their sweetness; all things fair, their beauty; all things bright, their splendor; all things that live, their life; all things sentient, their sense; all that move, their vigor; all intelligences, their knowledge; all things perfect, their perfection; all things in any wise good, their goodness."[33] In the so trying hours and days in which we now live, what more satisfying contemplation may we have than the all-sufficient goodness and surpassing beauty of the Lord?

---

[33] E. B. Pusey, *op. cit.*, p. 412, quoted by him without name.

CHAPTER II

4. Additional Blessings for Israel, 10:1-12.

THIS CHAPTER is so closley related to the preceding one that some expositors have suggested that verse one (others say verse two also) belongs to chapter nine. Although the tenth chapter does enlarge upon the theme of the ninth, there is no real necessity to transpose any of the verses of the present chapter. To do so would disrupt the continuity of thought between verse 2 (b) and verse 3. It is sufficient to recognize that the prophet, having foretold blessings for Israel through the coming of her King of Peace, dilates upon the subject of Israel's promises, contrasting at the same time their future blessedness with their past miseries due to their disobedience.

Zechariah, predicting the fruitfulness of the land in the Messianic era in 9:17, speaks in the same vein: "Ask ye of Jehovah rain in the time of the latter rain, *of* Jehovah that maketh lightnings: and he will give them showers of rain, to every one grass in the field" (v. 1). The way of blessing is clear: they are to ask and God is both ready and willing to give them their request. Does the passage speak of literal rain or is the rain merely a symbol of spiritual blessings? Both positions have their advocates. The literal signification is taken by Wright, Dods, Pusey, Baron, Keil, and others. They do not deny, however, that the words may have a spiritual application also. Keil summarizes this position well: "The prayer for rain, on which the successful cultivation of the fruits of the ground depends, simply serves to individualize the prayer for the

177

bestowal of the blessings of God, in order to sustain both temporal and spiritual life."[1]

On the other hand, Chambers, Hengstenberg, Ironside, Dennett, and others understand the rain in a spiritual sense, or as a representative of all blessings. Dennett restricts the reference to two specific events: he takes Pentecost as the former rain and the prophecy of Joel (3:1-2, Hebrew; Acts 2:17, 18) as the latter rain. The figurative meaning is explained by Ironside thus: "We need not be surprised [considering the land's need of the former and latter rains] to find the prophets using the rain in a figurative sense. Spiritually, Israel has had her former rain, but a long season of drought has since come in. Now they are bidden to look up in hope, and ask of the Lord 'rain in the time of the latter rain'; in response to which He pledges Himself to give showers of blessing. This is undoubtedly the outpouring of the Spirit predicted by Joel, which will surely take place at the time of the end."[2] It appears to us that the literal sense is the preferable for several reasons: (1) the connection with 9:17 points in this direction; (2) the promises to Israel for obedience took into account literal rain upon the land (cf. Deut. 11:14-17; Jer. 3:3; 14:22; Joel 2:23. Note especially Deuteronomy's use of 'eth and its occurrence here.); (3) the time of the rain has point here, preparing the crop for the harvest; (4) lightnings, the forerunners of rain, are mentioned; (5) the result of the rain in vegetation is also set forth. This view does not preclude that actual spiritual blessings were also in store for Israel, because she could not and would not receive these abundant rains were not the prerequisite conditions of faith and obedience present. See also 14:17.

But it is God alone who is the source of Israel's help, for

---

[1] *Op. cit.,* Vol. II, p. 345.
[2] *Op. cit.,* p. 396.

past experience has shown her the disaster of turning to idols and soothsayers. "For the teraphim have spoken nothingness, and the soothsayers have seen a lie; and they tell false dreams, they comfort in vain: therefore they departed like sheep, they are afflicted, because there is no shepherd" (v. 2). Cause and effect could not be more clearly stated than here. Israel, seeking the blessings indicated in verse 1 through the use of pagan and heathen enchantments and divinations, had been deceived, had brought about her own downfall, and had suffered humiliating exile. The etymology of the word *teraphim,* used some fifteen times in the Old Testament, is uncertain. Gesenius in his lexicon derives the word from the Arabic *tarafa,* "to live in comfort." Davidson in his concordance prefers an unused root meaning "to nourish." Both, however, translate the word in question as "household gods." (So also Keil, Dods, Baron, Wright, Chambers, and many others.)

Hengstenberg thinks they were intermediate deities who aided in foretelling events of the future; he denies that they were exclusively household gods. According to his view protection and blessing are never attributed to them, only deliverance in distress and anxiety. (Cf. Ezek. 21:26 [Heb.]; Judg. 17:5; Hos. 3:4; in the last two citations the teraphim are joined with the ephod.)[3] Keil and others, on the other hand, believe the teraphim were worshipped as the source of earthly prosperity. They are said to be similar to the *lares* and the *penates* of the Romans. Wright thinks they were human in form and often life-size. See I Samuel 19:13-16. Sometimes they were smaller as in Genesis 31:34 (the teraphim of Laban stolen by Rachel). He thinks it not unlikely that they were "originally actual human heads, though in process of time they were formed of gold, silver, etc." (*in loco*). Though they were explicitly forbidden in

---

[3] *Op. cit.,* Vol. III, p. 390, footnote.

Israel, they are found repeatedly (Gen. 35:2, 4; I Sam. 15:23;
II Kings 23:24). As to the etymology of the word Albright has
interestingly suggested that: "The verb *trp* is evidently a secondary formation from *rpy,* which means 'sag, slacken,' etc., in
Hebrew ... it appears in Arabic as *trf,* 'to live slackly, indolently.'
This may possibly help to explain the etymology of the mysteri-
ous word 'teraphim.' "[4]

With reference to the passage in 1 Samuel, Baron has concluded that there were two types of teraphim: larger ones
for temple use and smaller ones for private use. The results of
archaeological research have helped somewhat to clarify the
situation. Albright holds that "archaeology can now give a
negative answer to the traditional view that the teraphim of I
Samuel 19:12-17 were an 'image' or images of idols. That the
word sometimes had this sense is undeniable, but the context
absolutely precludes it in this passage. No 'idols' of comparable
size have ever been found in Palestinian excavations, and the
representations of divinity from Canaanite temples are all carved
outlines on stelae; all known copper or clay plaques and figurines
are much too small. Since neither the true meaning of the
word 'teraphim' nor the expression translated 'pillow of goats'
hair' in the Authorized Version is clear, there is no reason to
suppose that any cult object is referred to." What form, then,
did the deception of Michal take in order to save David from
the relentless Saul? Albright maintains that "It is very hard
to separate the expression used here, *kebir ha-'izzim,* from the
parallel *sefir ha-'izzim,* used in several passages in the clear
sense of 'he-goat.' The first word is derived from the verb *kbr,*
which means 'to be large, old' in Aramaic and Arabic, and 'to
be fat' in Accadian. If it meant 'old he-goat,' it would be easy

[4] *Bulletin of the American Schools of Oriental Research,* No. 83, Oct.
1941, p. 40, footnote.

to see how effective the latter's half-concealed head, with black beard and burning eyes, would be as a substitute for a sick man. As for 'teraphim' in this passage, I suggest the possible rendering 'old rags'; in Canaanite *trp* is now known to have meant 'to wear out,' or the like."[5]

Because of the mention in our verse of teraphim and divination some have taken the passage as a proof of pre-exilic date. The prophet is undoubtedly speaking of the sins of earlier times. Wright decisively puts it: "No distinct reference is here made to idolatry as a sin common among the people of the prophet's own time. The belief in diviners and in teraphim, a belief which existed even in Israel's purest days, though always opposed by the prophets, was one of those beliefs which probably lingered long among the people, just as similar superstitions have frequently prevailed among Christian nationalities. Recent investigations have, at least, made it probable that traces of the old idolatrous practices exist to the present day among the fellaheen of Palestine. It cannot, therefore, be thought strange that a prophet of the restoration should casually refer to the vanity of all such superstitions."[6]

We understand *haqqosemim* as the subject of all three verbs that follow it. The LXX, however, translates *ta 'enupnia psuede 'elaloun*: "dreams spake lies (or, the dreams were speaking lies)." The objection to this view is the absence of the article with *halomoth* (if it were intended as subject), whereas the usage is clear when taken as a construct with its genitive. Because of Israel's pursuit of lies and the vain comfort of soothsayers, they were made to depart into the Babylonian captivity just ended.

---

[5] *Archaeology and the Religion of Israel,* pp. 114 and 207 (note 63). The contention is that the Israelites used the expression "old rags" contemptuously.

[6] *Op. cit.,* p. 267.

The figure in the verb *nasa'* is taken from the pulling up of the stakes of a tent. Cf. Arabic *nz'* (*to pluck up,* that is, the tent-pins or stakes for moving). The resultant oppression continued down to the time of the prophet (note use of imperfect in the verbal form *'nh*), for the loss of the Davidic monarchy was a bitter reality to all. In this forlorn condition did David's greater Son, the Lord Jesus Christ, find them in His sojourn upon earth (cf. Matt. 9:36).

Whenever Israel, the chosen people of God, are afflicted we may be sure that God takes full note of it. So we read: "Against the shepherds is my anger kindled, and I will punish the he-goats; for Jehovah of hosts has visited his flock, the house of Judah, and will make them as his majestic horse in the battle" (v. 3). The English words *punish* and *visited* are translations of the same Hebrew verb. The paronomasia with *paqadh* gives us a good example of the use of this verb with its two different meanings: (1) with direct object of the person, a visiting with favor, and (2) with the preposition *'al* and the person, denoting a visiting with disfavor or punishment. The prophets repeatedly use the figure of shepherds to denote princes, priests, and prophets in Israel. See Jeremiah 23 and Ezekiel 34 for classic passages. But is such the intention here? Baron is of this opinion, and understands the he-goats to refer to the rich oppressors of the poor in Israel. Dods feels that God is angry with both shepherds and he-goats because they have misled the people.

They are probably correct who see in these categories the foreign rulers, persecutors, and tyrants over Israel (cf. Isa. 14:9; Jer. 6:3, 4). Kimchi goes so far as to identify them. Says he, "These are the kings of Greece, who oppress Israel before the day when the house of Hasmoneans rose up against them."[7] Zechariah passes easily from the picture of a flock of sheep, op-

---

[7] *Op. cit.,* p. 112.

pressed and downtrodden, to that of a "richly caparisoned battle-horse" which executes the fierce judgment of God upon the ungodly. God will punish, but He will use His persecuted people as the instruments of His sore visitation. He will not only liberate them, but give them joyous victory over their enemies. Why the mention of Judah alone? "The house of Judah only is mentioned in verse 3, not in distinction from Ephraim, however (cf. verse 6), but as the stem and kernel of the covenant nation, with which Ephraim is to be united once more."[8] Moreover, the name of Judah was coming to be the designation for the whole nation. The prediction is thus clear that Israel "will rule over their oppressors" (Isa. 14:2), but only when they are so ruled over by God's Messiah that they are His pliable instruments.

Whereas in former days of disobedience Israel knew the tyrannical oppression of foreign shepherds (compare verses 2 and 3), they shall enjoy in future days, in the time of God's restored favor, the beneficent and benevolent rule of their own rulers, particularly that of the Messiah. Zechariah predicts: "From him *shall be* the corner-stone, from him the nail, from him the battle-bow; from him shall go forth every oppressor together" (v. 4). The word *mimmennu* is undoubtedly of great importance for it is found four times in this verse. Wright (so also Von Orelli) refers it to the Lord. His arguments are: (1) a similar sense in Hosea 8:4 refers to Jehovah; (2) the proximity of the suffix of the word *hodho* to *mimmennu;* (3) Judah is treated as a plural in *'otham* (verse 3) and all the verbs of verse 5. In answer to the first contention it must be readily admitted that the cases are not parallel; it is evident that the Lord is speaking of Himself in the Hosea passage, whereas that cannot be easily claimed for our text in Zechariah. The suffix in *hodho* may indeed be

---

[8] Keil, *op. cit.*, p. 346.

close to the word under discussion, but the subject emphasized in verse 3 (b) is God's flock and God's majestic horse, namely, Judah. Lastly, it is true that Judah is spoken of in verses 3 and 5 by the use of the plural, but surely Judah is also referred to in the words *flock* and *horse* which are singular. Hebrew usage shifts easily from the singular to the plural in the discussion of the same subject, so that no argument can be based entirely upon this factor.

With the majority of interpreters of the passage, therefore, we understand Judah to be meant. It will be from Judah herself that One will come to rule righteously and will both empower them to the conflict and assure of ultimate victory over the enemy. Note the important confirmation of our position in Jeremiah 30:21. Hengstenberg, in summarizing, says: "The meaning is this: having attained to perfect freedom by the help of the Lord, who gives success to their arms, they will now receive rulers and officers from among themselves, and a military force of their own; and whereas they were formerly a prey to strange conquerors, they will now terrify even foreign nations."[9]

But to what does the prophet refer in the use of the four subjects of this verse? Keil takes the corner-stone, the nail, and the war-bow as the war-like equipment, figuratively set forth, whereby Judah gains the victory over her adversaries, whereas the second clause is said to state the same truth literally. In short, for Keil the corner-stone and the rest are figures for the "ruler" of the latter part of the verse. The corner-stone is supposed to represent the firm foundation that Judah will have; the nail, the mainstays of the political structure; and the war-bow, the military power and furnishings.[10] No mention is made

---

[9] *Op. cit.*, Vol. III, pp. 391, 392.
[10] *Op. cit.*, Vol. II, pp. 347, 348.

by him of any Messianic reference in our passage. On the other hand, Baron finds that every subject in the text points to the Messiah. He is more certain of the first three than of the fourth, but feels that the fourth must have in mind the same person as the previous ones. This cannot be considered a conclusive argument. We prefer to understand the cornerstone, the nail, and the battle bow of the Messiah, while the second clause presents the result of His activities. Because the Messiah intervenes in the manner to be noted, every oppressor will depart from Judah. Cause and effect are clearly stated.

Although *pinnah* is not here qualified by a descriptive modifier, as in Isaiah 28:16 (where *'ebhen* is used) or Psalm 118:22 (where *ro'sh* is employed), it is taken to refer to the corner-stone. This designation of the Messiah conceives of Him as "a prince, on whom as a corner-stone the burden of the state rests."[11] When this figure for the Messiah is followed throughout the Scriptures, the result is much gain in a fuller understanding of the manifold relationships which the Lord Jesus Christ sustains to Israel, the Gentiles, and the Church of God (cf. I Cor. 10:32). First, this metaphor relates Him to the unbelieving in Israel. Isaiah prophesied: "And he shall be for a sanctuary; but for a stone of stumbling and for a rock of offence to both the houses of Israel, for a gin and for a snare to the inhabitants of Jerusalem. And many shall stumble thereon, and fall, and be broken, and be snared, and be taken" (Isa. 8:14, 15). The prophet mentions that He shall be a sanctuary, but he does not dwell upon this aspect of the truth. In another passage he elaborates on the other phase of Messiah's coming to Israel: His relationship to the believing in Israel. Says the prophet, "Thus saith

---

[11] Gesenius-Robinson, *op. cit.* (1882), pp. 856, 857, He adduces the following references: Psa. 118:22; Isa. 28:16; also Isa. 19:13; our passage; 1 Sam. 14:38; Judg. 20:2.

the Lord Jehovah, Behold, I lay in Zion for a foundation a stone, a tried stone, a precious corner-stone of sure foundation: he that believeth shall not be in haste" (Isa. 28:16). Third, this figure is employed to set forth the truth that God has set His seal of approval upon the finished work of Christ. Peter, filled with the Holy Spirit, testified in Jerusalem to the rulers, elders, scribes, the high priest, and the kindred of the high priest that "He [Christ] is the stone which was set at nought of you the builders, which was made the head of the corner" (Acts 4:11).

Fourth, the symbol of the stone is used again by Peter to reveal the bond between believers of this age and the Lord Jesus. In exhortations for the present wilderness experience of the children of God we read: "Putting away therefore all wickedness, and all guile, and hypocrisies, and envies, and all evil speakings, as newborn babes, long for the spiritual milk which is without guile, that ye may grow thereby unto salvation; if ye have tasted that the Lord is gracious: unto whom coming, a living stone, rejected indeed of men, but with God elect, precious, ye also, as living stones, are built up a spiritual house, to be a holy priesthood, to offer up spiritual sacrifices, acceptable to God through Jesus Christ. Because it is contained in Scripture, Behold, I lay in Zion a chief corner stone, elect, precious: And he that believeth on him shall not be put to shame. For you therefore that believe is the preciousness: but for such as disbelieve, The stone which the builders rejected, The same was made the head of the corner; and, A stone of stumbling, and a rock of offence; for they stumble at the word, being disobedient: whereunto also they were appointed."[12] Fifth, in speaking of his rejection by Israel our Lord Jesus Christ made use of this figure in such a way as to predict the future relationship of the nations to Him. Said the Lord: "And he that falleth

---

[12] I Peter 2:1-8.

on this stone shall be broken to pieces:[18] but on whomsoever it shall fall, it will scatter him as dust" (Matt. 21:44). The same truth is set forth at greater length in Daniel 2:31-45.

Out of Judah will the Messiah come, not only as the cornerstone with its manifold implications, but also as the nail or the peg. Our word is found both for the peg of a tent (Judg. 4:21, 22) or the large nail for hanging household utensils on the wall of the house (cf. Ezek. 15:3). The key to the meaning here is found in Isaiah 22:15-25. The prophet foretells that Shebna the treasurer, the arrogant and insolent one, is to be cast out from his position of honor, and Eliakim the son of Hilkiah is to be entrusted with the government. The key of authority to the realm will be given him, and he will be as a nail upon which all the glory of his father's house will be suspended. But it, too, in its turn will give way and all will fall with it. But our Lord Jesus Christ, the dependable Nail, will have entrusted to Him all the glory of His Father's house in that coming day, and will not fail. Think of how much wealth today hangs on nails: masterpieces of art, costly clothing, and valuable objects of every description. An incalculable commitment has been placed upon Christ by the Father: He is entrusted with all authority in heaven and upon earth (Matt. 28:18).

The third figure for the One coming from Judah is that of the battle-bow, signifying the warrior. He is the Warrior *par excellence*. Moses and all Israel had sung that "Jehovah is a man of war" (Exod. 15:3). The sons of Korah foresaw that His sharp arrows, in His second coming, would lodge in the heart of the king's enemies, and they would fall under Him (Ps. 45:6 Hebrew). David celebrated Him as the coming incomparable world Conquerer (Ps. 110:5-7; note well that it is

---

13 Such was the result of His coming upon Israel. See 1 Corinthians 1:23.

the Lord at God's right hand, verse 5). By inspiration of the Spirit the apostle John looked down the range of the centuries and saw Him judging and making war in righteousness (Rev. 19:11).

Because the Messiah will be such to Israel, every oppressor will go forth from their midst. The American Standard Version, with some commentators, translates *noghes* as "ruler," although "exactor" is given in the margin. The Authorized Version, with the support of many commentators, renders the word "oppressor." True, the temptation is strong, having three designations of the Messiah, to make the last noun convey the same meaning. But other factors militate against such a course. Baron translates it "every ruler together" or "he that will exercise all rule." The former meaning may be possible (but even this is doubtful), but the latter rendering is grammatically impossible. He admits: "I am guided more by the context and obvious sense [?] than by strict principles of Hebrew grammar."[14] Keil voices the judgment of many in stating that *"Noges,* an oppressor or task-master, is not applied to a leader or ruler in a good sense even here, any more than in Isaiah 3:12 and 60:17. . . . The fact that *negus* in Ethiopic is the name given to the king . . . proves nothing in relation to Hebrew usage."[15] Hengstenberg's opinion is that the passages adduced in favor of the translation "ruler" are inconclusive. He sees no reason to depart from the usual meaning, if we regard the harshness, not against Israel but against their foes. In any event, the reference cannot possibly be to the Messiah, because *yahdaw* proves definitely that more than one oppressor will go forth. Through Messiah's activity all oppressors, every one of them together, will depart from Israel.

---

[14] *Op. cit.,* p. 355.
[15] *Op. cit.,* pp. 347, 348.

But for the victory the Lord will empower His people. Kelly has well said: "He will fight not merely for them, but in and by them. It is a great mistake to suppose that all will be accomplished by Jehovah single-handed."[16] So we read: "And they shall be as mighty men, trampling *their enemies* in the mire of the streets in the battle; and they shall fight, for Jehovah is with them; and the riders of horses shall be put to shame" (v. 5). The thought of enabling and empowering is prominent throughout this passage, for we find the root *gabhar* besides here, also in verses 6, 7, and 12. We take it that Judah is the subject of the first clause. The decisiveness of their victory is brought out in two expressions, the trampling of their enemies in the mire of the streets and the confounding of the cavalry. Keil (*in loco*) and others see the Qal participle of *bus* as an intransitive and make the dirt of the streets represent the enemy. Passages given in support of this contention are II Samuel 22:43 and Micah 7:10. Both references, however, have a different preposition from the one found here. Besides, Keil admits that our verb in this stem "is construed in every other case with the accusative of the object."[17] The accusative to be understood here is the enemies of Judah, as we have given it in our translation. It is not only that they will fight, but they will do so with such success that even the cavalry will be put to the worse in the conflict. Asiatic rulers made the cavalry their principal strength, whereas Israel had no comparable force.[18]

After the successful issue of the conflict Israel will be restored and blessed in the land. The prophet predicts it thus: "And I will strengthen the house of Judah, and the house of

---

[16] *Lectures Introductory to the Minor Prophets,* p. 472.

[17] See, for example, Isaiah 63:6.

[18] This fact gave point to the taunt of Rabshakeh of Sennacherib's army in the time of Hezekiah. *Cf.* 2 Kings 18:23 and Isa. 36:8.

Joseph will I save; and I will cause them to dwell, for I have
mercy upon them; and they shall be as though I had not cast
them off, for I am Jehovah their God, and I will hear them"
(v. 6). If Judah has been to the fore thus far, it is not that
Joseph (meaning Israel, so called from the leading tribes—
Ephraim and Manasseh) is to be excluded from these purposes
of God for His people. Both will share in the deliverance
(physical) and salvation (spiritual) which the Lord is promis-
ing in this prophecy. Much discussion has centered about the
unusual form *wehoshebhothim*. Kimchi (with Aben Ezra, Baron,
Pusey, *et al.*) regards the verb as a *forma composita* or conflate
from the Hiphils of *shubh* and *yashabh*. Kimchi explains, "The
two ideas are here both implied, that is to say, He will cause
them to return to their land, and will cause them to dwell there
in peace and security."[19] The Authorized Version conforms to
this view, translating the word "and I will bring them again
to place them." The American Standard Version favors the
Hiphil of *shubh* in the text but the Hiphil of *yashabh* is given
in the margin.

Keil finds no analogy for the conflate, and points out that
Jeremiah 32:37 is sufficient evidence that the Hiphils of both
verbs are found in one and the same verse. The Jeremiah passage, then, cannot be adduced to support the view of a composite
form, as Pusey does. We agree with Keil (*in loco*) that the
form we have in our text is a confusion of the verbs *mediae
waw* and *primae yodh*. Together with the LXX, Hengstenberg,
and others, he understands the verb to be the Hiphil of *yashabh*.
The Targum, Vulgate, and others prefer the Hiphil of *shubh*.
The former is the more expressive, because to bring back does
not affirm as much as to make to dwell, in which latter case
they would be as though they had not been cast off. The verb

---

[19] *Op. cit.*, p. 114.

zanaḥ brings vividly before us God's great hatred for sin. The root meaning of the word is that which is foul or rancid (compare the kindred verb in Arabic used of foul water). No longer will Israel be such to the Lord; He will be their God in reality, answering their every need for help.

What is said of Judah in verses 5 and 6 is here noted of Ephraim. The promise is: "And Ephraim shall be like a mighty man, and their heart shall rejoice as through wine; and their sons shall see it, and rejoice; their heart shall be glad in Jehovah" (v. 7). Some commentators feel that from this verse on the prophet's attention is centered on Ephraim. The text itself does not compel us to restrict the reference to Ephraim alone in the remainder of the chapter. The verse before us sets forth that just as Judah was to be empowered to the conflict, so Ephraim will fight by the enablement of the Lord. They with their sons will rejoice in the victory granted them of God. Both father and son will exult in the presence of God with them. For the same figure compare Psalm 78:65, 66. Chambers explains why the reference is especially (but not exclusively) to Ephraim. He notes: "In this verse and the following, the prophet refers particularly to Ephraim (but not to the exclusion of Judah), for the reason that heretofore the ten tribes had not participated as largely as it was intended they should, in the return from exile."[20]

How will God's people be in the land to participate in the Lord's triumph over His foes? This regathering, as well as other details incident to the return of the people to the land is now brought before us. The Lord says, "I will hiss for them, and will gather them, for I have redeemed them; and they shall increase as they have increased" (v. 8). The verb *sharaq* is onomatopoetic and alludes to the ancient method of swarming bees (cf. Isa. 5:26; 7:18). The perfect in *padhah* is a prophetic per-

---

[20] Lange's Commentary, Minor Prophets, *op. cit.*, p. 78.

fect. The last clause cannot be taken as an idiomatic expression—
"They will be as numerous as ever they wish" (so Wright *in
loco*) nor "They shall increase to any extent" (so Lowe *in loco*),
because the manner of Israel's former deliverance (verses 8-12)
from Egyptian bondage is the pattern of the one yet future.
The increase referred to is that of Exodus 1:7, 12, which is
alluded to again and again, as in Deuteronomy 26:5.

Strange as it may seem, this increase will be the result of
their being sown among the nations. The record reads: "And
I will sow them among the peoples, and in the far countries
they shall remember me; and they shall live with their children,
and shall return" (v. 9). *Zara'* is never used in the sense of
scattering (*in sensu malo*) but always of sowing. Just as there
is an increase from sowing in the field, there will be a multiply-
ing of the nation when sown among the nations of the earth.
Unquestionably, this is a reference to a then future sowing, for
that in Babylon was past to Zechariah. The LXX bears out
the view that the verb does not convey the thought of banish,
scatter, or destroy; it uses *spero*. (Cf. Hos. 2:24, 25; Jer. 31:27;
Ezek. 36:9, 10.) Their increase in foreign lands would cause
them to recall the protecting hand of God and thus lead them
to return. See Deuteronomy 30:1-3. Remembering the Lord they
will come alive (cf. Ezek. 37:14, 25) and enjoy the permanent
blessings of God with their children.

Whereas the human side of the return of Israel is given in
verse 9, the divine operation is stressed in verse 10 thus: "And
I will return them from the land of Egypt, and from Assyria
will I gather them; and unto the land of Gilead and Lebanon
will I bring them; and *place* shall not be found for them." We
concur in the position of Keil that Egypt and Assyria are representative. He writes: "Egypt . . . is rather introduced in all
the passages mentioned simply as a type of the land of bondage,

on account of its having been the land in which Israel lived in
the olden time, under the oppression of the heathen world.
And Asshur is introduced in the same way, as the land into
which the ten tribes had been afterwards exiled. This typical
significance is placed beyond all doubt by verse 11, since the redemption of Israel out of the countries named is there exhibited
under the type of liberation of Israel out of the bondage of
Egypt under the guidance of Moses."[21] (Cf. Isa. 11:11 ff.) Hengstenberg asks why there is no mention of the Chaldeans. His
answer is that since Ephraim especially is now in view, for them
Egypt and Assyria (and not Babylon) had been the only foes.
(Cf. Isa. 52:4; Hos. 11:11.) The mention of Gilead and Lebanon—both sides of the Jordan in northern Palestine—should not
be restricted to the former abode of the ten tribes (which it was),
but, as with the remainder of the passage, be understood to include all of Israel's homeland (cf. Isa. 49:20, 21).

If God is to return them to their land, He will have to
remove the barriers. How He does this the prophet portrays:
"And he will pass through the sea, affliction, and will smite the
waves in the sea, and all the depths of the river shall dry up;
and the pride of Assyria shall be brought down, and the rod of
Egypt shall depart" (v. 11). The imagery is clear for it is
taken from the exodus of Israel from Egyptian servitude. Events
of Israel's past history are in themselves prophecies of God's
future dealings with them (cf. Isa. 11:11-16). Neither the
Authorized Version (with its "through the sea with affliction")
nor the American Standard Version (with its "through the sea
of affliction") does justice to the words *bayyam tsarah*. The
simplest and best rendering is to take the words as nouns in
apposition (see translation above), in the sense of the sea which

---

21 *Op. cit.*, p. 351.

caused affliction or distress. The LXX translation *'en thalasse stene* is untenable, for, says Pusey, "(1) *yam,* as the sea nowhere occurs as fem.; in II Kings 16:17 it is 'the brazen sea' which is spoken of; (2) the narrowness of the sea, if physical, would facilitate the crossing, not aggravate it; (3) omitting the article, *bayyam tsarah* would be 'in a sea of affliction,' but would drop the reference to the sea, or 'the red sea,' 'sea' becoming a mere metaphor."[22] The word *ye'or* always refers to the Nile (except Dan. 12:5); such is its meaning here. When God goes before Israel, both the rod of Egypt's taskmasters and the pride of insolent Assyria will be brought to nought (cf. Isa. 10:7ff.).

Just as oppression (cf. Exod. 1:8 ff.) is characteristic of Egypt, so Assyria is well described by pride. In the records written after the sixth campaign of Sennacherib we find the following: "Palace of Sennacherib, the great king, the mighty king, king of the universe, king of Assyria, king of the four quarters (of the world); favorite of the great gods; the wise and crafty one; strong hero, first among all princes; the flame that consumes the insubmissive, who strikes the wicked with the thunderbolt. Assur, the great god, has intrusted to me an unrivaled kingship, and has made powerful my weapons above (all) those who dwell in palaces. From the upper sea of the setting sun to the lower sea of the rising sun, all princes of the four quarters (of the world) he has brought in submission to my feet."[23] God knows how to bring such pride very low, and He will do it that day.

The prophet Zechariah closes with a picture of the condition of restored and vindicated Israel: "And I will strengthen them

---

[22] *Op. cit.,* Vol. II, p. 418, footnote.

[23] D. D. Luckenbill, *Ancient Records of Assyria and Babylonia,* Vol. II, p. 140, par. 300.

in Jehovah; and they shall walk up and down in his name, saith Jehovah" (v. 12). Strength for enjoyment of God, as well as strength for battle, must come from God. They will walk in the light of all His revealed excellence. The LXX suggests *katakauchesontai* ("in his name shall they boast"—evidently reading *yithhallelu*). The proposal is not necessary for we have the parallel to the Masoretic text in Micah 4:5, where the LXX translates *halakh* by *poreuomai*. Israel strengthened of the Lord and walking in conformity with His name—such is the prospect which Zechariah places before Israel as the culmination of their history.

If students of prophecy differ upon restricted context and points of grammar, they are none the less at variance when they come to place a given prophecy in its intended setting. For example, Wright and Chambers believe the predictions of this chapter were realized in the conflicts and victories of the glorious age of the Maccabees. Keil finds a partial fulfillment of the promises of 9:11-10:12 in the past: the return from captivity, the large population in Galilee, the care of God over His people in their conflicts with world powers for Palestine. But, says he, "The principal fulfillment is of a spiritual kind, and was effected through the gathering of the Jews into the kingdom of Christ, which commenced in the time of the apostles, and will continue till the remnant of Israel is converted to Christ its Saviour."[24] Kimchi, speaking of the entire chapter, claims "My own decided opinion is, that it is entirely future, as well as that which preceded."[25] He places it in the days of the Messiah. Those who have been following our comments on this and the preceding chapter are aware that we have taken the setting of the prophecy in 9:10-10:12 to be that of the latter days for Israel in the

---

[24] *Op. cit.*, pp. 353, 354.
[25] *Op. cit.*, p. 116.

coming again to them of their Messiah King. Toward Israel
He will make every gracious blessing to abound. May that glad
day be hastened for distressed Israel, distressed of men but
beloved of God.[26]

---

[26] We suggest as a helpful exercise for the student of prophecy the
making of a chronological outline of this chapter (Zech. 10). He will
soon be convinced, we warrant, of the marvelous gamut over which the
Holy Spirit moved men of old in the writing of the Scriptures.

CHAPTER III

5. The Rejection of the Good Shepherd and the Rule of the Wicked One, 11:1-17.

THE CONTRAST between the present chapter and chapters 9 and 10 is quite marked. They speak of blessing and prosperity, while here a sad picture of sin and punishment is brought before us in most vivid language and dramatic events. Compare chapters 3 and 4 of this prophecy with chapter 5 for a similar sequence. Chapter 11 explains why the blessings and promises of the previous chapter are in abeyance for Israel. Preceding the fulfillment of the prophecies of blessing are the apostasy of Israel and their rejection of the Good Shepherd, their Messiah, with the consequent visitation of God upon them in dire punishment. This concluding chapter in the first burden is easily divisible into three parts: (1) the visitation of God in wrath, verses 1-3; (2) the cause of this manifestation, verses 4-14; and (3) the ultimate outcome of the sin of Israel in the final scourge upon them, verses 15-17.

There is no strictly poetic portion in chapters 1 through 8 of this prophecy. In chapters 9 to 14, however, there are poetic sections in each chapter, chapters 9 and 10 being poetic practically throughout. The first division of the present passage is in poetry as well as the last verse (mainly, but not uniformly, 3:3 metre). Probably the most poetic section of the whole book of Zechariah is 11:1-3.

In beautiful apostrophic language the prophet declares:

"Open thy doors, O Lebanon,
And let fire devour thy cedars!
Wail, O fir-tree, for the cedar is fallen,
For the glorious ones are destroyed;
Wail, O oaks of Bashan,
For the fortified forest has come down!
The loud wailing of the shepherds,
For their glory is destroyed;
The loud roaring of young lions,
For the pride of Jordan is destroyed!" (verses 1-3)

Of what is the prophet speaking? Unquestionably, he is depicting for us the complete desolation of the land; it is a scene of judgment. Upon this all are agreed, although there is diversity upon certain details. Chambers states it well thus: "The first three verses describe the ruin of the entire land, in words arranged with great rhetorical power, full of poetic imagery and lively dramatic movement."[1] There are those who are inclined to take the description of the prophet in a figurative sense; that is, the cedars, fir-trees, and the oaks are understood to refer to earthly rulers and individuals of varying ranks. Thus, the cedars would indicate the highest in the land, while the others would be gradated under these. (So Hengstenberg, Dennett, Baron, *et al.*) It is better to see here the physical desolation of the land which, to be sure, would involve the people dwelling in it. (So Keil, Wright, Von Orelli and many others.) The storm of judgment is seen sweeping on from the high lands to the lowlands. North and south alike are affected. The mention of Lebanon in verse 1 naturally carries our thought back to 10:10, where with Gilead the entire land is designated. In this passage Lebanon, Bashan, and Jordan represent the land of Israel. Pusey, following the Jewish commentators, finds in the mention of

---

[1] Lange's Commentary, *op. cit.*, p. 83.

Lebanon a reference to the temple, but the passage necessitates no such position.

As though the fate of the one foreshadowed the doom threatening the other, the cypress or fir-tree is called upon to bewail the destruction of the cedar. The phrase *ya'ar habbatsur* of verse 2 has the Qeri *habbatsir,* changing the reading from "defenced, impenetrable, or inaccessible forest" to "forest of the vintage." The Kethibh is the better. The absence of the article with the noun and its presence with the modifying participle used adjectivally, is by no means rare nor infrequent.[2] The shepherds wail because their pasture lands have been destroyed by the overflowing scourge. Compare Jeremiah 25:34, 36. The young lions roar lamentably because the pride of Jordan is laid waste. The "pride of Jordan" has reference to "the stately oaks on its banks, which shroud it from sight, until you reach its edges, and which, after the captivity of the ten tribes, became the haunt of lions and their chief abode in Palestine"[3] (see Jer. 12:5; 49:19; 50:44).

To what historical event or series does this passage have reference? Chambers finds here the destruction of the kingdom of the Jews, without specifying more closely (see *in loco*). Wright feels that the expressions employed are far too vague to allow us to view them as the prediction of any special invasion of the land of Israel. For him the language could cover any invasion of the Holy Land if it began in the north and spent itself in the south (*in loco*). Dennett contents himself with the general observation that "The first three verses describe the condition of the land after some great public calamity, the

<hr />

[2] Gesenius-Kautzsch's *Hebrew Grammar* (1910 ed.), p. 408, par. 126 w.

[3] E. B. Pusey, *op. cit.*, Vol. II, p. 420.

effects perhaps of some invasion by the Gentiles."[4] We prefer
to understand the passage as a specific reference (although in
very general terms, it is true) of the judgment of God upon
Israel in the time of the Second Temple at the hand of the
Romans. This is the position of Ironside ("the solemn announcement of wrath upon the land and people because of the
tragedy of the cross"),[5] Keil, and Dods. Says the latter rightly,
"It is extremely difficult to establish that this prophecy had any
definite preliminary fulfilment previous to the rejection of our
Lord, and the consequent ruin of the Jews."[6] Such outpouring
of God's wrath had been occasioned by the sin of His people,
and the prophet now depicts for us in narrative form the
enormity of that defection from the Lord.

The greatest of the three sections of the chapter is now
before us, and its detail is designed to bring before us in vivid
portrayal the stages of Israel's great sin, the manifold implications of it, and the tragic consequences of it. The passage with
which we now occupy ourselves is one of the outstanding
prophetic passages in the Old Testament on the ministry and
message of the Messiah. Every verse, though the general import
is clear, is difficult and marked by great diversity of opinion
among those who have given themselves to the study of the
prophecy. By a sharp transition from the scene of devastation
and ruin that has just been before us we hear the Lord's commission of the prophet: "Thus said Jehovah my God: Feed the
flock of slaughter; whose buyers kill them, and account themselves not guilty; and those who sell them say, Blessed be
Jehovah, for I am rich; and their shepherds have no pity upon
them" (vv. 4-5). Two questions are immediately brought before

---

4 *Op. cit.*, p. 131.
5 *Op. cit.*, p. 402.
6 *The Post-Exilian Prophets*, p. 106.

us: (1) in what way was the word of the Lord carried out by
the prophet? and (2) in what capacity did he act?

Our text gives us the answer to both these important
queries. From the range of the prophecy (note such details as
shepherding the whole nation as a flock, the covenant with
the peoples, the cutting off of the three shepherds, the breaking
of the bond between Judah and Israel, and especially the time
of the fulfilment of the prophecy as seen from verses 1-3) we
are driven to the conclusion that we have here a symbolical
act of the character of a vision. In no wise is the message less
forceful on this account. Most commentators are agreed that
the prophet is acting in the capacity of, or representatively for,
the Messiah, the Shepherd of Israel *par excellence*. Compare
chapter 6 and our chapter, verse 15, where the prophet represents the wicked shepherd. Further proof is given in verse 8
and even more so from verse 10. Wright does not feel that
Zechariah acts representatively for the Messiah, but only in his
prophetic capacity for the Lord. This position, it seems, is
modified by his later statement that "The prophecy is, we believe, one of a peculiarly Messianic character. What Jahveh is
said to perform through his prophet, was done in very deed by
the Messiah."[7] That such passages as Psalm 23:1; Isaiah 40:10,
11; Ezekiel 34:11-19 refer ultimately to the Messiah is patent
from Old Testament passages such as Ezekiel 34:23, 24, to
say nothing of the New Testament confirmation to be found in
John 10:1-18; Hebrews 13:20, 21; I Peter 2:25 and 5:14.

Acting for the Messiah, then, the prophet was to feed the
flock of slaughter. The people are so designated either because
they were already being slaughtered or yet to be so. Perhaps
the latter is preferable because, although their condition was
already precarious (see 10:2), it was to be even more so in

---

[7] *Op. cit.*, pp. 304, 305.

the period of the prophecy's realization. Compare Psalm 44:23 (Heb.) for a similar designation of Israel. All that the phrase implies is to be gleaned from the vivid explanation of verses 5 and 6. Israel was bought and sold as so much merchandise by those who used her for their own selfish ends. Who are these buyers and sellers? Some understand these oppressors to be foreign rulers, while a lesser number believe the reference is to the civil and religious leaders of Judah and Israel who abused their position for their own gain. While Ezekiel 34 and other passages denounce the heartless shepherds of Israel, they are not depicted as wantonly bartering Israel for their profit or actually slaying her. However, the foreign oppressors of Israel are so denoted.

Furthermore, they are so hardened in their ways that, instead of realizing their wickedness, they congratulate themselves upon their successes, mockingly and blasphemously blessing God for the results of their transactions. So little do they account themselves guilty in the matter. Compare Jeremiah 50:6, 7. Keil translates *ye'shamu* as "bear no blame"; that is, they have thus far gone unpunished (see *in loco*). He cites in support of this translation Hosea 5:15 and 14:1. Whatever may be said for the latter passage, the former is scarcely susceptible of the meaning he attaches to it. Despite such warnings from God as those in Jeremiah 2:3 and 30:16 the enemies of Israel, then as now, have felt they could molest Israel with impunity. But if the oppression of foreign rulers was culpable, that of their own leaders, their own shepherds, was all the more blameworthy. These had no compassion upon the sheep, thus leaving the miserable sheep without human defender either from within the nation or from without.

But Zechariah goes on to a climax when he predicts: "For I will no longer pity the inhabitants of the land, saith

Jehovah; but, behold, I will deliver the men each into the
hand of his neighbor and into the hand of his king; and they
shall smite the land, and I will not deliver from their hand"
(v. 6). Sad was the lot of Israel when foreigners made merchandise of them; worse was their condition when their
own leaders showed them no pity; but worst of all when God
Himself declares He will no longer pity them. Their plight
has reached its climax. Keil takes what to us seems a rather
strange position.[8] He understands by the inhabitants of the
land (which word he translates in its broader meaning of
"earth") those in whose midst the flock of slaughter are living.
The former are the world-powers and our prediction foretells
their destruction by civil wars and despotic kings because of
their affliction of Israel. His reasoning is this: if verse 6 is still
speaking of Israel, then why the need to feed them as in verse
7? But the same argument would hold for verse 4 as well.

Why should God tell the prophet (in his representative
character) to feed the flock in verse 4, if their condition is
rightly set forth in verses 5 and 6? The answer to the problem
is to be found in the nature of the prophetic oracles: repeatedly
we find a condition described the reason for which is elaborated
later. Thus it is here. It is precisely because Zechariah was
charged of God to feed the flock and it is because of the result
of this ministry in the ingratitude of the people, that the consequences are noted again and again in this passage. God is not
stating in the same breath that He desires to have the flock
of slaughter fed and then that He has no pity upon them. There
is a time element involved and this is gleaned from viewing
the passage (verses 4-14) in the large. Because of the events
related in verses 8 and following it is stated here that God
determined that He would no longer pity Israel. What such a

[8] *Op. cit.*, Vol. II, p. 360.

declaration involves is seen immediately in the remainder of the verse. Internecine warfare, despotism, and desolation of the land are the outcome. Such conditions they had already experienced in their past history (see 8:10). The king indicated is not a king of Israel. We agree with Hengstenberg that mention is made of a foreign despot. He explains: "That we are to understand by the king a foreign oppressor, and not a native ruler, is evident from the fact that the covenant nation had no native king in the time of the prophet, and that he never speaks of any such king in his descriptions of the future, with the exception of the Messiah."[9] Dennett states simply that it "will probably be Caesar" (*in loco*). Though this ruler will not be of Israel, he is still designated as their king—in the sense that they would have no king but Caesar. It is thus clear from our foregoing remarks that we judge verses 5 and 6 in the manner of a parenthesis, showing the result of the ministry of the true Shepherd. History demonstrates that these conditions did take place after Israel's rejection of their Messiah.

In verse 7 there is a resumption of the thought of verse 4 in these words: "So I fed the flock of slaughter, in truth the poor of the flock. And I took unto me two staves; the one I called Beauty, and the other I called Bands; and I fed the flock." In vision the prophet performs the commission of the Lord which he states both at the beginning of the verse and at the end. The illative *lakhen* specifies more closely those to whom the ministry of the Shepherd came. Gesenius cites our passage as an instance where an adjective, followed by a partitive genitive, acquires the sense of a superlative.[10] The LXX has erroneously joined *lakhen* with the following noun and translated *eis ten Chanaanitin* "unto the Canaanite," omitting also the

---

[9] *Op. cit.*, Vol. IV, p. 19.
[10] *Op. cit.*, p. 431, par. 133 h.

word *hatstso'n*. The Vulgate renders it correctly: *propter hoc, o pauperes gregis*. Horst follows the LXX reading and translates: "So weidete ich die Schlachtschafe für die Schafhandler" (So I pastured the sheep of slaughter for the sheep merchants.).[11]

For the performance of his duties as shepherd the prophet took two staves. Compare the rod and staff of Psalm 23:4. These were to protect the sheep against a twofold danger, as is clear from this passage, namely, from outward enemies and inward strife. See verses 10, 14. The first staff is called "pleasantness, favor, or beauty." There are but seven references in the Old Testament to this word; the name Naomi is from the same root. The second staff bears the name of "bands" or "binders," the plural of excellence. Neither the *schoinisma* of the LXX nor the *funiculus* of the Vulgate does justice to the second name, although both translate the first correctly. The names of the staves imply the blessings flowing from the ministry of the Shepherd: the favor of God toward Israel in keeping their enemies from destroying them, and the bonds whereby He kept brother and brother united within the nation.

In a passage of the Ras Shamra literature (published in *Syria,* XVI, pp. 29-45) mention is made of two "smd." H. L. Ginsberg suggests a kind of weapon. Each has a name answering to its purpose. He notes: "We are immediately reminded of Zechariah 11:4ff. It is the shepherd's (the king's) duty to maintain well-being, hence his staff No'am; it is his duty to maintain concord (the antithesis of 'they shall eat each other's flesh,' vs. 9, or, in the case of the king, sectional strife, vs. 6), hence his staff Habalim ('ropes', 'ties')." In explaining the reference in the aforementioned literature he says: "Perhaps what is meant is a mace with a stone head drilled through to admit the wooden

---

[11] T. H. Robinson and F. Horst, *Die Zwölf Kleinen Propheten* (Tübingen, 1938), *in loco*.

shaft, to which it is lashed tightly with thongs; and hence the name from the root *smd* 'to bind.' Such mace heads are found frequently in excavations."[12] It should be added that the weapons just referred to, though they do remind us of the staves of our prophecy, are not identical with them, for the word in our text is *mql*.

But from the very first the gracious shepherd care of the good Shepherd was met with opposition. So we read: "And I cut off the three shepherds in one month; for my soul was weary of them, and their soul also loathed me" (verse 8). Perhaps no other passage in the Old Testament has been so variously interpreted as this. Chambers (*in loco*) counts forty different solutions to the identity of the three shepherds. We shall not burden the reader with the enumeration of them. The oldest, and probably the correct, view is that of Cyril and Theodoret, which is followed by Hengstenberg, Chambers, Baron, Dods, Gaebelein, and others. This interpretation sees in the three shepherds not three individuals, but three orders or classes of individuals: the king, the priest, and the prophet (compare Jer. 2:8, 26). There seems to be a valid objection to this view as it stands. If the passage is set in the time of the Second Temple and the earthly ministry of the Messiah of Israel, then the prophetic order had ceased to exist before that time. Hengstenberg explains that "in accordance with the essential character of prophecy, the prophet represents the future by means of the analogous circumstances of his own time."[13] For him the place of the prophet was taken by the scribe of our Lord's time. But this is not necessary for the New Testament

---

[12] "The Victory of the Land-God over the Sea-God," *Journal of the Palestine Oriental Society*, Vol. XV, 1935, p. 328 and footnote 1.

[13] *Op. cit*, p. 23.

knows of prophets, John the Baptist himself having been accounted as one (compare Matt. 11:9, 10).

Some students of the prophecy regard the cutting off as a gracious intervention of God on behalf of His people, an indication of His shepherd care over them. It is better to view the act as God's displeasure against those who would not have the rule of the Shepherd over them. The cutting off of the three shepherds (for the use of the numeral see Exodus 26:3, 9) will take place in a comparatively short time, one month. Whether this period extends through the earthly ministry of our Lord or shortly after it, it is not necessary to determine. Upon Israel's rejection of Christ, the three mediatorial offices of prophet, priest, and king (all of which were represented in their fullest and highest sense in Him) were abolished, showing the cessation of God's direct communication with them, the suspension of covenant relationships. Whereas the patience of the Shepherd became exhausted with the godless ways of the shepherds, they in turn loathed Him. The verb *baḥal* expresses loathing to the point of nausea. Compare the Syriac *behila.*

The setting at naught of the Messiah was followed by sorrow upon sorrow for Israel, as history well confirms. This the prophet describes for us thus: "Then I said, I will not feed you: that which dieth, let it die; and that which is to be cut off, let it be cut off; and let them that remain eat each the flesh of the other. And I took my staff Beauty, and cut it asunder, that I might break my covenant which I had made with all the peoples. And it was broken in that day; and thus the poor of the flock that watched me knew that it was the word of Jehovah" (vv. 9-11). Three types of calamity came speedily upon God's wayward people: death from famine or pestilence, violence at the hand of a foreign foe, and civil strife. What is plainly set forth in verse 9 is symbolically stated in verse 10. Wright, starting

with his view that the passage speaks of Maccabean times, holds
rather strangely that "The 'beauty' had indeed departed from
the people when the high priesthood was made with their con-
sent a political institution."[14] Graver issues than these were
involved. The covenant was made with the nations and peoples
of the world on behalf of Israel. Compare Sennacherib's invasion
of Judah in the reign of Hezekiah for an example, Isaiah 36 and
37. Keil states it simply: "This covenant consisted in the fact
that God imposed upon the nations of the earth the obligation
not to hurt Israel or destroy it, and was one consequence of
the favour of Jehovah towards His people."[15] In the coming day
of Israel's return to the Lord this covenant will be enlarged;
see Hosea 2:20-22 (Heb.). In the meantime the fulfillment of
the prophet Zechariah's words is to be found in Luke 19:41-44
and 21:24. The full import of the act of the prophet was understood by the godly in Israel, especially, but the message in the
act was not wholly lost upon the remainder of the nation.

But the base ingratitude of the nation and the dark hue of
their sin must be brought out in bolder relief. The Shepherd,
through the prophet, addresses His people: "And I said unto
them, If ye think good, give me my wages; and if not, forbear.
So they weighed for my wages thirty pieces of silver. And
Jehovah said unto me, Cast it unto the potter, the precious price
that I was prized at by them. And I took the thirty pieces of
silver, and cast them unto the potter, in the house of Jehovah"
(vv. 12, 13). That the Shepherd asks His wages of the sheep
reveals them to be men. The matter was entirely voluntary, and
not of constraint, for they could refuse to give Him anything if
they so chose. The response of the people was calculated in
this instance to bring out more forcefully than any words exactly

---

[14] *Op. cit.*, p. 322.
[15] *Op. cit.*, p. 366.

their appreciation and appraisal of the ministry of the Shepherd
of Israel. Almost unbelievable but true, they weighed out to
Him thirty pieces of silver! He was requesting of them fruitage
from His ministry, such as piety, godly fear, devotion, and love,
and they gave Him instead that which was far worse than a
direct refusal (compare Matt. 21:33-41). Under the Mosaic law
thirty pieces of silver were compensation for a slave gored to
death by an ox (compare Exod. 21:32). Says Dods, "To offer
this sum was therefore equivalent to telling the Shepherd of
Israel that they could any day buy a common slave who would
be as useful to them as He had been."[16] God will not and does
not allow this affront to His beloved Son to go unrebuked. The
prophet is told to cast this "precious price" to the potter, which
he does in the house of the Lord. In the words *'edher hayeqar*
we have an example of exquisite irony, which is not common
in Scripture. (Compare Job 12:2.)

Why should this contemptible price be cast to the potter?
It must be noted that some, following the Syriac version, believe
yotser is an error for *'otsar*. The Syriac renders it *bit gaza*, "the
treasury." Horst concurs in this, translating the command: "Wirf
es in den Schatz" (*in loco*). The verb itself *hishlikh* is opposed
to the thought of putting the money into a treasury, and in
actual fulfillment (Matt. 27:3-10) it never was. The LXX with
its *eis to choneuterion* (into the melting-furnace) is nearer to
the truth, while the Vulgate is the best of the versions, rendering
it "statuarius." Once we feel certain that the money was to be
cast to the potter, the question must still be answered as to the
connection of the potter with the money. "Throw it to the
potter" was probably equivalent to our own "Throw it to the
dogs" when speaking of something contemptible. The casting
to the potter is taken by some (following Hengstenberg) to be

---

[16] *Op. cit.*, p. 109.

equivalent to casting a thing into an unclean place. He argues
that there was a potter employed about the temple whose work-
shop was in the Valley of Hinnom, a place of pollution in every
way from the time of Josiah (compare II Kings 23:10; Jer.
18:2; 19:2).

There are several strong objections to Hengstenberg's position: (1) the passages in Jeremiah do not prove that the potter
lived in the Valley of Hinnom; (2) if he did live there, it
would not have made him personally unclean; (3) if the potter
were unclean, he would not have worked in the temple where
he was found by the prophet. Moreover, this view necessitates
Hengstenberg's adding to the end of the verse: "to be carried
thence to the potter" without any foundation whatever. It is
clear from the Mosaic law that dishonorable money could not
remain in the temple, Deuteronomy 23:19 (Heb.). Wright gives
us the best solution (so Keil, Baron, and others): "The price so
insultingly offered to the shepherd was to be flung to a potter
as one of the lowest of the labouring classes, to be cast to a poor
worker in clay, whose productions were of so little value that
when marred by any accident they could easily be replaced at a
trifling expenditure of cost or toil."[17] The potter was undoubtedly serving in the temple when the prophet, still in vision, mark
you, came to cast away the money. The temple was chosen so
that the act of repudiation by God might be as public as possible.

The last breach between God and Israel remains to be
symbolized (see verses 6 and 9 also) and we have it in these
words: "Then I cut asunder my other staff, namely, Bands, that
I might break the brotherhood between Judah and Israel" (v. 14),
Those who assign to Zechariah a pre-exilic date find here the
disruption of the kingdom after the death of Solomon. But this
is to fly in the face of all too many clear proofs of the post-exilic

---

[17] *Op. cit.*, p. 329.

composition of the entire book. The word *ha'ahawah* is a *hapax-legomenon* and was mistaken by the LXX for *ha'ahuzzah,* translating it *ten kataschesin,* "the possession." Compare the correct Vulgate *germanitas.* The word is actually from '*ah* and is found in later Hebrew in the Mishna, Sanhedrin 58b, Sabbath 20a, and elsewhere.[18] Chambers rightly says: "The breaking up of the nation into parties bitterly hostile to each other, was one of the most marked peculiarities of the later Jewish history, and greatly accelerated the ruin of the popular cause in the Roman war."[19]

With real insight Dods notes the chronological sequence of the events: "It will be observed that the breaking of the first staff preceded, while the breaking of the second staff succeeded, the final and contemptuous rejection of the Shepherd by the people. This, too, is the historical order. The Jews had long been under foreign rule, Idumaean and Roman, before they were scattered and lost coherence as a nation."[20] Now that we have concluded this section it will be all the more readily seen that the passage unquestionably speaks of the spiritual condition of Israel during the time of the Second Temple, and especially in the period of Christ's ministry, which eventuated in the catastrophic rejection by Israel of their Messiah and the subsequent breakup of the Jewish commonwealth. The Romans did come and take away both their place and nation. See John 11:48.

Between verses 14 and 15 comes the whole of the present Church period. Israel's tragedy has a sequel and it is given in short compass. The prophet is recommissioned by the Lord in the following words: "And Jehovah said unto me, Take unto thee again the instruments of a foolish shepherd. For, behold,

---

[18] M. Jastrow, *Dictionary of the Targumim,* Vol. I, p. 39, col. 1 (New York, 1943).

[19] *Op. cit.,* p. 86.

[20] *Op. cit.,* p. 110.

I will raise up a shepherd in the land, who will not visit those that are cut off, neither will he seek those that are scattered, nor heal that which is broken, nor feed that which is sound; but he will eat the flesh of the fat, and will tear their hoofs in pieces. Woe to the worthless shepherd that leaves the flock! A sword shall be upon his arm, and upon his right eye: his arm shall surely be dried up, and his right eye shall be utterly darkened" (vv. 15-17). Just as Zechariah represented the true Shepherd, he is now commanded of the Lord to portray the wicked shepherd. We need not assume that the instruments of the foolish shepherd differ from those of the true Shepherd, because the difference is primarily one of the heart. This foolish shepherd is not Herod or Agrippa (Kimchi), nor all the rulers of Israel from the decline of the Maccabean period to the rejection of Christ (Lowe), nor the Roman Empire (Wright), but the personal Antichrist (Jerome, Pusey, Baron, Dennett, and others). In verse 15 we have the character of this shepherd; in verse 16 his works; and in verse 17 his punishment. The adjective *'ewili* is a *hapaxlegomenon,* the substantive of which is often used. Folly in the Old Testament is sin. Compare Psalm 14:1. He is foolish in the moral sense.

The grievousness of the situation is brought out by the fact that God is said to raise up this shepherd in the land. God will allow him to have his full way for a time. For this sinister figure see the leading passages in Daniel 11:36-38; our passage; John 5:43; II Thessalonians 2:1-12; I John 2:18, 22, 26; 4:1-3; II John 7; Revelation 13:11-18. He will be a religious leader in the land of Palestine (the false prophet of the Book of Revelation) in confederation with the Roman Beast at Rome, who will head the revived Roman Empire of prophetic times. Verse 16 pictures for us the evil works of this diabolical figure. He is the opposite in every particular of that which he should be.

Contrast with Isaiah 42:3 and compare with Jeremiah 23:1 ff.;
Ezekiel 34:1 ff.; and John 10:12, 13. Hengstenberg is against
the majority of commentators in rendering *hanna'ar* by "tender,"
and attaches little import to the fact that the word is never used
of animals. It is the abstract for the concrete. The LXX renders
it rightly by *to 'eskorpismenon,* so also the Vulgate by *dispersum*
and the Syriac by "the scattered ones." Von Orelli puts the
verse in the form of a climax: "The neglect of the bad shepherd
is pictured in the form of climax: The sheep in peril he saved
not by incurring danger himself; the lost he seeks not, because
this would fatigue him; the injured he does not lovingly care
for; for the sound there is not the slighest regard; the fat he
even feeds on; and the lively he maims, that he may keep good
eating for the future without trouble."[21] He has, however, mis-
understood the *ro'i* and *'ozebhi* of the next verse by taking the
yodh as a suffix referring to God. These are instances of the
yodh compaginis with the construct state. The word *'elil* is used
of idols as being valueless and worthless. The arm (symbol of
power) and the eye (the symbol of intelligence) are the objects
of punishment (standing for the entire body), because instead
of fulfilling the office of shepherd, they falsified and outraged
it. Judgment will ultimately fall upon the Antichrist, the wicked
shepherd, but not until he has wrought much havoc in Israel.
If it be thought impossible that Israel will receive him, we need
only remember that they did prefer Barabbas to Him in His
first coming.

The judgment here (v. 17) brings to a close the cycle of
prophecy which began with judgment (9:1). Judgment has
gone from the circumference (the nations) to the center (Israel);
Zechariah will yet reveal that in blessing the direction will be
from the center (Israel) to the circumference (the nations) as

---

[21] *Op. cit.,* p. 360.

in chapter 14. Chapter 11 of this prophecy reveals the darkest chapter in Israel's history. But thank God, out of this darkness God has caused light to shine to the ends of the earth through the glorious death and sacrifice of the Son of God, a death whose virtues and efficacy will yet enthrall the hearts of Israel as we shall see in a future study.

EXCURSUS ON ZECHARIAH 11:12, 13 AND MATTHEW 27:3-10

The passage in Matthew narrates the remorse of Judas Iscariot after his betrayal of the Lord Jesus, his casting of the money into the sanctuary, his suicide, and the buying by the priests with this money of a potter's field in which to bury strangers. The evangelist then continues: "Then was fulfilled that which was spoken through Jeremiah the prophet, saying, And they took the thirty pieces of silver, the price of him that was priced, which they of the children of Israel priced; and they gave them for the potter's field, as the Lord appointed me." No little difficulty has been occasioned by the mention in verse 9 of the prophet Jeremiah when the name of Zechariah appears to be called for. How shall we explain this phenomenon?

First of all, even a cursory reading of Zechariah 11:12, 13 in the Hebrew, the same passage in the LXX, and the Greek of Matthew 27:9 will reveal that the LXX is not an exact rendering of the Hebrew, and that the Greek in Matthew differs from both. The Gospel account, though revealing accurately how the prophecy in Zechariah was carried out, gives the general sense of the Old Testament prophecy. It is clear that Matthew has reference to the transaction predicted in Zechariah. Why did he assign it to Jeremiah? Or did he assign it or did another?

Let us see what light can be thrown upon the problem from the versions. As is known, there is no LXX on the New Testa-

ment. But the Syriac Peshito and the Latin Vulgate do translate
the New Testament. The Vulgate renders Matthew 27:9 thus
(in the first part of the verse): "Quod dictum est per Ieremiam
prophetam dicentem . . .", which is identical with the Greek
text. The Syriac reads: "beyad nebiya demar," which is to be
translated "by the prophet who said" without mentioning the
name of the prophet. Thus there is no agreement between the
versions. Cod. 22 does read *Zachariou,* but this is an inferior
MS.[22]

Among attempted solutions are the following. It was an
oral statement of Jeremiah. Manifestly, this cannot be proved,
so we are advanced no farther. Eusebius claimed the Jews deleted
the passage from Jeremiah's writings. Considering the well-
known reverence of the Jews for the Scriptures, this opinion
must be rejected at first glance. Origen conjectures that the
passage is found in an apocryphal book of Jeremiah. Again,
there is no proof forthcoming. Augustine, Luther, Beza, Keil,
Wright, and almost all moderns consider it a simple slip of
memory. This position does not take a very high view of the
inspiration of the passage, if the slip of memory can be attributed to the evangelist. If it be assigned to a later scribe,
as some do, the case is possible. If it be viewed as a copyist's
error, it must be very old, before any of the MSS. that have come
down to us.

Plummer suggests that "The prophecy, though attributed
to Jeremiah, is evidently Zechariah 11:13, but it may be influenced
by Jeremiah 18:2 and 19:1, 11, and hence be quoted as from
Jeremiah."[23] His expressed preference is to regard it as probably

---

[22] Nestle's Greek New Testament, 16th ed. (1936), p. 77.
[23] *Exegetical Commentary on the Gospel according to St. Matthew,*
p. 386.

a slip of memory. Hengstenberg holds that as far as the main features are concerned, Zechariah's prophecy in chapter 11 was only a repetition of Jeremiah 19. This is not true, as a reading of the Jeremiah passage will show, but Edersheim seems to incline to this position. He speaks of "St. Matthew, targuming this prophecy in form as in its spirit, and in true Jewish manner stringing to it the prophetic description furnished by Zechariah, sets the event before us as the fulfillment of Jeremy's prophecy."[24] It can easily be verified that Jeremiah's prophecy speaks of no rejection of the Messiah and weighing for Him thirty pieces of silver. Some early commentators supposed that the Matthew passage was compounded from both Jeremiah and Zechariah (as appears to be the view of Plummer, Hengstenberg, and Edersheim), and that Jeremiah was mentioned as being the more distinguished of the two. Compare Mark 1:2, 3 for a case in point. But it still cannot be proved that the Matthew passage has any affinities to Jeremiah apart from the mention of the potter. Other prophets mention the potter also, namely, Isaiah.

To Hengstenberg we are indebted for the interesting fact that in all other quotations from Zechariah in the New Testament, no mention is ever made of the name of the prophet. Compare John 19:37 (Zech. 12:10); John 12:14 (Zech. 9:9); Matthew 26:31 (Zech. 13:7); and Matthew 21:4,5 (Zech. 9:9). Though interesting, this fact causes us to wonder all the more why Matthew, when he does assign a prophecy of Zechariah by name, connects it with the name of Jeremiah.

Many have maintained that Matthew had in his original text *Zriou* (*Zachariou*) but an early copyist mistook it for *Iriou* (*'Ieremiou*). Wright gives the sufficient refutation to this at-

---

[24] *The Life and Times of Jesus the Messiah*, Vol. II, p. 576.

tempted solution. He notes that such contractions do not occur in the oldest MSS.[25]

The best solution appears to us to be that of Lightfoot (so Scrivener also). The Talmudic tradition shows that the prophetic writings in the order of their place in the sacred books were Jeremiah, Ezekiel, Isaiah, etc. This order is found in many Hebrew MSS. (Wright *in loco*). Matthew, then, quoted the passage as from the roll of the prophets, which roll is cited by the first book. Compare the use of "psalms" in Luke 24:44 where the entire third division of the Hebrew canon is meant.

---

[25] *Op. cit.*, p. 337; see also the footnote: "It is safer to acknowledge the difficulty as yet unsolved."

CHAPTER IV

II. The Second Burden, 12-14.

1. Israel's Conflict and Deliverance, 12:1-14.

THE LAST section of the latter part of Zechariah's prophecy deals with events in the distant future. The only exception is 13:7. As a portion of the prophetic Scriptures it is second to none in importance in this book or in any other Old Testament book. It is indispensable to an understanding of the events of the last days for Israel—the time of the Great Tribulation and the establishment of God's kingdom on earth.

The events of the second burden take place within the same prophetic period, designated repeatedly by *bayyom hahu'*. Compare 12:3, 4, 6, 8 (*bis*), 9, 11; 13:1, 2, 4; 14:4, 6, 8, 9, 13, 20, 21. The time element must be of great significance if it be reiterated with such frequency, and we shall see that it is. Says Dods, "It is obvious that from the beginning of the twelfth chapter to the end of the book it is one period that is described."[1] In these chapters the city of Jerusalem holds a prominent place, being mentioned in 12:2 (*bis*), 3, 5, 6 (*bis*), 7, 8, 9, 10, 11; 13:1; 14:2, 4, 8, 10, 11, 12, 14, 16, 17, 21. The Tetragrammaton is found with marked frequency in this last burden of Zechariah. The nations of the earth (designated as *'ammim, goyim,* and *mishpahoth*) play a major role in the events set forth. See 12:2, 3 (two synonymous words), 4, 6, 9; 14:2, 3, 12, 14, 16, 17, 18, 19. If we gather these important elements together, we find that in

---

[1] *Op. cit.,* p. 112.

the end time God will be dealing with both Israel and the nations of the earth relative to the city of the great King, Jerusalem.

The actual events, world-embracing in character, which are presented include the world confederacy against Jerusalem; the victory of God's people, empowered of the Lord; the conviction of Israel nationally by the Spirit of God; the presentation of Christ as their rejected Messiah; the national Day of Atonement; the cleansing of the hearts of the nation; the purging of the land from idolatry and false prophets; parenthetically, the crucifixion of the Messiah; the time of Jacob's trouble; the partial success of the nations invading Palestine and besieging Jerusalem; the appearance of the Messiah for His people; their rescue and His coming with His saints; the changed and renovated Holy Land; the establishment of the Messianic kingdom; the punishment of the nations for their futile assault on Israel; the celebration of the kingdom feast, the Feast of Tabernacles; and the complete restoration of the people of God to a holy nation. It is impossible to find outside the Scriptures and difficult to discover in the Bible itself a portion of prophecy more vital or revealing. Only the Spirit of God can unveil its fullness to our hearts and minds.

The prophecy of Zechariah manifests a symmetry between its two major divisions (chaps. 1-8 and 9-14) which cannot be considered accidental. Hengstenberg notes: "We must call attention here to the strict agreement between the first and second portions of Zechariah. . . . Chap. IX and X correspond exactly to chap. I-IV. In both we have a description of the blessings to be bestowed upon the covenant nation previous to the coming of Christ, but still more especially of those to be enjoyed in consequence of His coming. Chap. XI answers to chap. V. In both we find an account of the divine judgments which would

be inflicted upon the unbelieving and ungodly portion of the
covenant nation after its ungodliness had been most openly
displayed in the rejection of the Messiah. Chap. VI:1-8 contains a brief notice of the events which are more fully described
in the prophecy before us and in chap. XIV."[2]

The opening words of the chapter are the same as those in
9:1. The burden of the word of the Lord concerns Israel rather
than the nations, although they are seen in their relation to
the covenant people. Says Zechariah: "The burden of the word
of Jehovah concerning Israel. Jehovah, who stretches forth the
heavens, and lays the foundation of the earth, and forms the
spirit of man in him, says: Behold, I will make Jerusalem a basin
of reeling unto all the peoples round about, and against Judah
also shall it be in the siege against Jerusalem" (vv. 1-2). The
designation of the prophecy as a *massa'* reveals its minatory
character. See our discussion under 9:1. Although the burden
concerns itself almost wholly with the city of Jerusalem and the
kingdom of Judah, in the larger sense it has reference to the
nation as a whole. The three participles reveal the Lord to be
the omnipotent One in heaven, upon earth, and among men.
Compare Isaiah 42:5; 44:24. He is the all-sufficient assurance that
these things will be performed. The use of the participial form
instead of the finite manifests the immanence of the Lord in His
creation. Hengstenberg (followed by Wright and others) holds
that "in direct opposition to the mechanical view of the works
of God, as standing when once created in just the same relation
to him as a house to the builder, the upholding of these works
is represented in the Scriptures as being, in a certain sense, a
continuous creation. Every day God spreads out the heavens,
every day he lays the foundation of the earth, which would

---

[2] *Op. cit.*, p. 53.
[3] *Op. cit.*, p. 55.

wander from its orbit and fall into ruins if it were not upheld by his power."[4] See the Epistle to the Hebrews 1:3.

It is this omnipotent One who warns that He will make Jerusalem a basin of reeling to all the nations round about. Both the LXX and the Vulgate translate *saph* as "threshold." It does have this meaning in Judges 19:27; I Kings 14:17; Zephaniah 2:14, *et al*. But what would be the import of a threshold of reeling? Undoubtedly, the other meaning of this word, namely, "bowl" or "basin," is called for here. Compare also Exodus 12:22; II Samuel 17:28; I Kings 7:50; II Kings 12:14; and others. The figure is a common one in the prophets to express the visitation of God in judgment. See Isaiah 51:17, 21, 22 (although the words employed are different from the one used in Zechariah, the figure is the very same); Jeremiah 25:15-28; 49:12; 51:7; Ezekiel 23:31-33; Psalm 60:5 (Heb.); 75:9 (Heb.); note also Revelation 14:10; 16:19. God's wrath will be poured out upon all the peoples coming against Jerusalem in siege. The two world wars in a little over a quarter of a century have shown us that it is not difficult for the nations of the earth to become embroiled in global catastrophe.

The last clause of verse 2 is somewhat ambiguous, and has been interpreted by Kimchi (among others) to mean: "Judah will be joined with the enemies in the siege against Jerusalem."[4] This position is wholly untenable (no matter what may be the subject of the verb), because the entire chapter shows Judah to be in alliance with Jerusalem, the princes of Judah relying upon the support of the inhabitants of Jerusalem against their common enemy (verse 5) and being used of God to destroy the confederacy of the nations in order to deliver Jerusalem (verse 6). So Keil, Wright, Hengstenberg, Chambers, Baron, and others. There will not be opposition between the capital city

---

[4] *Op. cit.*, pp. 151-52.

and the surrounding country, but mutual help and a common defense against the invading hordes. The clause, then, informs us that Judah too (note the force of *wegham*) will share the fate of Jerusalem. In the time of our passage all the nations of earth will be bitten by the virus of anti-Semitism. From a comparison of prophetic Scriptures we ascertain that the confederacies will be aligned after this manner: (1) the revived Roman Empire (Dan. 2 and 7; Rev. 13 and 17); (2) the Assyrian power (Dan. 11); (3) the northern confederacy (Ezek. 38 and 39); and (4) the kings of the East (Rev. 16).

The passage now before us deals with Armageddon, as does Zechariah chapter 14. In the light of these Scriptures it is useless for Hengstenberg to contend that " a real conflict between the city of Jerusalem and all the nations of the earth is in itself a very improbable thing. We have evidently here a comprehensive view of that which appears in history in a long series of events, the victorious course of the militant Church through the many centuries of the world's history, dating from the appearance of the Good Shepherd."[5] Joel 4:2 (Heb.) is the sufficient refutation of this position. The nations of the earth, in coming to destroy Jerusalem and the people of God, will only be positioning themselves for the stroke of God's unmixed wrath upon them.

So real is the judgment that will fall upon the enemies of Israel that the prophet amplifies thus: "And it shall come to pass in that day, that I will make Jerusalem a stone of burden to all the peoples; all that burden themselves with it shall surely be wounded; and all the nations of the earth will be gathered together against it. In that day, says Jehovah, I will smite every horse with terror, and his rider with madness; and I will open my eyes upon the house of Judah, and I will smite every horse of the peoples with blindness" (vv. 3-4). There is a distinct

---

[5] *Op. cit.*, p. 59.

gradation in thought between verse 2, verse 3, and verse 9: the enemy will be rendered powerless; they will be lacerated; they will be completely annihilated and destroyed. The prophet is not referring to the stone (Christ) of Matthew 21:44 (so Dennett), but any indefinite burdensome stone. Nor is Jerome's suggestion necessary that reference is being made to the custom prevalent in Judea of young men in competition testing their strength by lifting stones provided for that purpose. The verb *sarat* is used in the Pentateuch of the cuttings made for the dead by mourners. Compare Leviticus 19:28; 21:5. What this judgment will consist of in the hour of battle is now stated in prose terminology. The seriousness of this blow to the armies of the enemy will be readily understood when it is remembered that cavalry held a large place in Eastern warfare. Imagine the confusion in the ranks of the beleaguering armies when their horses are thrown into deadly fright and are blinded, and the horsemen are smitten with madness. For the same three plagues see Deuteronomy 28:28. In the same hour that God blinds the eyes of Israel's enemies, He will open His own upon the house of Judah in love and compassion to protect them. See I Kings 8:29; Jeremiah 24:6; Psalm 32:8; Nehemiah 1:6 for similar expressions.

God will give victory over the foe in a twofold way: (1) He will *empower* Israel to triumph over their adversaries, and (2) He will personally *overpower* the enemies of His people. Says the prophet: "And the chieftains of Judah shall say in their heart, The inhabitants of Jerusalem are my strength in Jehovah of hosts their God. In that day I will set the chieftains of Judah as a pan of fire among wood, and like a flaming torch among sheaves; and they shall consume all the peoples round about, on the right hand and on the left; and Jerusalem shall again dwell in her place in Jerusalem" (vv. 5, 6). The Vulgate renders *'alluphe* by *duces,* while the LXX, more in keeping with the derivation of the word, translates by *chiliarchoi.* Hengstenberg correctly notes that "the use of the noun *'alluph* in this passage, and also in chap. 9:7, to denote the princes and leaders of the covenant nation, is very remarkable. Elsewhere it is merely applied to the hereditary princes of Idumea (Gen. 36:15 ff.; Exod. 15:15; I Chron. 1:51 ff.)."[6] In the word *'amtsah* we have a *hapaxlegomenon.* Contrast the unity of the nation (*li* shows that the leaders express the conviction of the entire people as the deputation did in 7:3) with the confused and disrupted condition of their enemies (v. 4).

God will so work in the hearts of the leaders that they will realize it is not their own strength. They will own their dependence upon the people of the land who in turn are strengthened of the Lord of hosts for the conflict. When the princes in Israel are so empowered the issue of the battle is certain. By a vivid figure the prophet depicts the devastation that will be inflicted by Israel upon their foes. The devouring power of fire is well known, especially among sheaves. See Judges 15:1-5 (the case of Samson) and II Samuel 14:28-30 (the instance of Absalom). In verse 6 the first mention of Jerusalem is of the people and the second is of the city. The preposition *tahath* is used here with the same force as in 6:12 and 14:10. The LXX translates all three occurrences in a different way and not in conformity with the Hebrew idiom. The Vulgate renders 6:12 contrary to Hebrew usage, but 12:6 and 14:10 are given correctly.

That the battle and its outcome are not dependent upon Israel and their leaders in the final analysis is clear from the next verse: "And Jehovah shall save the tents of Judah first, that the glory of the house of David and the glory of the inhabitants of Jerusalem be not magnified over Judah. In that day Jehovah

---

[6] *Op. cit.,* p. 60.

shall defend the inhabitants of Jerusalem; and he that stumbles
among them in that day shall be as David; and the house of
David shall be as God, as the angel of Jehovah before them.
And it shall come to pass in that day, that I will seek to destroy
all the nations that come against Jerusalem" (vv. 7-9). The
salvation spoken of in verse 7 is deliverance in the physical realm
from their enemies. The tents of Judah will be saved first.
Pusey thinks "he probably indicates their defenselessness."[7] God
will work so that human pride will not be indulged. Compare
I Corinthians 1:29, 31; II Corinthians 10:17. The Lord will deliver the defenseless country before the fortified and well-
defended capital, so that both may realize that the victory is of
the Lord. Wright understands the double use of *tiph'arah* as indicating martial glory. Probably what is meant is the natural
tendency on the part of the lineage of David to boast of their
choice by God and on the part of the inhabitants of Jerusalem
to glory in their city as the city of the king and his throne.

In their utter helplessness before the unprovoked onslaught
of the enemy all alike will be endowed with superhuman power
and strength. The one who can scarcely walk, let alone wage
effective warfare, will become as the greatest warrior in all
Israel's history, David. And the royal house itself will become
as the mighty Angel of Jehovah who went before Israel in their
desert march. Von Orelli probably sees too little in the latter
comparison when he suggests taking *'Elohim* as an appellative,
as in Psalm 8:6 (Heb.), but Hengstenberg doubtless sees too
much when he maintains that "the true equality of the house
of David with God, and, as it is here stated by way of climax,
with the angel of the Lord, could only be effected by such an
union of the human nature and the divine as was really accomplished in Christ. Humanity in itself could never be exalted

---

[7] *Op. cit.,* p. 436.

to such a height as this. That it is not a mere resemblance which
is spoken of here, but a literal equality, is evident from the
expression, 'as David' in the previous verse."[8] Since no union
with the nature of David is required to understand how God
could empower the feeble in Israel for battle, no such union with
the nature of God need be postulated, because God lays all His
power at the disposal of the rulers of David's house. The greatest
possible power on earth and in heaven will be theirs. Power
belongeth unto the Lord, atomic bombs to the contrary notwithstanding. Compare Psalm 62:12 (Heb.).

In verse 9 we have a summary of the previous verses of
this chapter. Wright, drawing unwarranted conclusions from
the use of *biqqesh* says: "This passage is not an absolute promise
of the utter destruction of the nations. For the phrase which
here occurs, and which is often used in prose and poetry, does
not necessarily denote that that which is sought for is ultimately
obtained."[9] This observation can carry no weight here, for of
what use would the power of God be to Israel in the hour of
her trial, if He Himself could not achieve the objects He sets
for Himself to accomplish? Wright does admit that the verb
is used both of successful, as well as unsuccessful seeking. He
goes on to say, however, "The prophecy does not speak of all
nations (*sic!*) being gathered together against Jerusalem, but
merely announces that those nations or peoples that were round
about Jerusalem should gather themselves together against her."[10]

His difficulty is a two-fold one: (1) he restricts unwar-
rantedly the force of the adverb *sabhibh* in verses 2 and 6. When
we remember that the Scriptures view Palestine as the heart
of the earth (Ezek. 38:12), the nations round about can well

---

[8] *Op. cit.*, p. 63.
[9] *Op. cit.*, p. 380.
[10] *Op. cit.*, p. 369.

mean all the nations of the earth. His suggestion of a time
between the restoration from captivity and the coming of our
Lord, during which time attempts against the land were made
by Idumaeans, Philistines, Arabians, Ammonites, Moabites,
Tyrians, Syrians, and Greeks, his suggestion, I say, just does not
meet the requirements of the case. (2) He cannot conceive of
such a colossal gathering, which he terms "an impossibility."
Such an array of armed forces would not necessitate that every
individual of each nation be present, for in this past war, though
the United States of America participated fully in the war, more
than 115,000,000 of our population never took up arms. But in
the truest sense of the word we fought both Germany and Japan.
Chambers has caught the true meaning of the idiom when he
notes, "This does not mean to seek out in order to destroy,
but is spoken, *more humano,* to express the energetic purpose of
the speaker."[11]

It is in point now to ask of what period of time the
prophet is speaking in verses 1-9. Many commentators refer
the passage to the time of the Maccabees. Dods is not too certain
in the matter, for he suggests: "We look in vain for any historical
occurrences in which the letter of this prophecy has been fulfilled to Israel after the flesh, unless it be in the Maccabean period."[12] Hengstenberg is frank to admit that "we are introduced
here to a state of things such as never existed under the Old
Testament."[13] Wright feels certain of his ground, for his position is that "the prophecy . . . is a prediction of what actually
occurred in the glorious days of Israel's revival under the Mac-
cabee chieftains."[14] We invite the reader to peruse the deeds
and events of Maccabean days in order to find there a fulfillment

---

11 *Op. cit.,* p. 92.
12 *Op. cit.,* p. 112.
13 *Op. cit.,* p. 57.
14 *Op. cit.,* pp. 368-69.

of the things predicted here. The only manner in which the two can be made to speak of the same thing, is to spiritualize in large measure the actual statements of the text. Such men demand of us a more than rigid literalism (such as the actual gathering of all the populations of all peoples against Jerusalem), and yet will in no wise abide by a consistent literal interpretation of the text themselves. As we have intimated above in the course of our remarks, we place the entire passage in the time of the Great Tribulation and more specifically in the War of Armageddon, when the nations of the earth will make their last frantic effort to blot Israel out of existence, only to be met by the most crushing defeat at the hands of the Lord of hosts Himself.

The transition which Zechariah makes now from a physical deliverance to spiritual salvation for God's people is one which is in accord with the whole prophetic testimony of the Old Testament. God never contents Himself with effecting mere physical and temporal rescue; He ever desires truth in the inward parts. The root of the matter must be present. So we read: "And I will pour out upon the house of David and upon the inhabitants of Jerusalem, the spirit of grace and supplication; and they shall look unto me whom they have pierced; and they shall mourn for him, as one mourneth for his only son, and shall be in bitterness for him, as one that is in bitterness for his first-born" (v. 10). This Scripture is of vast importance for an understanding of the future of Israel. It is closely related to the passage in Romans 11:25-27. Just as God pours out refreshing showers upon the parched and thirsty ground, so He will pour out the spirit of grace and supplication upon needy Israel. The verb *shaphakh* is employed in Joel 3:1 ff. (Heb.) also to express this transforming spiritual transaction. For the same truth see Isaiah 44:3; Ezekiel 36:26, 27; and 39:29.

The pouring out of the spirit of grace upon the house of David and the inhabitants of Jerusalem reveals two features: (1) the whole nation from the highest to the lowest will be included; and (2) where the Lord was rejected, there He begins His work of restoration. Keil notes correctly: "The fact that only the inhabitants of Jerusalem are named, and not those of Judah also, is explained correctly by the commentators from the custom of regarding the capital as the representative of the whole nation."[15] The words *hen* and *tahanunim* are from the same Hebrew root, and the paronomasia is a most happy one, for, as Dods observes, "The former of the two words is commonly and rightly rendered *favour* or *grace,* and if used in this sense here it must refer to a new disposition towards God springing up in the people, a spirit of relenting, of contrition for rejecting God, of willingness to accept Him, in a word, of love, but of love that has in it the element of tender compunction about its past treatment of God. The second verb refers rather to the expressions of love, the trustful cries for help and acknowledgments of dependence which accompany this relenting."[16] In short, the spirit of grace is the Holy Spirit who, when poured out upon Israel, will awaken their hearts to supplication for the bestowal of God's favor upon them. Compare *to Pneuma tes charitos* of Hebrews 10:29.

Then they shall look upon Him whom they have pierced. How many have been the times that the missionary to Israel, weary in his task but not weary of it, has sighed as he said, "Oh, if they could only see Him, and be brought face to face with Him!" This longing will be realized as our text plainly indicates. As Dennett points out (*in loco*), this is ever the divine order: first, the conviction of sin, and then, the presentation of

---

15 *Op. cit.,* p. 387.
16 *Op. cit.,* p. 114.

the crucified Saviour. We remember a similar working in the
lives of Joseph and his brethren: first, their broken-down condition, then his disclosure of himself to them. The verb *nabhat*
is used of both physical and spiritual sight and is not infrequently
"coupled with the idea of confidence in the object beheld; like
theorein, for example, in John 6:40."[17] See Numbers 21:9 (with
reference to the brazen serpent). The more difficult *'elay* is to
be preferred to *'elayw,* because the former (so Chambers *in loco*)
is found in all the ancient manuscripts, in the best and most
numerous of the later ones, the LXX, Vulgate, Targum, Syriac,
Arabic, Aquila, Symmachus, and Theodotion.

The prophet intentionally would bring the matter upon a
more intimate basis, between the Messiah and Israel, and that
directly. Keil notes: " *'eth 'asher* is chosen here, as in Jeremiah
38:9, in the place of the simple *'asher* to mark *'asher* more clearly
as an accusative, since the simple *'asher* might also be rendered
'who pierced (me).' "[18] There are some who would make
daqaru mean "wound by insulting, by revilings." The LXX,
strangely enough, uses the verb *katorcheomai,* "to insult." Of
the eleven occurrences of this verb in the Old Testament, not
one is susceptible of this interpretation. Compare 13:3 and the
correct translation of the Vulgate, *confixerunt.* Besides, if the
thought is merely insulting, why such deep and unprecedented
sorrow on the part of the people? Did Israel, actually and historically, only insult the Messiah? Or did they reject Him and
deliver Him to the Romans to be crucified and pierced to death?
Our verb has the same force as *meholal* in Isaiah 53:5.

And let us remember that Isaiah 53 is the inspired confession that repentant Israel will voice on this important occasion.
If Calvary be the tragic hour of Israel's age-long history, then

---

[17] E. W. Hengstenberg, *op. cit.,* p. 65.
[18] *Op. cit.,* p. 387.

this national Day of Atonement will be the hour of their penitent sorrow to be followed by rejoicings ineffable. In that hour,
with enlightened hearts and broken spirits, they will inquire of
one another, "Which ones of us believed the report made to
us? To which ones of us did the mighty power of God disclose
itself? So few of us, because He appeared so lacking in promise;
He had no outward attraction that our carnal hearts could then
delight in. So we desired Him not, with the result that He was
despised and cut off from our company, knowing only griefs
and pains, as we went our way turning our gaze from Him.
But marvel of it all, He was bearing and enduring our sorrows
and our griefs, and all the while we thought He was being
stricken, smitten of God, and afflicted because He was so sinful
and we so good. No, He was smitten because we were so sinful,
for He was wounded because we had transgressed the law and
will of God; He was crushed to death because of our iniquitous
ways; the scourge of God was upon Him so that we might have
spiritual healing and peace with God. We all went senselessly
on in our sins, deliberately and wilfully, and God caused to
come upon Him as an avalanche the sins of us all. What op-
pressions and merciless treatment He suffered, yet He endured
them so patiently and submissively. And yet we did not lay it
to heart that He was suffering all this because it was due us."

As unbelieving Thomas they will not believe until they
see the prints in His hands. The picture in the verb *saphadh*
is that of smiting on the breasts in mourning. Compare Isaiah
32:12. The suffix in *'alayw* is not neuter but masculine ("for
him"), because the preposition is always connected with the individual for whom the mourning is made (so Hengstenberg).
See II Samuel 11:26; I Kings 13:30. It is not so much a mourning
for the act committed, but for the Person involved. Compare
John 19:37; Revelation 1:7. To emphasize the intensity and

wholeheartedness of the grief, never before experienced in the nation's history, though they have learned well through the centuries how to weep and mourn, the prophet likens the lamentation to that for the only child, and the bitterness of heart for the loss of the first-born. These sorrows are the deepest that can enter the private life. (See Exod. 11:6; Jer. 6:26; Amos 8:10.)

Now the prophet would show us how universal as well as individual will be that sorrow, so he writes: "In that day the mourning shall be great in Jerusalem, as the mourning of Hadadrimmon in the valley of Megiddon. And the land shall mourn, every family apart; the family of the house of David apart, and their wives apart; the family of the house of Nathan apart, and their wives apart; the family of the house of Levi apart, and their wives apart; the family of the Shimeites apart, and their wives apart; all the families that remain, every family apart, and their wives apart" (vv. 11-14). As Chambers rightly states, "It is a picture of penitence as vivid and accurate as any found anywhere in the Scriptures."[19] This is the experience of Psalm 51 on a national scale. In verse 10 the mourning is likened to the worst domestic grief; in verse 11 the sorrow is compared to a great public calamity. The mourning of Hadadrimmon (Maximianopolis) in the valley of Megiddo was on the occasion of the slaying of the godly king Josiah by Pharaoh-Necho of Egypt. Compare II Chronicles 35:22-27. The Chronicles passage reveals how great was the lamentation over this king. And rightly so, for "this was the greatest sorrow, which had fallen on Judah. Josiah was the last hope of its declining kingdom. . . . In Josiah's death the last gleam of the sunset of Judah faded into night."[20]

---

19 *Op. cit.*, p. 94.
20 E. B. Pusey, *op. cit.*, p. 440.

Of the three proper nouns in verse 11 the LXX translates only the first as a name, erroneously rendering the other two as appellatives. Because of the overwhelming sorrow, each family will weep apart. It will be an intense and sincere sorrow; private and public; national and individual; personal and family. The mourning will extend from the highest to the lowest in the land. The mention of the house of David shows the kings to be guilty; the house of Nathan (if this be Nathan the prophet and not Nathan, son of David), prophets guilty; the house of Levi, the priests guilty; and the house of Shimei, the ordinary Levites (Num. 3:21) guilty. The old Jewish view held that Nathan represented the prophetic order, while the Shimeite stood for the teachers (so Chambers *in loco*). Luther, followed by Keil and many others, held: "Four families are enumerated, two from the royal line under the names of David and Nathan (son of David), and two from the priestly line, Levi and his grandson Shimei; after which he embraces all together."[21] Suffice it to say, all will mourn. Even husbands and wives will lament apart. Kelly observes with insight: "The closest relationship is as nothing in presence of sin and God as its judge. Each must be alone."[22] The deepest grief seeks seclusion. Meyer comments, "All the people that remain shall be bowed in one common act of contrition. It is much to see one prodigal stricken with remorse—what will it be when a whole nation beats on its breast, and bewails its sins!"[23] Nothing can excite to repentance like a view of the crucified Saviour.

How has this important passage been treated by Jewish and Christian students in the past? Early Jewish opinion favored the Messianic interpretation of this portion of Zechariah. After

---

21 Chambers, *op. cit.*, p. 96.
22 *Op. cit.*, p. 486.
23 *Op. cit.*, p. 129.

the Christian era the theory of two Messiahs, the first, the son
of Joseph, and the second, the son of David, came into vogue.
Such is the position of the Talmud and many Jewish commentators, even to this day. But M'Caul rightly asks, "Why should
the house of David and the inhabitants of Jerusalem mourn so
bitterly for a son of Joseph, especially as, according to Abarbanel,
his death is to make way for the object of their hopes and prayers,
Messiah, the son of David?"[24] There can be no Messiah, son
of Joseph, because (so M'Caul): (1) they, the two Messiahs,
cannot exist contemporaneously in view of Ezekiel 34:22, 23
("one shepherd") and 37:21-24 ("one king"); and (2) the son
of David cannot succeed the son of Joseph in view of Hosea
3:4, 5, for they will have no king until they seek the son of
David. However, still other Jewish commentators denied any
Messianic reference whatsoever (so Kimchi). The latter says,
in commenting on our passage, "Our rabbis, of blessed memory,
have interpreted this of Messiah, the son of Joseph, who shall
be killed in the war. But I wonder, according to their interpretation, how he is here spoken of unconnectedly, without any
previous mention at all."[25]

Among Christians the prevailing view was that Zechariah
spoke of Christ, and so most of the Reformers. Calvin was the
exception, for he held that God was vexed (figuratively said to
be pierced) by the Jews. His contemporaries repudiated his view.
Later writers referred it to some Jewish leader or martyr. That
interpretation which refers the passage to the Lord Jesus Christ
is the correct one because, as M'Caul has pointed out, (1) the
Jewish tradition referred the passage to the coming Messiah, even
if it did err in assigning it to the son of Joseph; (2) all Jewish
commentators acknowledged that the chapter spoke of the days

---

[24] D. Kimchi, *op. cit.*, p. 159.
[25] *Op. cit.*, p. 155.

or times of the Messiah; and (3) this view agrees with other
Scriptures which represent this mourning as that of repentance.
Compare Ezekiel 36:25-31. There must be a sufficient cause
to answer to the profundity and universality of the grief. The
heart that is in line with the purposes of God will pray fervently
that the hour may not be far off when repentant Israel will look
upon their pierced Messiah and own Him as their Shepherd,
their Lord, their King, and their Saviour.

CHAPTER V

2. Israel Cleansed of Her Sin, 13:1-6.

THE connection between chapters 12 and 13 is so close that a chapter division is really uncalled for. The same people, the same subject, and the same time are in view in both chapters. The relationship between 12:10-14 and 13:1-6 is not only logical but chronological as well. Once Israel is brought to a penitent condition and is brought face to face with her crucified Messiah, then the provision of God for cleansing will be appropriate.

The prophet Zechariah foretells that glad day in the following words: "In that day there shall be a fountain opened for the house of David and for the inhabitants of Jerusalem for sin and for uncleanness" (v. 1). The godly sorrow of Israel will not be in vain. The prophetic period under consideration is the same as that in chapter 12. The root of the word *maqor* is the verb "to dig," hence a place dug out, a spring, a fountain. Compare Jeremiah 2:13 and 17:13 where the same noun refers to the Lord Himself as the Fountain of living waters. A fountain is considered shut up as long as it is concealed in the rock, but opened when it gushes forth (so Hengstenberg *in loco*). See Isaiah 35:6 and 41:18 for similarity of thought; the grammatical constructions are not the same, however. Pusey has pointed out (*in loco*) that the periphrastic construction has the force of permanence: the fountain will not only be opened, but remain open. What is promised for the house of David and the people of Jerusalem is applicable to the whole nation.[1] Compare Eze-

---

[1] It is of interest to note that Cowper's famous hymn, "There is a fountain filled with blood . . ." is based on this verse.

kiel 36:24, 25. The fountain will avail for the cleansing of sin and uncleanness.

The last words of the verse recall the terminology of the Levitical ceremonies and cleansings. There may be allusion here in the first instance to the water whereby the Levites were consecrated to their priestly office, specifically, the *me hatta'th* of Numbers 8:7. In the second case there may be a reference to that water for cleansing—the *me niddah* of Numbers 19:9—because of the ever present possibility of defilement through contact with the dead. The word *niddah* is employed not only in the general meaning of uncleanness, but of the periodic uncleanness of women (Lev. 12:2; 15:19-33). This fact accounts for the seemingly strange renderings of the LXX (with its *chorismon*) and the Vulgate (with its *menstruatae*).[2] Purification from bodily defilement stands here for cleansing from moral pollution. The spiritual condition of Israel in 13:1 is similar to that in 3:3, 4. The blessed fountain is none other than Israel's pierced Messiah. On the Day of Calvary that fountain was opened potentially for Israel and all the world; on the national Day of Atonement for Israel it will be opened experientially. In the light of the context and the larger movement of the prophetic events here noted, Chambers' contention that the passage is applicable to no particular period but to every instance where the gospel is received with repentance toward God and faith in our Lord Jesus Christ, is untenable.[3]

---

[2] In Talmudic usage the word is practically limited to the second meaning, one of the tractates of the Talmud being entitled *Niddah*. See M. Jastrow, *Dictionary of the Targumim*, Vol. 11, p. 878, col. 1; also R. Grossman, *Compendious Hebrew-English Dictionary* (Tel-Aviv, 1938), p. 222, col. 2. The root idea of the word is removal or separation. It is obvious from the context in Zechariah that our reference is to the general sense of uncleanness.

[3] *Op. cit.*, p. 100.

The cleansing of the hearts of God's people will be followed necessarily by a thoroughgoing purging of the land which Zechariah describes thus: "And it shall come to pass in that day, saith Jehovah of hosts, that I will cut off the names of the idols from the land, and they shall no longer be remembered; and the prophets also and the spirit of uncleanness will I cause to pass from the land" (v. 2). The two besetting sins of Israel in the days before the exile were idolatry and false prophecy. Where idolatry existed, false prophets were always present. In the apostate age of Ahab and Jehoshaphat there were four hundred false prophets, but only one prophet for God. On Mt. Carmel there appeared four hundred and fifty prophets of Baal and but one Elijah. The prophets spoken of in our text are undoubtedly the false prophets as both the LXX and Vulgate confirm. To state that the names of the idols will be cut off is a declaration of their complete destruction. (Compare Exod. 23:13 and Hos. 2:19.) The designation "spirit of uncleanness" is in marked contrast to the spirit of grace and supplication of 12:10. The words of the original text occur only here in the Old Testament. Compare *pneuma 'akatharton,* Matthew 12:43; Mark 5:8; Luke 8:29; 11:24; Revelation 16:13; 18:2. The spirit of uncleanness is of Satanic origin and was ever present in the mouths of lying prophets. See I Kings 22:21-23.

How are we to explain a reference to idols in the post-exilic period when there was no idolatry? There are those who see here an indication of pre-exilic authorship. This position is scarcely necessary, nor is it tenable. We need not assume that the mention of these sins in the time of the prophet proves their existence in his day. There is here a portrayal of the future in the terms of the past (so Chambers, Wright, Dods, Keil, and others). Then, too, we must remember that, though idolatry did not exist, the possibility of its resurgence was always present.

The danger of falling into idolatry was always real, especially in view of the mixed marriages contracted in exilic times. Compare Ezra 9:2; Nehemiah 6:10 (a heathen practice); 13:23-24. Besides all this, Kohler is doubtless right in seeing here a reference to the revival of idolatry before the consummation of all things for Israel (II Thess. 2:4; Rev. 9:20; 13:1 ff.).

In the verses immediately following we have an elaboration of the prediction that all idolatry and especially false prophecy will be abolished. The prophet declares: "And it shall come to pass that, if a man prophesies any more, his father and his mother who begat him shall say to him, Thou shalt not live, for thou hast spoken falsehood in the name of Jehovah; and his father and his mother who begat him shall pierce him through when he prophesies. And it shall come to pass in that day, that the prophets shall be ashamed every one of his vision, when he prophesies; neither shall they wear a hairy mantle to deceive. But he shall say, I am no prophet, I am a tiller of the ground; for a man bought me from my youth. And if he shall say to him, What are these wounds between your hands? Then he shall answer, Those with which I was wounded in the house of my friends" (vv. 3-6). The prophet reveals how great will be the zeal for the Lord in that day and how dire will be the consequences for anyone presuming to indulge himself in false prophecy. His own mother and father will put the guilty one to death. Jealousy for the truth of God will outweigh the most intimate and dearest relationships of earth. Note Deuteronomy 13:6-12, also 18:20.

The verb *daqar* is the same as in 12:10. Strangely enough, the LXX has translated the verb here by *sumpodiousin,* "to bind hand and foot," a different translation for this word than it has given for the same word in 12:10, neither being the exact equivalent of the Hebrew word, which means "to thrust through, pierce through."[4] The sense in which the verb is to be taken is amply clear from the preceding words, "thou shalt not live." Like Phinehas of old (Num. 25:7, 8) considerations of the Lord's honor will be paramount with all the people in that hour.[5] So ashamed of the former falsehoods will the false prophets be in that period, that they will no longer wear the true prophet's garb to deceive. The false prophets assumed this mark of the true prophet in order to perpetrate their deceptions upon the unsuspecting people. Compare II Kings 1:8. Dods notes: "This garb was either an untanned sheepskin, or a cloak, like the Bedouin blanket, made of camel's hair, as the Baptist's was."[6] Hengstenberg, with customary insight, has pointed out that "in every one of the three verses we have a distinct sign, which serves to mark the prophet as a false one; in verse 2, the association of the unclean spirit along with the notice of the prophet; in verse 3, his speaking lies; and in verse 4, his deceiving."[7]

In verses 5 and 6 we have a vivid portrayal of the manner in which one of these false prophets will attempt, when faced with the charge of false prophecy, to escape detection. When confronted with the indictment that he has practiced the deceptive art, he will disavow any claim to the prophetic office. The disclaimer of this hypothetical false prophet has been likened by some to the statement of Amos in his answer to Amaziah (Amos 7:14, 15). The purpose of the two passages is quite different:

---

[4] The Vulgate has correctly translated the verb in 12:10 and here by *configo*, "to pierce through with a weapon."

[5] A curiosity in interpretation is that of Lowe who says: "Here we propose to read chapter 12:10-14. We admit that we have no authority for so doing either of MSS., versions, or commentaries (*sic!*)" (*op. cit.*, p. 114). He further understands verse 3 as referring to the rejection of the true prophet, the application to the Lord Himself being the most remarkable fulfillment, howbeit not the only one.

[6] *Op. cit.*, p. 117.

[7] *Op. cit.*, p. 91.

Amos was laying claim to a true call from the Lord to the
office of prophet; this suspected one in the passage before us is
repudiating any claim to prophetic ministry whatsoever, because
he wants to avert suspicion from himself. He declares rather
that he is of the humblest class of society and not one to arrogate
to himself the prophetic office. In fact, he claims, a man bought
him from his youth. The *hapaxlegomenon hiqnani* has been
variously rendered by different writers. The *Qal* and *Niphal* of
this verb occur numbers of times in the Old Testament, but the
Hiphil appearing only here has occasioned difference of rendering. Pusey (*in loco*) prefers "a man taught me from my youth."
He contends: "Against the modern rendering 'sold' . . . or
'bought' . . . it seems decisive, that this would be contrary to
the Levitical law. For since, if bought or sold as a slave, he
would have been set free in the seventh year, he would not
have been sold or bought from his youth."[8] His observation can
be answered by the fact that the law all too often was violated
by the people. Proof can be found in Nehemiah 5:1-13 and Jeremiah 34:8-22. Our verb is not a denominative from *miqneh*, but
means to purchase for service.[9]

Thus the argument of the one accused of false prophecy is
that he is neither a prophet now, since he is a farmer, nor has
he ever aspired to prophetic ministry, because he has been pur-
chased from his youth for farming. Then the accused one is
interrogated as to the wounds between his hands; these, he
answers, are those which have been inflicted upon him by his
friends. Pusey, Kelly, Dennett, and others understand verse 6
to refer to Christ. Dennett admits that *"the transition is abrupt*

---

[8] *Op. cit.*, p. 443, footnote 9.

[9] Gesenius-Buhl (13th ed., 1899) renders it *jemand durch Kauf zum
Sklaven erwerben* ("to purchase, acquire someone as slave by purchase"), p. 735, col. 2.

in the extreme (italics ours), but there can be no manner of doubt, in the light of the following verses, that the Messiah is here introduced."[10] Most modern students of the passage understand the verse to be a continuation of the conversation between one accused of false prophesying and his accuser. In the latter opinion we concur. Our reasons are as follows:

1. The transition between verses 5 and 6, on the theory that verse 6 refers to Christ, is so abrupt as to be insupportable. There are no clear indications of a change of subject as we have between verses 6 and 7.

2. For Christ to state He was no prophet would be untrue. Compare Deuteronomy 18:15-18.

3. It is not true that Christ was a farmer.

4. It is not true that Christ was bought by a man from His youth.

5. It is not true that Christ had wounds "between thy hands."

6. Christ was certainly not wounded physically in the house of His friends.

7. There is no conceivable occasion upon which Christ would be subjected to such a cross-examination, as here indicated.

Doubtless, the reference is to the false prophet. We are not prepared to make such a sweeping accusation, however, as Dods has in his statement that "to apply such as allusion to our Lord from the mere circumstance of a mention of *wounds in the hands* is a careless and superficial mode of dealing with the Old Testament which cannot be too strongly reprehended. Were it adopted by an adversary of the faith, one would suppose it to be profanity."[11] Among those who view the statement as one made by the person accused of false prophecy, there are again two positions. There are some who take the statement as

---

10 *Op. cit.*, pp. 170-71.
11 *Op. cit.*, p. 118.

an admission of guilt, a final confession that the accusation is valid. Hengstenberg is of this opinion and understands the wounds to be those inflicted in connection with idol worship. Compare I Kings 18:28; see also Deuteronomy 14:1; Jeremiah 16:6 and 41:5 (in the last instances the cuttings are connected with mourning for the dead). Much of Hengstenberg's argument is based on the use of the word *me'ahabhim*. He denies its use in a good sense, contending that "from the nature of the Piel as an intensive form, it is always used to denote impure and sinful love, either carnal or spiritual, and especially that of idols. It occurs in this sense not less than fourteen times; first of all in Hosea; then in Jeremiah and Ezekiel; and these are the only books in which it is found. It is evident that it must have the same meaning here."[12]

It is difficult to gainsay the argument based on the usage of this word which does have an important place in the passage. Wright, however, answers in this fashion: "though it be true that the special conjugation of this verb (piel) is used in all other cases of dishonorable love, there is nothing in the form of the verb to render that meaning necessary, intensity of love being all that is expressed thereby, and the expression might, as far as the form is concerned, be used with reference to parents, or any friends, whether good or bad."[13] The position of Wright, Keil, and others is that the accuser, suspecting that the wounds of the false prophet were inflicted upon himself in arousing his prophetic ecstasy in idolatrous rites, asks the origin of the wounds, only to be told by way of evasion that they were received in chastisement, presumably in his youth, from loving parents or

---

[12] *Op. cit.*, p. 92. The references are Hosea 2:7, 9, 12, 14-15; Jeremiah 22:20, 22, 30:14; Lamentations 1:19; Ezekiel 16:33, 36-37; 23:5, 9,22 and Zechariah 13:6.

[13] *Op. cit.*, p. 429.

friends. Interesting are the different explanations given for the
words *ben yadhekha.* It has been suggested that the phrase relates to the palms of the hands and the arms (Keil), the hands
themselves and round about them (Hengstenberg), the breast
between the hands (Wright), and between the shoulders (Rashi).
This much is certain: it had to be a place where the accuser
could easily see it to inquire as to its cause. The best view is
gained by taking the words to mean upon the breast or chest.
Compare II Kings 9:24, where we have an analogous case.[14]

3. The Shepherd Smitten and the Sheep Scattered, 13:7-9.

Just as 9:9-10 is a passage in contrast to 9:1-8, so verse 7 of
this chapter follows verse 6 by way of contrast. Having dealt
with the deceit and falsehoods of a false prophet, the prophet
Zechariah turns to the true Prophet, the Messiah of Israel. The
death of the Messiah, which is regarded in 12:10-14 as the act
of Israel, is now seen as the sovereign act of God. Compare
Isaiah 53:10 as well as Psalm 22:16 (Heb.) and Acts 2:23. In
a vivid personification the Lord addresses the sword: "Awake, O
sword, against my shepherd, and against the man that is my
fellow, saith Jehovah of hosts: smite the shepherd and the sheep
shall be scattered; and I will turn my hand upon the little ones"
(v. 7). Ewald and others have felt that verses 7-9 are out of

---

[14] The Ras Shamra cuneiform tables (found in 1929 at Ugarit in
north Syria) have yielded the expression *bn ydm.* Virolleaud, the translator of the texts in the first editions, translates it *entre les deux mains,
c' est-à-dire sur la poitrine* ("between the two hands, that is to say,
upon the chest"). See his "La révolte de Koser contre Baal. Poème de
Ras Shamra (III AB, A)," *Syria,* 16, 1935, pp. 29-45, esp. p. 41. Zellig
Harris, however, interprets the words in the sense of "back." *Cf.* his
Ras Shamra: Canaanite Civilization and Language, Smithsonian Institution, 1938, Washington, D. C. Both these scholars cite the passage in
Zechariah 13:6 as a parallel passage in the Bible to the cuneiform expression. Evidently, there is no more agreement among the cuneiformists
on this point than there is among the Biblical commentators.

place and belong logically to the end of chapter 11 (verse 17), where a sword is to fall upon a shepherd also. Neither the manuscripts nor the versions support such a change, least of all the context. Jeremiah similarly addresses the sword which has been active in judgment (Jer. 47:6, 7). Zechariah reveals God as awaking the sword from its sleep in order to do His will. The sword is used in the broad sense of any weapon used for the taking of life. Compare II Samuel 11:24 and 12:9 where the life of Uriah was taken by arrows, yet the same expression is used. Note also Romans 13:4 and the Roman *jus gladii*. The imperative *hakh* is masculine where we should expect feminine, like *'uri* in this verse, but such enallage is not rare in Hebrew, as in Genesis 4:7. The Shepherd is the same as the One described in 11:4-14, not collective as the LXX has it. The word *'amithi* is of vast doctrinal importance. Besides its usage here the word is found only in Leviticus, where it occurs eleven times (Lev. 5:21 *bis*; 18:20; 19:11, 15, 17; 24:19; 25:14 *bis,* 15, 17), each time with a suffix. All the citations in Leviticus have reference to laws concerning injuries committed against near relatives "to show how great a crime it is to injure one who is related both bodily and spiritually by a common descent. It is used interchangeably as being equivalent to *brother;* a word which is invariably employed in the laws of Moses with reference to a common physical and spiritual descent."[15] When used in Zechariah it refers to One who is connected with God by a unity of essence. Compare John 1:18; 10:31.

Keil explicitly states it: "The idea of nearest one (or fellow) involves not only similarity in vocation, but community of physical or spiritual descent, according to which he whom God calls His neighbour cannot be a mere man, but can only be one

---

15 Hengstenberg, *op. cit.*, p. 97.

who participates in the divine nature, or is essentially divine."[16]
Jewish commentators—Abarbanel, Kimchi, and others—interpret
this as a false claim made by a mere man, but recognize that
the word means one equal with God. This cannot be a false
claim, because God Himself gives it to His Shepherd. In a real
sense the smiting of the Shepherd was a judgment upon the
flock which was worthy of punishment (cf. chap. 11). God has
overruled the smiting for blessing, but still the consequences
must follow such rejection of Messiah by Israel. See the New
Testament citations in Matthew 26:31, 32 and Mark 14:27, 28.[17]
The sheep were not only scattered on the night of His betrayal,
but have been scattered over the world since the destruction of
Jerusalem. But God will turn His hand upon the little ones, the
remnant of 11:7. The expression is usually employed for infliction of judgment and chastisement, as in Amos 1:8 and Psalm
81:15 (Heb.). Here it is employed for the salvation of God's
people. Compare Isaiah 1:25.

Between verse 7 with its smiting of the Shepherd and the
scattering of the sheep, and verse 8, comes the present age of
grace. The prophet now describes the time of Jacob's trouble
(Jer. 30:7) and its issue in these words: "And it shall come to
pass that in all the land, saith Jehovah, two parts shall be cut
off and die in it; but the third shall be left in it. And I will
bring the third part into the fire, and will refine them as silver
is refined, and will test them as gold is tested. They shall call
on my name, and I will answer them: I will say, They are my
people; and they shall say, Jehovah is my God" (vv. 8, 9). Zechariah describes the misery Israel's act brings upon them. Two
parts are to be destroyed. The phrase *pi shenayim* is used in

---

[16] *Op. cit.*, p. 397.

[17] The New Testament quotations are not from the LXX, but agree
essentially with the Hebrew, although not a literal translation.

Deuteronomy 21:17 of the double portion of the first-born. Death will have the right of the first-born with Israel. The verb *yighwa'u* shows that the thought in *yikkarethu* (cf. verse 2) is not merely exile, but death. In the case of "the third," literalness is not to be pressed, because Isaiah (6:13) speaks only of a tenth. The third is the remnant, the little ones. God's method of turning His hand upon the little ones will be to bring them through the fire to purge them of all dross. Compare Revelation 7 and 14 for the 144,000. The blessed result of all God's dealings will be the restoration of covenant relationship with Israel, now so long set aside but not broken. Compare Hosea 1 and 2; Jeremiah 32:38-41; Ezekiel 37:23-28. Only the omnipotent and gracious God can bring out vessels for His glory from vessels marred and ruined; He alone can produce gold of the purest kind from that which was dross. Israel's promises all await fulfillment, but they await the time and pleasure and plan of Him who cannot lie.

CHAPTER VI

4. The Great Consummation: Israel's Deliverance and God's Earthly Kingdom, 14:1-21.

THE LAST three verses of chapter 13 are amplified in this chapter. The beginning of the chapter takes us back to the time indicated in the first part of chapter 12. It is customary with the prophets to give a general statement and then expand the theme later by the addition of details. From other Scriptures we know that before the events outlined in this passage take place, the nation Israel is regathered to the land in unbelief and has made a covenant with the false Messiah, the foolish shepherd of 11:15-17. Few chapters, if any, in the Scriptures are of greater eschatological significance than the chapter before us, and few passages reveal more clearly the vast difference between the literal interpretation of prophecy and the figurative or spiritualizing. Lowe is prepared to confess: "We almost agree with De Wette that this chapter defies all historical explanation. . . . We are compelled therefore to interpret the chapter wholly in a figurative and Messianic sense."[1] Hengstenberg, interpreting the chapter by the same method, refers its events not "exclusively to the termination of the Church's history, but to the whole of the Messianic era from its commencement till its close."[2] Wright (*in loco*) understands the chapter to be an ideal description of the last things, that is, of the Jewish dispensation. When the passage is interpreted in the literal sense, it harmonizes with all that Zechariah has revealed thus far and with the prophecies

---

[1] *Op. cit.*, pp. 131-32.
[2] *Op. cit.*, p. 107.

concerning the consummation for Israel found throughout the Scriptures.

The first five verses outline the confederated attack upon Jerusalem by the nations, the spoiling of the city, and the interposition of the Lord for the deliverance of the remnant. The prophet commands our attention thus: "Behold, a day comes for Jehovah, and thy spoil shall be divided in the midst of thee" (v. 1). The day spoken of here is one in which He will manifest His power and glory, in which the Lord will vindicate His honor and His name in wrath upon His adversaries, and in which He will bring to a speedy climax His purposes of grace for Israel and all the earth. In keeping with many other passages the reference to a day here does not have in view a twenty-four hour day. The expression in the first clause of the verse is equivalent to that in Isaiah 2:12. The pronominal suffix in *shelalekh* refers to Jerusalem as is clear from the following verse and the remainder of the chapter. It is not the booty that she takes, but that which is plundered from her. The spoil, contrary to usual practice, is leisurely divided in the midst of the city, showing how completely she will be overthrown and how secure her enemies will feel in their victory over her. This is indeed the severest and most devastating of all Jerusalem's sieges. Evidently, the last great attack against Jerusalem on the part of the allied nations will issue in an initial success. We concur in B. W. Newton's observation: "As far as I am aware, this *first* verse of Zechariah xiv is the only place in Scripture in which this last *triumph* of the Gentiles over Jerusalem is described."[3] Other Scriptures dwell on the final stage of the battle when the Gentiles are defeated.[4] Kimchi

---

[3] *Expository Teaching on the Millennium and Israel's Future*, p. 161.

[4] *Cf.* Isaiah 29:1-8; Joel 4:1 ff. (Heb.); Zechariah 12:1-9. See our notes on chapter 12 for the alignment of the nations in this great campaign against the holy city.

(*in loco*) rightly refers our verse to the time of the attack by Gog and Magog as prophesied by Ezekiel.

Now that the early fortunes of the conflict have been set forth, the prophet furnishes us with the details implied in verse 1. Says he, "For I will gather all the nations to Jerusalem to battle; and the city shall be taken, and the houses rifled, and the women ravished; and half of the city shall go forth into captivity, and the remainder of the people shall not be cut off from the city" (v. 2). The *waw* of *we'asaphti* is *waw explicativum*, setting forth the antecedents of the spoiling of the city. It is to be noted that God gathers the nations as a scourge to chasten the ungodly among His people, and ultimately to punish them for the evil devices of their hearts against Israel. The twelfth chapter of our prophecy (vv. 2, 3, 9) gives the complement to this picture, showing that the nations come with evil intent to destroy the city of God's people. The enemy, then, is victorious and his victory is described relative to the city, the homes, the women, and the population. The description of the capture is reminiscent of Isaiah 13:16 where the expressions refer to Babylon. Jeremiah told of the capture of Jerusalem by Nebuchadnezzar; Josephus, of the siege of the Romans; but Zechariah, of the desolation toward the end of the Great Tribulation.

The prophecy has been understood by some of the Church Fathers to refer to the destruction of Jerusalem by the Romans. This cannot be the overthrow of the city of Titus, because he was not at the head of all nations, nor did he leave half of the population. Too, the passage cannot be speaking of the Babylonian conquest of Jerusalem, because the greater part of the people were exiled and later the remnant suffered the same treatment. Compare II Kings 25:11. Half of the population will go into captivity, but the other half will constitute the remnant. To the literal interpretation of this prophecy it has been objected

that it would be a physical impossibility for all nations to as-
semble in battle against Jerusalem. Newton correctly states:
"It should also be observed that when nations are described as
being gathered *as nations,* it is not meant that every individual
comes, but they who are governmentally and executively the
constituted representatives of their power."[5] It will be well to
bear this truth in mind when we come to the explanation of
verses 16-18 of this chapter.

The rabbis made current the saying, "When the straw fails,
then comes Moses." But in Israel's final struggle with the world
powers she will need One greater than Moses, the Lord of hosts
Himself, and He will be ready to succor. "Then shall Jehovah
go forth, and fight against those nations, as when he fought
in the day of battle" (v. 3). After the enemy has prevailed and
the hour is darkest, the Lord Himself espouses the cause of His
beleaguered people. "Jehovah is a man of war" (Exod. 15:3) and
the battle is not new to Him. Wright notes that "the expression
'to go forth' (*yatsa'*) is used almost technically for the going
forth of an army to battle."[6] Jehovah of hosts will muster His
hosts for the encounter, although the battle will be the Lord's.
Jerome, Hengstenberg, and Pusey, among others, take the reference to the day of battle as an allusion specifically to the conflict
at the Red Sea (Exod. 14:14). Perhaps it is better to take the
figure in the most general sense: the Lord will wage war as He
has on numerous occasions in the past. See Joshua 10:14, 42;
23:3; Judges 4:15; I Samuel 7:10; and II Chronicles 20:15 (the
references in Joshua use the same verb as in our passage).

Then the Lord will fulfill in His coming such passages as
Isaiah 64:1, 2 and Acts 1:11. Where the Messiah of Israel left
the earth, there He will return. Like Joseph of old, who made

---

[5] *Op. cit.,* p. 162. The same principle holds true for every war.
[6] *Op. cit.,* p. 464.

himself known to his brethren in the hour of their greatest straits, the Lord will manifest Himself to His own people. It is described majestically thus: "And his feet shall stand in that day upon the mount of Olives, which is before Jerusalem on the east; and the mount of Olives shall be cleft in the midst thereof toward the east and toward the west, *making* a very great valley; and half of the mountain shall remove toward the north, and half of it toward the south" (v. 4). The cleft mountain at the appearing of the Lord is reminiscent of the cleft sea when Israel escaped from the Egyptian host. The Mount of Olives was the most serious obstacle in the way of a quick escape from Jerusalem. It was such in David's hour of flight from Absalom (II Sam. 15:30). God will convert the obstacle into a way of escape. This is the only reference in the Old Testament to the name "Mount of Olives." In II Samuel 15:30 the phrase is "the ascent of Olives." The mountain is said to be split latitudinally, causing a great valley to run from east to west.

In view of the plain wording of the passage it seems strange that Wright should maintain: "No mention is made in this prophecy of any personal appearance of Jahaveh in glory to be seen by all those assembled at Jerusalem."[7] But that is precisely what the passage teaches in unequivocal language. That the valley formed by this cleaving of the mountain is intended for the escape of the remnant of Israel is distinctly stated in the following verse: "And ye shall flee by the valley of my mountains; for the valley of the mountains shall reach to Azal; yea, ye shall flee, as ye fled because of the earthquake in the days of Uzziah king of Judah; and Jehovah my God shall come, all the holy ones with thee" (v. 5). A few manuscripts, the LXX, Symmachus, and the Targum read *wenistam* ("stopped up") for *wenastem,* but this rendering would give the opposite idea to

---

[7] *Op. cit.,* p. 466.

that of escape. If the valley were suddenly stopped up, the fleeing remnant would not be benefited. In the words *ge' haray* we have the accusative of direction which does not require the preposition because of the verb of motion. *Ge'* does not refer to the Tyropoeon Valley, but to the one made by the splitting of the Mount of Olives. Inasmuch as the Lord formed them Himself they are designated *haray* ("my mountains").

How far will the valley extend? The text states "unto Azal." Jerome (with his *usque ad proximum*) and Symmachus take the prepositional phrase in the appellative sense: "to very near," i.e., to the place where the fugitives actually are. Wright, Dods, *et al* follow this view. But, as Keil has noted, this is too obscure a manner of speaking. Pusey, Keil, and others relate it to Beth-Azel of Micah 1:11, the latter pointing out that *beth* is often omitted from place names used with it. It is probably best to understand the proper noun as referring to a place near Jerusalem, the location of which is not now known.[8] The reason for the flight is twofold: (1) fear of the formidable enemy and (2) fear of the earthquake. Their precipitous flight is likened to that occasioned by the earthquake in the time of Uzziah king of Judah. This occurrence is not mentioned in the historical books of the Old Testament, but it is referred to by Amos (1:1). Earthquakes were quite common in Palestine, so this one must have been of special violence for the memory of it to linger some two centuries. Then the Lord God, in the Person of the long-rejected Messiah, will come, thus recapitulating what has been foretold in the previous two verses. So enraptured with the thought of the coming of the Lord is Zechariah that he turns from the third personal pronoun to the second personal pronoun: "all the holy ones with thee." Both the Vulgate (with

---

[8] *Cf.* G. E. Wright, and F. V. Filson, eds., *The Westminster Historical Atlas of the Bible* (Phila., 1945), p. 107, col. 5.

its *cum eo*) and the LXX (with its *met' autou*) have need-
lessly altered the meaning. Wright, Keil, Von Orelli, and
Chambers restrict the "holy ones" to angels. Passages like
Matthew 25:31 and II Thessalonians 1:10 indicate that in His
coming again to the earth the Lord Jesus Christ will be attended
by a retinue made up of both angels and saints. The first five
verses of our chapter, then, have given us the results for Israel in
Messiah's coming; verses 6-11 treat of the consequences for the
land of Israel in the coming of Messiah; verses 12-19 deal with
the results for the nations in Messiah's coming; and verses 20
and 21 portray the issue for holiness in the appearing of Messiah.
How much is dependent upon the blessed event of the return
of our gracious Lord! No wonder all creation, animal and
human, groans and longs for that hour (Rom. 8:18-25).

The coming of the Messiah to earth cannot but be attended
by remarkable changes in the realm of nature. Zechariah describes these for us thus: "And it shall come to pass in that
day, that there shall not be light; the bright ones will be congealed" (v. 6). The first portion of the verse has caused no
difficulty, and is abundantly set forth in other prophetic passages.
Compare Isaiah 13:10; Joel 4:15 (Heb.); Amos 5:18; Matthew
24:29. But the last two words have called forth various views
and differing interpretations. Keil translates: "the glorious ones
will melt away"; Hengstenberg renders it: "the precious will become mean" (in the sense of diminished); Kimchi gives: "the
light shall neither be precious nor thickness"; and Wright translates: "precious things (or, the lights) shall be contracted."

The difficulties are several: (1) the verb (if we take the
Kethibh), is masculine while the subject is feminine; (2) the word
used for the lights of heaven is found nowhere else in that
meaning; (3) if the second word is taken as a noun (so the
Qere), no such noun is found. It is probably best, on the basis

of the principle of parallelism so evident in the prophetic and
poetic books of the Old Testament as well as in the literature
of the Near East, to understand that last clause as a reiteration
in figurative language of that which is stated in prose in the
first clause. The LXX and Vulgate with others (reading
weqaruth weqippa'on) translate "cold and ice." But these are not
opposites to light, as Keil has shown. Gesenius-Buhl (13th ed.)
is non-committal, rendering the last word of the verse under
the verb form and the noun form. Gesenius-Robinson (1882)
prefers the *Kethibh,* as does Keil. We have stated our preference
in the translation above. Job 31:26 gives us a parallel use for the
noun, while Exodus 15:8 and Job 10:10 furnish the same verb
with the meaning of "curdle, contract, congeal." That day will
be characterized by absence of light, for the luminaries of heaven
will be congealed to give forth no brilliance.

That day will be so epoch-making that the prophet describes
it in further detail. "And it shall be one day which is known
unto Jehovah; not day and not night; but it shall come to pass,
that at evening time there shall be light" (v. 7). The numeral
'ehadh is employed in the sense of unique, peculiar, solitary,
unparalleled by any other. For the use of the cardinal in this
sense see verse 9; Ezekiel 7:5; and Song of Solomon 6:9. The
day will be known only to the Lord in its essential character,
for it will not be day nor night. It will not be a mixture of
day and night, a murky twilight (*nuchthemeron*), as Dods has
supposed, but will resemble neither. It will not be day, because
the natural sources of light will be withdrawn; not night, because of the supernatural light at evening and the glorious presence of the returned Lord. Compare Psalm 97:3, 4. Apparently, the
course of nature is changed, for the day is darkened to night
and the evening sees light. In the hour of deepest gloom and

blackness God causes the bright light of His deliverance to
shine forth for the distressed ones.

With the coming of the light there are poured out upon the
land living waters, which may be the result (with the physical
changes noted in verse 10) of the earthquake described in verses
4 and 5. Water to the Westerner as well as the Easterner means
refreshment, productivity, a need without which life cannot
continue. There will be life-giving streams. Zechariah predicts:
"And it shall come to pass in that day, that living waters
shall go out from Jerusalem; half of them toward the eastern
sea, and half of them toward the western sea; in summer and
in winter shall it be" (v. 8). Living waters are those which
spring from the ground and last; rain water finds its way to
the sea. Compare Joel 4:18 (Heb.); Ezekiel 47:1-12. The eastern
sea is the Dead Sea (or as the Hebrews call it, the Salt Sea),
for the Hebrews looked eastward. The western sea, or the hinder
sea, is the Mediterranean. The water will flow through all the
promised land bound on the east by the Dead Sea and on the
west by the Mediterranean. These streams will be full not only
in winter, when bodies of water are full everywhere in Palestine,
but in summer also, when natural streams are dry in the holy
land. The refreshing, abundant waters that God will give will
flow perpetually.

At this time, too, earth will know a righteous King. We
read: "And Jehovah shall be King over all the earth: in that
day shall Jehovah be one and his name one" (v. 9). The Lord
will be King not only in heaven, but recognized as King of
earth as well. He will be King not only *de jure* (by right), but
de facto (in fact). Strangely enough, Wright takes the phrase
'al kol ha'arets to refer to the whole of Palestine only. He argues: "In that which follows (verse 10) he mentions the land
of Judah under the same designation (*kol ha'arets*) for its limits

are expressly stated as reaching from Geba to Rimmon."[9] That
the Lord will be Sovereign over all the earth is clearly presented
to us in verse 16. Furthermore, we cannot overlook such passages as Isaiah 54:5; Psalm 72:8-11; and Zechariah 9:9, 10. All
polytheism will come to an end in that day. The Lord Jesus
Christ will be owned and recognized as sole Ruler of the earth.
Compare Isaiah 65:16.

The prophet once more reverts to the theme of the changes,
now topographical, wrought in the land by the appearing of the
Messiah. He predicts: "All the land shall be made like the
Arabah, from Geba to Rimmon south of Jerusalem; and she
shall be lifted up, and shall dwell in her place, from the gate
of Benjamin to the place of the first gate, to the corner gate,
and *from* the tower of Hananel unto the king's winepresses.
And they shall dwell therein, and there shall be no more curse;
but Jerusalem shall dwell safely" (vv. 10, 11). The Authorized
Version translates *ka'arabhah* "as a plain." This is inadequate,
for the article is emphatic. It denotes Arabah or el-Ghor, the
largest of the plains of Judea, running from Hermon to the Red
Sea and known as the deepest depression on the face of the
globe.[10] All the land will be depressed in order that Jerusalem
might be elevated. See Isaiah 2:2 and Micah 4:1. The directions
given cannot be determined with certainty, but they prove two
things: (1) the description must be taken literally (else why
the abundance of detail?) and (2) the city will be rebuilt in its
former extent. Compare Jeremiah 31:37, 38. Geba was on the
northern frontier of Judah, probably Gibeah of Saul (II Kings
23:8). Rimmon south of Jerusalem is to be distinguished from

---

[9] *Op. cit.*, p. 489. He later maintains the Lord's reign is universal
but begins in Judah.

[10] *Cf.* Deut. 1:1. See also Wright and Filson, *op. cit.*, pp. 17, 20, 48,
and 65; N. Glueck, *The River Jordan* (Phila., 1946), especially pp. 3-30.

the Rimmon of Galilee (Josh. 19:13) and that in Benjamin
(Judg. 20:45-47). The city here designated was on the border
of Edom given to Simeon by Judah. The subject of *wera'amah*
is Jerusalem. The verb is probably an expanded form of *weramah*
from *rum,* like *qa'm* in Hosea 10:14.

The city will be inhabited on its ancient site (for the same
use of the preposition see 12:6); it will possess its old boundaries.
The gate of Benjamin was in the north wall, facing the territory
of Benjamin (Jer. 37:13; 38:7). The first gate is probably the
old gate (Neh. 3:6). The corner gate was westward of the old
gate. Compare II Kings 14:13. The winepresses of the king were
probably in the royal gardens in the valley southeast of Jerusalem.
See II Kings 25:4; Jeremiah 39:4; 52:7; and Nehemiah 3:15. Not
only will the city have its former bounds but its population will
live therein, not to go out as captives or fugitives. They will need
to fear no further hostile attacks. There will be no more curse,
that complete devoting to destruction when given up by God
to a curse. The Vulgate has *anathema* and the LXX, *anathema.*
The verb is used in the sense of devoting to God what could
not be redeemed. Compare Deuteronomy 2:34; Revelation 22:3.
Isaiah 65:17-25 does not contradict this verse because the curse
in Isaiah (note the different word employed) is upon an individual; here it is national in scope. Newton observes: "The
outward changes are but symbolic indications of that which will
be morally and spiritually true in that day."[11] The description
is literal and conveys the interrelation of outward fact with inward condition, as Genesis 3 (thorns and thistles resulting from
the sin of man) and Romans 8.

In verses 12-15 the prophet returns to give in fuller detail
the judgment of God upon the enemies of His people. Chrono-
logically these verses follow verse 3. Zechariah vividly describes

---

[11] *Op. cit.,* p. 173.

thus: "And this shall be the plague wherewith Jehovah will smite all the peoples that have warred against Jerusalem: their flesh shall consume away while they stand upon their feet, and their eyes shall consume away in their sockets, and their tongue shall consume away in their mouth. And it shall come to pass in that day, that a great tumult from Jehovah shall be among them; and they shall lay hold every one on the hand of his neighbor, and his hand shall rise up against the hand of his neighbor. And Judah also shall fight at Jerusalem; and the wealth of all the nations round about shall be gathered together, gold, and silver, and apparel in great abundance. And so shall be the plague of the horse, of the mule, of the camel, and of the ass, and of all the beasts that shall be in those camps, as that plague" (vv. 12-15). The word *maggephah* always denotes a plague sent by God. Compare Exodus 9:14; Numbers 14:37; 17:15; I Samuel 6:4; II Samuel 24:21. The infinitive absolute *hameq* stresses the action of the verb and is a *hapaxlegomenon*. The singular suffixes in verse 12 are to be taken distributively of each one involved. Putrefaction and decay will set in while the body is still alive, indeed, still standing—an indication of the frightful suddenness of the visitation. "To strengthen the threat there is added the rotting of the eyes which spied out the nakednesses of the city of God, and of the tongue which blasphemed God and His people (cf. Isa. 37:6)."[12]

The plague is one form of visitation; another is mutual destruction through a supernatural panic. One will prevail over another and lift his hand to strike his friend dead. Compare 12:4; Judges 7:22 (Gideon and the Midianites); I Samuel 14:16-20 (Jonathan and the Philistines at Michmash); and II Chronicles 20:23 (Jehoshaphat and Ammon, Moab, and Edom). The third weapon God employs against the enemy is Judah

---

[12] *Keil,* op. cit., p. 410.

(v. 14). The Vulgate, Luther, and others translate the preposition *b* in *birushalayim* as "against." It must be admitted that this is the usual meaning, but the local sense is also well attested. Note verse 3 where the preposition is used as "against" and then "in" (temporally). The LXX translates "in" in verse 14. The local force is also found in Exodus 17:8; Judges 5:19; II Chronicles 35:20, 22. Fighting is not infrequently introduced without mentioning the object of the attack. Moreover, the context nor parallel passages warrant the assumption that there is opposition between Judah (here for the whole nation) and Jerusalem. Apparel formed a large part of Oriental wealth, so it is mentioned along with gold and silver. Compare Job 27:16; also II Chronicles 20:25; II Kings 7:2-8. The beasts are described as suffering the same plague as their owners. Animal creation was involved in man's judgment at the fall and in the flood. Note the case of Achan in Joshua 7:24, 25.

When the Lord's judgments are in the earth, the nations learn righteousness (see Isa. 26:9). Zechariah reveals that there will be a remnant among the nations also: "And it shall come to pass that every one that is left of all the nations that came against Jerusalem shall go up from year to year to worship the King, Jehovah of hosts, and to celebrate the feast of tabernacles. And it shall be that whoso of the families of the earth goeth not up to Jerusalem to worship the King, Jehovah of hosts, upon them there shall be no rain. And if the family of Egypt go not up, and come not, neither *shall the rain come* upon them; there shall be the plague wherewith Jehovah will smite the nations that go not up to keep the feast of tabernacles. This shall be the sin of Egypt, and the sin of all the nations that go not up to celebrate the feast of tabernacles" (vv. 16-19). For the remnant of the nations God has promised a rich feast (Isa. 25:6). There are many views as to why choice was made of the Feast of Tabernacles, but the most probable is that, speaking of the joys of the ingathering, it will celebrate the gathering of the nations to the Lord and especially His tabernacling among them. The millennial feast is the Feast of Tabernacles, because then God will tabernacle with men more fully than ever before in man's long history. Note especially Revelation 7:15-17, which is a harbinger of the endless tabernacling of God as found in Revelation 21:3.

Verse 17 reveals that the millennial conditions will not approximate conditions in the eternal state, because multitudes will give only feigned submission to the King Jehovah. Note the last verb in the Hebrew of Psalm 66:3. Just as Israel had been threatened with cessation of rain in times of apostasy (Deut. 11:16, 17 and I Kings 17:1ff.), so the nations will be warned of the same punishment. The need for rain shows that the millennial earth is not the new earth of the eternal state. Keil and others think Egypt is individualized in verse 18, because it showed in ancient times the greatest hostility to the Lord and His people, and yet will enjoy the blessings of salvation given to Israel (see Isa. 19:19ff). Probably Egypt is designated because, though it was dependent upon rains to fill the lakes which empty into the Nile, it would appear to be less dependent upon a balanced arrangement of rainfall (as in Palestine), and hence appear to be untouched by the warning of withholding of rain for disobedience. The statement of Hecataeus, the geographer, which was first repeated by Herodotus, was: "Egypt is a gift of the Nile."[13]

Breasted well described the conditions in Egypt thus: "While

---

[13] G. Steindorff, *The Religion of the Ancient Egyptians* (1905), p. 6, and G. Steindorff and K. C. Seele, *When Egypt Ruled The East* (1942), p. 7.

the climate of the country is not rainless, yet the rare showers of the south, often separated by intervals of years, and even the more frequent rains of the Delta, are totally insufficient to maintain the processes of agriculture. The marvellous productivity of the Egyptian soil is due to the annual inundation of the river, which is caused by the melting of the snows, and by the spring rains at the sources of the Blue Nile. Freighted with the rich loam of the Abyssinian highlands, the rushing waters of the spring freshet hurry down the Nubian valley, and a slight rise is discernible at the first cataract in the early part of June. The flood swells rapidly and steadily, and although the increase is usually interrupted for nearly a month from the end of September on, it is usually resumed again, and the maximum level continues until the end of October or into November."[14] For Egypt, then, there will be punishment too, namely, the plague. *Hatta'th* in verse 19 has in view the results of sin, the punishment for the disobedience. (Compare Num. 32:23.) There is an inseparable connection between sin and its punishment.

The last two verses of the prophecy may well close not only this book but the whole history of Israel, for it shows God's original purpose in Israel fulfilled (Exod. 19:6). The heart of Zechariah must have thrilled as he penned the words: "In that day shall there be upon the bells of the horses, Holy unto Jehovah; and the pots in Jehovah's house shall be like the bowls before the altar. Indeed, every pot in Jerusalem and in Judah shall be holy unto Jehovah of hosts; and all they that sacrifice shall come and take of them, and boil therein: and in that day there shall be no more a Canaanite in the house of Jehovah of hosts" (vv. 20-21). When all is cleansed and holy in Jerusalem and among God's people Israel, there will be no need for distinctions of holy and secular, and differences be-

---

[14] *A History of Egypt,* pp. 7-8.

tween holy and more holy. Sin brought in such necessary distinctions, but with the removal of all sin all will alike be holy. There will be holiness in public life (bells of the horses), in religious life (vessels of the Lord's house), and all private life (every vessel in Jerusalem and Judah). (See Newton *in loco*.)

What is the meaning of the reference to the Canaanite? It is immediately recognized that it cannot refer to the Canaanites who formerly inhabited the land, for they were never allowed access to the house of the Lord. They were under the curse (compare Deut. 7:2). The Canaanites (the Phoenicians) were renowned merchantmen (note the Vulgate *mercator*) and notorious for their unprincipled and wicked ways. In time they came to be symbolic of all that was deceitful, unclean, and ungodly (for proof note Hosea 12:8 in the Hebrew). God promises that in that day of holiness no unclean shall defile the house of the Lord. In short, what is stated positively in the first part of verse 21 is repeated negatively in the latter part of the verse. God's great object in Israel is holiness; His great aim in the Church is holiness; His great longing for your life and mine is holiness, and only holiness. Our chapter which began in darkness (as did, indeed, the entire prophecy of Zechariah) ends in the radiant and transparent light of holiness. And throughout the prophecy there is presented to us on every page the spotless, blemishless Holy One of Israel, the Lord Jesus Christ, the Messiah and King of Israel. See Him in

> Chapter one as the Riding One;
> Chapter two as the Measuring One;
> Chapter three as the Cleansing One;
> Chapter four as the Empowering One;
> Chapter five as the Judging One;
> Chapter six as the Crowned One;
> Chapter seven as the Rebuking One;

Chapter eight as the Restoring One;
Chapter nine as the Kingly One;
Chapter ten as the Blessing One;
Chapter eleven as the Shepherding One;
Chapter twelve as the Returning One;
Chapter thirteen as the Smitten One;
Chapter fourteen as the Reigning One.

Come, let us worship at His feet!

INDEX OF SCRIPTURE REFERENCES

Page

GENESIS

4:7	245
6:3	52
10:10	91
10:20,31	145
11:2	91
14:1,9	91
15:16	89
15:18	167
16:11,13	31
17:1	61
18:14	131
26:18	83
27:45	66
31:7	145
31:11	31
31:13	32
31:34	179
31:42	108
32:2,4	30
35:2,4	180
36:15ff	224
37:24	170
41:1,46	2
41:12	2
43:3	61
43:8	2
46:21	2
50:10	120
50:15	108

EXODUS

1:7,12	192
1:8ff	194
3:4-6	32

Page

4:22	171
9:14	259
10:23	103
11:6	232
12:22	221
14:14	251
14:19	31
15:3	187
15:8	255
15:15	160, 224
17:8	260
17:12	85
19:6	60, 262
20:12	130
21:32	209
23:13	238
24:8	169
25:31-40	71
26:3,9	207
26:13	85
26:15-25	84
27:20,21	72
28:9	65
28:36	65
28:36,38	61
30:7,8	72
32:15	85
32:27	160

LEVITICUS

5:21	245
12:2	237
13:55	90
14:45	86
15:19-33	237

Page

16 93
16:29 119
18:20 245
19:11,15,17 245
19:28 223
21:5 223
24:19 245
25:14,15,17 245
26:4 136
26:26 145
26:44 ....27, 56

NUMBERS

3:21 233
8:7 237
12:6,8 29
14:37 259
17:15 259
19:9 237
21:9 230
22:24 85
23:24 174
25:7,8 240
27:2 54
32:3,34,35 101
32:23 262
35:12 54

DEUTERONOMY

2:34 258
4:20 51
4:40 130
5:16,30 130
7:2 263
7:7,8 57
7:13,14 130
8:19 61
9:26,29 51
10:8 54
11:9 130
11:14-17 178

Page

11:16,17 261
12:5 194
12:6 41
13:6-12 239
14:1 243
17:8-10 61
18:15-18 242
18:20 239
19:17 54
21:15-17 171
21:17 247
23:3 159
23:19 210
26:5 192
27:26 85
28:15,45 21
28:28 223
30:1-3 192
32:7 130
32:8 69
32:9 51
32:10 ....49, 50
32:46 61
33:8-10 118
33:28 136
33:29 165

JOSHUA

7:24,25 260
10:14,42 251
13:3 158
16:5,7 101
18:13 101
19:13 257
20:6 54
23:3 251

JUDGES

3:11,30 33
4:15 251
4:21,22 187

Page

5:19	260
5:31	33
6:11	31
7:22	259
8:3	99
8:28	33
15:1-5	224
17:5	179
19:27	221
20:28	54
20:45-47	257

I SAMUEL

2:34	66
6:4	259
7:10	251
14:16-20	259
15:22,23	121
15:23	180
15:27	145
17:28	221
19:12-17	180
22:7	131
25:29	174

II SAMUEL

7	102
11:24	245
11:26	231
12:9	245
12:13	60
12:20	75
14:27	2
14:28-30	224
15:30	252
18:5	2
19:13-16	179
21:20	71
22:43	189
24:10	60
24:18	160
24:21	259

Page

I KINGS

3:16	54
4:25	67
6:3	84
7:50	221
8:29	223
9:20,21	160
13:30	231
14:17	221
17:1ff	261
18:28	243
20:29	66
22:21-23	238

II KINGS

1:8	240
1:11,13	83
7:2-8	260
9:24	244
12:14	221
16:17	194
17:7-23	19
18:23	189
19:28	35
21:13	37
23:8	257
23:10	210
23:24	180
24:2	135
25:1	118
25:4	258
25:8,9	117
25:11	250
25:25,26	118

I CHRONICLES

1:51ff	224
2:54	101
5:1,2	171
20:6	71

Page

II CHRONICLES

2:13	65
20:15	251
20:23	259
20:25	260
26	102
26:6	158
28:6	66
29:11	54
35:20,22	260
35:22-27	232
36:14-16	19
36:22,23	2

EZRA

1:1-4	2
2:28	116
3:10	133
3:11	76
3:11-13	2
3:12	77
4	134
4:5	2
5:1	1
5:1,2	133
5:16	113
6	113
6:14	1
6:15	113
9:2	239
9:6ff	21
10:18	58

NEHEMIAH

1:3	33
1:6	223
2:3	33
3:15	258
4	134
5:1-13	241
6:7	168

Page

6:10	239
7:4	33
7:32	116
9:29	124
9:36	33
11:31	116
12:4	1
12:12-16	1
13	129
13:10	86
13:20,21	45
13:23,24	239

JOB

1,2	54
2:2	29
8:4	80
10:10	255
12:2	209
27:16	260
29:14	61
30:12	55
31:26	255
31:36	101
42:10	172

PSALMS

2:7	20
2:8	167
6:3	34
8:6	225
9:6	56
11:3	104
14:1	212
16:8	55
22:16	244
23:1	201
23:4	205
27:13	108
32:8	223
33:16	165

Page

36:7 95
44:23 202
45 175
45:6 187
45:7,8 164
50:1 132
60:5 221
62:12 226
65:2 144
66:3 261
67:2,3 51
67:7 136
68:15 47
68:18 95
71:7 62
72 68
72 168
72:3-11 ....167, 257
72:7 51
73:24 49
74:6 65
75:5,6,11 42
75:9 221
76:5 5
76:7 56
78:57 19
78:65,66 191
80:7 56
81:15 246
89 102
89:20 165
96:6 104
97:3,4 255
104:1 104
104:4 98
104:15 75
109:6 55
109:31 55
110:4 103
110:5,7 187
113:3 132

Page

118:22 ....65, 185
121:5 55
122 144
128:3-5 130
133:2 75
142:5 55
148:8 98

PROVERBS

16:32 99
18:21 80
30:12 59

ECCLESIASTES

10:4 99

SONG OF SOLOMON

6:9 255

ISAIAH

1:11-17 123
1:21,26 128
1:25 246
2:1-3 144
2:1-4 ....45, 51
2:2 257
2:2-4 ....103, 143
2:12 249
3:12 188
3:22 60
3:26 85
4 106
4:1 145
4:2 ....63, 64
4:4 59
4:5,6 46
5:26 191
6:11 34
6:13 247
7 3
7:14-16 5

	Page		Page
7:18	191	31:3	52
8:2	1	32:12	120, 231
8:3	5	33:21	45
8:14	65	35:6	236
8:14,15	185	36	208
8:18	62	36:8	189
9:4-6	166	37	208
9:5	128	37:6	259
9:6,7	164	40-66	8
10:5,7	36	40:2	172
10:7ff	194	40:10,11	201
11:1	64	41:16	41
11:2	66	41:18	236
11:3-5	164	42:1	63
11:11	91	42:5	220
11:11ff	193	42:8	31
11:11-16	193	43:5,6	132
13:1	153	44:3	228
13:10	254	44:24	220
13:16	250	45:14	146
14:1	38	47:1-7	90
14:2	50, 183	47:6	36
14:9	182	48:10	57
15:1	153, 154	48:20	47
17:1	153	49:3,5	63
17:13	56	49:5,6	72
19:1	153	49:19,20	45
19:19ff	261	49:20,21	193
19:23-25	51	50:8,9	55
19:25	51	51:17,21,22	221
20:3	62	52:4	193
21:1	174	52:11	47
21:1,11,13	153	52:13	63
22:1	153	53:2	64
22:15-25	187	53:5	104, 230
25:6	260	53:10	64, 244
26:9	260	53:11	63
27:6	47	54:5	257
28:16	65, 185, 186	55:10,11	21
29:1	155	56:6,7	103
29:1-8	249	56:7	144

Page

57:15	82
58:3-8	121
58:3-9	122
60:1-3	51, 72
60:2,6,9	107
60:4-9	38
60:17	188
60:19	46
61:1-3	40
61:2,3,7	141
61:3	75
61:6	60
61:7	172
61:10	68
62:1,2	72
62:1-5	90
62:3	61
63:1	97
63:1,2	28
63:6	189
64:1,2	251
64:5	59
64:6	80
65:15	136
65:16	257
65:17-25	258
65:18,19	141
65:20	130
65:20-22	130
66:15	95

JEREMIAH

1:13,14	47
1:14,15	99
2:3	202
2:13	236
2:21	136
3:3	178
3:6-4:4	19
3:8,26	206
6:3,4	182

Page

6:26	232
7:3,5	19
7:4-7	122
11:11,14	125
12:5	199
14:11,12	125
14:12	121
14:22	178
15:7	41
16:6	243
16:18	172
17:13	236
18:2	210, 215
18:4	83
18:11	19
19	216
19:1,11	215
19:2	210
22:18	47
22:20,22	243
23	106, 182
23:1ff	213
23:5	63, 164
23:5,6	64
23:33ff	154
24:6	223
24:9	136
25:9	99
25:11,12	34
25:15,28	221
25:20	158
25:26	156
25:34,36	199
26:13	19
29:10	34, 129
29:22	136
30:7	246
30:11	27
30:14	243
30:16	202
30:21	184

	Page
31:27	192
31:36	56
31:37,38	257
31:38-40	38
32:27	131
32:37	190
32:38-41	247
33:15	63
34:8-22	241
37:13	258
38:7	258
38:9	230
39:1	118
39:2	117
39:4	258
41:1	118
41:5	243
47:6,7	245
48:25	39
49:12	221
49:19	199
49:36	98
50:6,7	202
50:44	199
51:6	47
51:6,9,45	47
51:7	221
51:41	156
52:6,7	117
52:7	258
52:12,13	117

LAMENTATIONS

1:19	243
2:17	21

EZEKIEL

1:4,7,16,22,27	90
2:9,10	83
5:2,10	41
5:5,6	69

	Page
5:12	99
7:5	255
8:3,4	128
9:6	84
10:4,18	128
11:19	124
11:22,23	128
12:6,11	62
15:3	187
16:33,36,37	243
16:42	99
17:21	47
21:26	179
22:16	51
23:4	156
23:5,9,22	243
23:31-33	221
24:13	99
24:24,27	62
26:7	158
28:1ff	156
33:11	19
34	182, 202
34:1	213
34:11-19	201
34:22,23	234
34:23,24	63, 201
35:7	11, 160
36:9,10	192
36:24,25	237
36:25-31	235
36:26,27	228
37:14,25	192
37:21-24	234
37:23-28	247
38	222
38:11	45
38:12	226
39	222
39:29	228
40-48	38, 102

Page

40	43
40:3	43
43:2	46
44:15	54
47:1-12	256
47:7	85
48:35	38

DANIEL

1:2	91
2	222
2,7	39, 40
2:31-45	187
2:34	65
2:35	65
2:37	17
4:32	40
7	222
7:2	98
8	31, 40
8:18	70
8:20,21	39
9	31
9:1,2	34
9:4	21
10:9	70
11	222
11:36-38	212

HOSEA

1,2	247
1:2	29
2:7,9,12,14,15	243
2:19	238
2:19-22	132
2:20-22	208
2:24,25	192
3:4	179
3:4,5	234
4:16	124
5:15	202

Page

6:6	123
8:4	183
10:14	258
11:11	193
12:6	31
12:7	263
13:15	174
14:1	202

JOEL

1:13	120
1:13,14	119
2:23	5, 178
3:1ff	228
3:1,2	178
4:1ff	249
4:2	222
4:2,12,16	95
4:6	173
4:15	254
4:16	166, 171
4:18	256

AMOS

1:6-8	158
1:6-9	173
1:8	246
3:2	84
4:11	57
5:16	47
5:18	254
6:13	39
7:14,15	240
8:5	89
8:10	141, 232

MICAH

1:11	253
2:14-16	143
4:1	257
4:1-5	143

Page

4:1-7 103
4:4 67
4:5 195
4:16-19 143
5:9ff 168
6:6-8 123
6:10 89
6:16 19
7:10 189

NAHUM

1:7 171

HABAKKUK

1:3 83
2:1 29
2:20 52
3:8 95

ZEPHANIAH

2:2 20
2:4 158
2:14 221
3:13 128

HAGGAI

1:1 2
1:4-16 113
1:6,9,11 134
1:14 ....113, 133
1:14,15 25
2:3 77
2:7,22 33
2:11 118
2:15-18 133
2:15-19 134
2:22 95

MALACHI

1:1 154
1:11 132

2:3 56
2:5-7 118
3:8 86

MATTHEW

5:14,16 72
8:11,12 132
9:36 182
11:9,10 207
12:43-45 93
12:43 238
13:33 90
21:4,5 216
21:33-41 209
21:42 65
21:44 ....187, 223
23:32 89
24:4,5 168
24:15 16
24:29 254
25:31 ....104, 254
26:28 169
26:31 216
26:31,32 246
27:3-10 ....209, 214
27:9 ....214, 215
27:9,10 10
28:18 187

MARK

1:2,3 216
5:8 238
10:27 131
14:27,28 246

LUKE

1:32,33 164
1:37 131
1:78 105
1:78,79 72
2:32 72

Page

4:16-21 40
8:29 238
9:32 70
10:34 74
11:24 238
12:35 72
19:41-44 208
21:24 ....17, 208
24:44 217

JOHN

1:14 50
1:18 245
4:22 145
5:43 212
6:40 230
8:12 72
9:5 72
10:1-18 201
10:12,13 213
10:31 245
11:48 211
12:12-16 168
12:14 216
16:12-15 74
17 ....33, 34
19:30 104
19:37 ....216, 231

ACTS

1:11 ....42, 251
2:17,18 178
2:23 244
4:11 ....65, 186
10:10 26
11:5 26
15 144

ROMANS

7:12 45
11:25-27 228

Page

13:4 245

I CORINTHIANS

1:23 187
1:29,31 225
2:9-12 74
10 15
10:11 15
10:31 120

II CORINTHIANS

5:21 68
7:1 94
10:17 225
10:32 185

EPHESIANS

1 68
2 144
2:13 18
2:17 167
2:20-22 65
3:10 68
5:8,9 72

PHILIPPIANS

2:5-11 158
2:7 126
2:15 72

II THESSALONIANS

1:10 254
2:1-12 212
2:4 239
2:6-8 91

II TIMOTHY

2:12 109

HEBREWS

1:3 ....104, 221

	Page
7:1,2	17
7:1-3	103
7:27	66
8:1	104
9:12	66
10:10	66
10:29	229
10:31	83, 158
12:2	104
12:29	17, 83, 158
13:20,21	201

JAMES

| 4:8 | 18 |

I PETER

2:2-7	65
2:25	201
4:17	84
5:8	29, 76
5:14	201

II PETER

| 1:21 | 124 |
| 2:5,9 | 109 |

I JOHN

2:18,22,26	212
2:27	74
4:1-3	212

II JOHN

| 7 | 212 |

JUDE

| 9 | 57 |
| 23 | 57 |

	Page
REVELATION	
1:5	81
1:5,6	109
1:7	231
1:20	72
2:5	81
2:20	90
3:14	81
3:15,16	81
3:21	104
5:5	76
5:6	66
7:1	98
7:15	17, 261
9:20	239
11	43
12:10	54
13	222
13:1ff	239
13:11-18	212
14:10	221
16	222
16:13	238
16:19	221
17	222
17,18	93
17:5	90
18:2	238
18:24	93
18:30	61
19:11	28, 81, 188
19:12	101
19:16	17
21:3	50, 261
22:9	50, 258

INDEX OF SUBJECTS

Aaron, 72
Abarbanel, 5, 31, 106, 168, 234, 246
Aben Ezra, 168
Abraham, 32, 37
Absalom, 2, 252
Achan, 260
Agrippa, 212
Ahab, 238
Ahaz, 9
Akiba, 118
Alexander the Great, 9, 10, 11, 42, 151, 152, 157, 160, 161
Amaziah, 240
Ammonites, 134, 227
Amos, 6, 240, 241
Angel, interpreting, 28, 29, 34, 41, 43, 44, 53, 70, 73, 90
Angel of Jehovah, 26, 27, 28, 29, 30, 32, 33, 34, 36, 38, 43, 44, 48, 54, 55, 56, 57, 58, 67, 108, 225
Anti-Christ, 76, 169, 212, 213, 248
Antiochus Epiphanes, 9, 156, 169, 173
Anti-Semitism, 222
Apostasy, 86
Arabah, 257
Arabians, 134, 227
Araunah, 160
Armageddon, 222, 228
Ashdod, 159
Ashdodites, 134
Ashkelon, 153, 159
Assyria, 27, 36, 40, 42, 89, 92, 192, 194, 222

Augustine, 215

Babylon, 1, 3, 6, 27, 33, 35, 36, 37, 40, 42, 47, 48, 50, 57, 88, 91, 92, 93, 96, 99, 100, 107, 108, 117, 138, 171, 193, 250
Babylonian Captivity, 12, 34, 37, 53, 57, 87, 88, 91, 132, 140
Babylonians, 36, 37, 50
Barabbas, 213
Bar Cochba, 118
Bashan, 198
Battle of Issus, 152, 153
Benjamin, 2, 88, 89
Beth-Azel, 253
Bethel, 11, 32, 115, 116, 118, 140, 144
Beza, 215
Bither, 118
Branch, 7, 63, 64, 77, 103, 104, 105, 106

Caesar, 204
Cain, 78
Calvary, 66, 77
Calvin, 34, 234
Cambyses, 42, 134
Canaan, 87
Canaanite, 263
Candlestick, 71, 72, 73
Chaldaisms, 4
Chaldeans, 193
Christ, High Priest, 64, 67, 68
Christendom, 93, 145
Church, 65, 72, 74, 75, 81, 87, 103, 147, 185

Church age, 143, 168, 211
Church Fathers, 65, 250
Cyrus, 2, 3, 35, 42, 113, 133, 170

Damascus, 153, 155
Daniel, 16, 28, 31, 34, 95, 96, 173
Daniel's empires, 39, 40
Darius Hystaspes, 2, 3, 16, 33, 37,
    47, 50, 113, 162
David, 37, 225
Davidic dynasty, 64, 69, 101, 102,
    225, 229, 233, 236
Day of Atonement, 93, 117, 119,
    219, 231, 237
Day of Jehovah, 8
Dead Sea, 256
Diaspora, 132

Edessa, 155
Edom, 160, 173, 257
Egypt, 40, 42, 92, 99, 134, 192,
    261, 262
Ekron, 153, 160
Eliakim, 187
Elijah, 42, 238
Ephraim, 166, 183, 190, 191, 193
Epiphania, 156
Esther, 27
Euphrates, 3, 167
Eusebius, 215
Ezekiel, 1, 8
Ezra, 116

Fasting, 113
Feast of Tabernacles, 219, 260,
    261

Gabriel, 31
Galilee, 195
Gaza, 153
Geba, 256
Gedaliah, 118
Gentiles, Times of, 16, 17, 41

Gibeah, 257
Gilead, 193
Gog and Magog, 250
Great Synagogue, 2
Great Tribulation, 8, 169, 218,
    228, 246, 250
Greece, 10, 96, 173
Greeks, 10, 172, 227

Hadadrimmon, 232
Hadrach, 154, 155
Hadrian, 118
Haggai, 2, 3, 16
Hagiographa, 16
Hamath, 155
Hasmonean, 168, 182
Heldiah, 107
Helem, 107
Hermon, 257
Herod, 58, 59, 212
Hezekiah, 9, 208
Holy Land, 86
Homs, 155
Holy Spirit, 71, 73, 74, 75, 76, 77
Hosea, 6

Iddo, 1
Idumea, 224, 227
Isaac, 32
Isaiah, 6, 7, 34
Israel, remnant of, 15, 16, 37, 195,
    249
Israel, return of, 37, 192, 208, 248

Jacob, 32, 78
Jaddua, 161
Jarchi, 5
Jebusite, 160
Jehoshaphat, 238
Jeremiah, 1, 6, 7, 10, 34
Jeroboam, 116
Jerome, 5, 26, 48, 145, 223

Jerusalem, 7, 8, 33, 34, 35, 36, 37, 38, 41, 43, 44, 45, 46, 47, 48, 55, 106, 113, 114, 116, 127, 128
Job, 54
Joel, 5
John the Apostle, 82
John the Baptist, 18, 207
Joiakim, 1
Joseph, 190
Josephus, 11, 58, 161, 250
Joshua, the high priest, 1, 3, 53, 54, 55, 56, 58, 59, 60, 61, 62, 63, 64, 67, 68, 69, 77, 78, 80, 81, 100, 108
Josiah, 107, 210
Judah, 5, 66, 88, 89, 184, 191, 308
Judaism, 93
Judas Iscariot, 36, 214

Kimchi, 30, 246 *et passim*
King—Priest, 103, 104, 108
Kosri, 32
Kyle, Melvin Grove, 10

Language, symbolical, 3
Leah, 78
Lebanon, 193, 198
Levi, 102
Levites, 17, 66, 86
Livy, 59
Luther, 6, 215

Maccabees, 169, 176, 195, 208, 212, 227
Maimonides, 32, 117
Malachi, 9
Manasseh, 190
Matthew, 10
Maximianopolis, 232
Mediterranean Sea, 167, 256
Medo-Persia, 40, 96
Megiddo, 232

Melchizedek, 17, 103, 105
Mesopotamia, 92
Messiah, 5, 7, 8, 11, 42, 45, 56, 64, 72, 80, 92, 100, 105, 113, 128, 140, 145, 163, 185, 188, 195, 200, 201
Messiah, throne of, 7, 38, 86, 87, 104, 114, 152
Messianic times, 37, 146
Micah, 6
Michael, the Angel, 26, 57
Michmash, 259
Middoth, 107
Millennium, 130, 131, 137, 176, 177
Mishnah, 159, 211
Moab, 154, 227
Moriah, 128
Moses, 57, 58, 69
Moses, law of, 32, 78, 85, 93, 209, 210
Mount Carmel, 238
Mount of Olives, 7, 95, 252, 253
Mount Zion, 36, 38, 48, 95, 128, 139, 141

Naomi, 205
Nebuchadnezzar, 17, 40, 42, 117, 250
Nehemiah, 37, 116, 129, 168
Nile, 167, 194, 261

Oil, 74, 75
Orontes, 156

Palestine, 1, 10, 47, 64, 87, 95, 167, 174, 193, 195, 199, 212, 226, 253, 256
Pelagianism, 56
Pentateuch, 10, 95, 151, 223
Pentateuch, Mosaic authorship of, 8

Pentecost, 121, 178
Persia, 27, 40, 42, 50, 76, 155
Peter, Apostle, 21, 25
Pharaoh-Necho, 232
Philistia, 158, 160, 227
Philo, 78
Phinehas, 240
Phoenicia, 158, 173
Priestly Code, 8
Prince of Peace, 68
Prophecy, 4, 5, 10
Prophecy, Messianic, 7, 8

Rachel, 78
Rashi, 66, 97
Ras Shamra, 205, 244
Red Sea, 251, 257
Reformers, 234
Rimmon, 256, 257
Romans, the, 36, 200, 211, 222, 230, 250
Rome, 96, 212
Rufus, Turnus, 118

Saadiah Gaon, 168
Sabbath, 129
Saladin, 117
Samaria, 144
Samaritans, 134
Sameas, 58
Sanballat, 76
Sanhedrin, 58
Satan, 29, 54, 55, 56, 58, 76
Sennacherib, 194, 208
Servant of the Lord, 63, 64, 67, 68
Shalmaneser, 157
Shebna, 187
Shechinah, 65

Shinar, 85, 88, 91, 93
Sidon, 153, 156
Solomon, 67, 160, 210
Stone, 7, 65, 66, 77
Symbolism, 76
Syrians, 227
Syro-Ephraimitic War, 5

Tabernacle, 65, 72, 73, 96
Talmud, 10, 32, 217, 234
Targum of Jonathan, 39, 63, 101, 135
Tatnai, 3
Temple, 2, 3, 7, 18, 33, 54, 65, 72, 84, 100, 107, 113, 115, 128, 200, 211
Temple, millennial, 77, 103
Theology, Persian, 4
Titus, 250
Twelve, The, 1, 11
Tyre, 153, 156, 227
Tyropoeon Valley, 253

Uriah, 245
Uzziah, 9, 102, 250

Valley of Hinnom, 210
Valley of Jehoshaphat, 95

World-empires, 65, 95, 96, 98

Zechariah, date of, 9
Zedekiah, 117, 118
Zemach, 63, 64, 67, 68
Zerubbabel, 1, 3, 53, 63, 69, 73, 75, 76, 77, 78, 80, 81, 101, 102, 103, 105, 108
Zohar, 65, 168
Zopyrus, 50

SELECTED BIBLIOGRAPHY

(Note: a study volume, such as this purports to be, must of necessity point the reader to other reference sources of information. A selected bibliography is *not* meant to be an exhaustive one. To the student who wants further references we recommend the bibliography in Lange's *Commentary on Zechariah*, pp. 18-19 where can be found entries from the Patristic and Jewish writers, from the Reformers and later writers, and more than a score of works from the last century. The entire critical problem has been splendidly treated by G. L. Robinson in his doctoral dissertation at the University of Leipzig (1896), and a fine coverage of the literature appears on pages 5-9. C. H. H. Wright in his *Zechariah and His Prophecies* includes a bibliography of the critical material available to him, pp. xlii-xlviii and citations in the General Index, p. 603 ff. R. H. Pfeiffer in his *Introduction to the Old Testament* (Harper, 1941) cites seven entries under Zechariah, all of them magazine articles none later than 1930. Our bibliography has in mind primarily the student of Hebrew who is beginning his exegetical studies. At a future date we hope to issue an exegetical commentary on Isaiah for students farther advanced in Hebrew exegesis.)

D. Baron, *The Visions and Prophecies of Zechariah.* 3rd ed. London: Morgan & Scott, 1919.

> A Hebrew Christian commentator of ability, he brings to the study a knowledge of rabbinic sources and a fine perception of the place of Israel in the prophetic plan of God.

J. A. Bewer, *The Book of the Twelve Prophets.* Vol. II. New York: Harper & Bros., 1949.

> A recent work in the accepted Wellhausen tradition; a good example of how exegetical work should not be done.

A. C. Gaebelein, *Studies in Zechariah.* New York: Our Hope Publishers, n.d.

> A study of the prophecy from the dispensational, premillennial position by one of the foremost teachers of prophecy in his generation.

E. Henderson, *The Minor Prophets*. Andover: Warren F. Draper, 1860.
One of the finest commentaries on the minor prophets, making splendid use of the cognate Semitic languages.

E. W. Hengstenberg, *Christology of the Old Testament*. Vol. III, pp. 264-401, and Vol. IV, pp. 1-138. Edinburgh: T. & T. Clark, 1875. Lengthy but always thorough and on a high spiritual plane. A great defender of the faith.

H. A. Ironside, *Notes on the Minor Prophets*, Loizeaux Brothers, New York, 1928.

Popular exposition of Scripture at its best is to be found in the works of this writer.

Jamieson, Fausset, & Brown, *A Commentary, Critical, Experimental, and Practical on the Old and New Testaments*. Vol. IV. Philadelphia: J. B. Lippincott & Co., 1868.

Accurate and thorough, though somewhat brief. Always on a high spiritual level. Application of Scripture truth for the Christian today is always helpfully set forth.

C. F. Keil, *The Twelve Minor Prophets*. J. Martin, trans. Vol. II. Edinburgh: T. & T. Clark, 1889.

He is one of the most dependable of all Old Testament commentators. His grasp of the original language and its cognates, his spiritual approach, and his thorough work make his volumes indispensable in Old Testament exegetical studies.

D. Kimchi, *Commentary upon the Prophecies of Zechariah*. A. M'Caul, trans. London: James Duncan, 1837.

This commentary from the noted twelfth century rabbinical grammarian and commentator is valuable both for its setting forth of the accepted Jewish interpretations of the prophecy, and for the comments of the translator on the controversial Messianic passages.

J. P. Lange, *A Commentary on the Holy Scriptures*, T. W. Chambers, *The Book of Zechariah*. New York: Charles Scribner's Sons, 1899.

A commentary of many values from which help is constantly forthcoming. A thorough introduction to the prophecy is followed by comments textual and grammatical, exegetical and critical, doctrinal and ethical, homiletical and practical. Always well-balanced and never off on a tangent.

F. B. Meyer, *The Prophet of Hope: Studies in Zechariah.* New York: Fleming H. Revell, 1900.

A short work by a past master of devotional literature.

H. G. Mitchell, J. M. P. Smith, & J. A. Bewer, *A Critical and Exegetical Commentary on Haggai, Zechariah, Malachi, and Jonah. (I.C.C. Series).* Edinburgh: T. & T. Clark, 1937.

This is the critical school at its best and at its worst: at its best in treating the Hebrew text thoroughly from the angle of Hebrew grammar, syntax, and ancient versions, and the cognate languages; at its worst in handling the sacred text as the zoologist dissects a toad. The reverent student of Scripture revolts at such spiritless, lifeless, and negative treatment of the living Word of God.

E. B. Pusey, *The Minor Prophets.* Vol. II. New York: Funk & Wagnalls, 1886.

A reverent and scholarly treatment of the book. Care must be exercised to distinguish application from interpretation. His numerous quotations from the Church Fathers enhance the value of the work.

G. A. Smith, *The Book of the Twelve Prophets.* Vol. II. New York: A. C. Armstrong & Son, 1898.

A good example of the critical and divisive approach to the Old Testament; he is of the emendation school of critics with little food for the spirit.

Conrad Von Orelli, *The Twelve Minor Prophets.* J. S. Banks, trans. Edinburgh: T. & T. Clark, 1893.

Brief but valuable for treatment of the Hebrew and parallel passages.

C. H. H. Wright, *Zechariah and His Prophecies.* (Bampton Lectures, 1878). London: Hodder & Stoughton, 1879.

A masterpiece on the prophecy of Zechariah. This writer differs from the premillennial and dispensational view set forth in this volume, but his work is very valuable. Especially useful to the student is the critical and grammatical commentary at the end of the volume. Wright is at home in the Biblical languages and the Semitic cognates. No one can claim to be well read on the prophecy of Zechariah who has not pondered this tome. He does honor to the prophecy by treating it at such great length.

BIBLIOGRAPHY UPDATE: 1977

Joyce G. Baldwin, *Haggai, Zechariah, Malachi.* Downers Grove, Ill.: InterVarsity Press, 1972 (Tyndale Old Testament Commentaries).

Paul D. Hanson, *The Dawn of the Apocalyptic.* Philadelphia: Fortress Press, 1975. Covers only chapters 9-14.

Douglas R. Jones, *Haggai, Zechariah and Malachi.* London: SCM Press Ltd., 1962 (Torch Bible Commentaries).

On occasion he assumes a "glossator." He encounters many difficulties in seeking to find fulfilments of prophecies of the future in past history. The work contains minimal exegesis of the original.

H. C. Leupold, *Exposition of Zechariah.* Grand Rapids: Baker Book House, 1965.

In the traditional covenant amillennial position with the obstacles attendant upon a use of a dual hermeneutic.

A. A. Van Ruler, *Zechariah Speaks Today.* New York: Association Press, 1963.

This work covers only chapters 1-8. It is a translation from the Dutch; the material was used in a series of broadcast talks. There is a strong devotional emphasis, but a loss of exegetical and eschatological elements.

Merrill F. Unger, *Zechariah: Prophet of Messiah's Glory.* Grand Rapids: Zondervan Publishing House, 1963.

A pupil of ours in Old Testament studies, he follows the standard grammatico-historical method with dispensational, premillennial guidelines.